Financial Modeling with Crystal Ball and Excel

Founded in 1807, John Wiley & Sons is the oldest independent publishing company in the United States. With offices in North America, Europe, Australia and Asia, Wiley is globally committed to developing and marketing print and electronic products and services for our customers' professional and personal knowledge and understanding.

The Wiley Finance series contains books written specifically for finance and investment professionals as well as sophisticated individual investors and their financial advisors. Book topics range from portfolio management to e-commerce, risk management, financial engineering, valuation and financial instrument analysis, as well as much more.

For a list of available titles, please visit our Web site at www.WileyFinance.com.

Financial Modeling with Crystal Ball and Excel

JOHN CHARNES

BICENTENNIAL
1807
WILEY
2007
BICENTENNIAL

John Wiley & Sons, Inc.

Published by John Wiley & Sons, Inc., Hoboken, New Jersey.
Published simultaneously in Canada.

For general information on our other products and services or for technical support, please contact our Customer Care Department within the United States at (800) 762-2974, outside the United States at (317) 572-3993 or fax (317) 572-4002.

Wiley also publishes its books in a variety of electronic formats. Some content that appears in print may not be available in electronic books. For more information about Wiley products, visit our Web site at www.wiley.com.

Library of Congress Cataloging-in-Publication Data:

Charnes, John Martin.
   Financial modeling with crystal ball and Excel / John M. Charnes.
      p. cm.—(Wiley finance series)
   "Published simultaneously in Canada."
   Includes bibliographical references.
   ISBN 13: 978-0-471-77972-8 (paper/cd-rom)
   ISBN 10: 0-471-77972-5 (paper/cd-rom)
 1. Finance–Mathematical models. 2. Investments–Mathematical models. 3. Crystal ball (Computer file) 4. Microsoft Excel (computer file) I. Title.
   HG106.C485 2007
   332.0285′554—dc22

                                   2006033467

Printed in the United States of America.

10 9 8 7 6 5 4 3 2 1

In Memory of Gerald Daniel Charnes, 1925–2005

Contents

Preface

I wrote this book to help financial analysts and other interested parties learn how to build and interpret the results of Crystal Ball models for decision support. There are several books that exist to inform readers about Monte Carlo simulation in general. Many of these general books are listed in the References section of this book. This book focuses on using Crystal Ball in three main areas of finance: corporate finance, investments, and derivatives.

In 1982, University of Minnesota–Duluth Business School professor Henry Person introduced me to IFPS, computer software designed for financial planning, that we ran on VAX mainframe computers for an MBA class in quantitative methods. IFPS used a tabular layout for financial data similar to Excel's, although it was more abstract than Excel's because one had to print the data to see the layout in IFPS instead of working with Excel's tabular display of the data on the screen. Gray (1996) describes what is evidently the latest, and perhaps final, version of this financial planning software. It is significant to me because IFPS included a Monte Carlo command that gave me my first glimpse of using a computer as a tool for financial risk analysis.

I was hooked. The next term, I took Henry's class in discrete-event simulation based on Tom Schriber's (1974) red GPSS textbook. I found the notion of system simulation fascinating. It made experimentation possible in a computer lab on models of real-world situations, just as the physical scale models of dams in the University of Minnesota–Twin Cities hydraulic laboratory made experimentation possible for the civil engineering professors during my days as an undergraduate student there. I saw many places where systems simulation could have been applied to the construction industry when I worked as a field engineer, but was unaware at the time of what simulation could accomplish.

More graduate school beckoned. After a year of teaching finance at the University of Washington in Seattle, I returned to the Twin Cities to eventually earn my doctorate in what became the Carlson School of Management. There I met David Kelton in 1986. His coauthored textbook, now in print as Law and Kelton (2000), got me started on my dissertation research that was done largely at the Minnesota Supercomputer Institute, where I ran FORTRAN programs on Cray supercomputers and graphed the resulting output on Sun workstations. It is amazing to me that anyone can do the same tasks today faster and more easily by using Crystal Ball on a personal computer. I wish that I had had today's version of the personal computer and Crystal Ball available to me when I worked as an economic analyst at a Fortune 50 banking conglomerate in 1985.

As assistant professor in the management sciences department at the University of Miami in Coral Gables, Florida, I taught simulation to systems analysis and industrial engineering students in their undergraduate and graduate programs. When I moved to the University of Kansas in 1994, I had hopes of offering a similar course of study, but learned quickly that the business students here then were more interested in financial risk analysis than systems simulation. In 1996, I offered my first course in risk analysis at our suburban Kansas City campus to 30 MBA students, who loved the material but not the software we used—which was neither IFPS nor Crystal Ball.

I heard many complaints that term about the "clunky software that crashed all the time," but one student posed an alternative. She asked if I had heard of Crystal Ball, which was then in use by a couple of her associates at Sprint, the Kansas City–based telecommunications company. I checked it out, and the more I read in the Crystal Ball documentation, the more convinced I became that the authors were influenced by the same Law and Kelton text that I had studied in graduate school.

At the 1997 Winter Simulation Conference, I met Eric Wainwright, chief technical officer at Decisioneering, Inc. (DI), and one of the two creators of Crystal Ball, who confirmed my suspicions about our shared background. Thus began my friendship with DI that led to creation of *Risk Analysis Using Crystal Ball*, the multimedia training CD-ROM offered on the DI Web site. That effort, in collaboration with Larry Goldman, Lucie Trepanier, and Dave Fredericks, was a wholly enjoyable experience that gave me reason to believe—correctly—that the effort to produce this book would also be enjoyable.

About the same time I met Eric, I had the good fortune to work with David Kellogg at Sprint. His interest in Crystal Ball and invitation to present a series of lectures on its use as a decision support tool led to my development of training classes that were part of the Sprint University of Excellence offerings for several years. I am grateful to David and all the participants in those classes over the years for their helping me to hone the presentation of the ideas contained in this book. I am also grateful to Sprint and Nortel Networks for the financial support that led to development of the real options valuation tool described in Chapter 13. Other consulting clients will go unnamed here, but they also have influenced the presentation.

Microsoft Excel has become the *lingua franca* of business. Business associates in different industries and even some in different divisions of the same company often find it difficult to communicate with each other. However, virtually everyone who does business planning uses Excel in some capacity, if not exclusively. Though not always able to communicate in the same language, businesspeople around the globe are able to share their Excel spreadsheets. As with everything in our society, Excel has its critics. Yet the overwhelming number of users of this program make it foolish to deliberately shun its use.

My main criticism of Excel is obviated by use of the Crystal Ball application. Excel is extremely versatile in its ability to allow one to build deterministic models in many different business, engineering and scientific domains. Without Crystal Ball, it is cumbersome to use Excel for stochastic modeling, but Crystal Ball's graphical input and output features make it easy for analysts to build stochastic models in Excel.

In the 1970s, Jerry Wagner and the other founders of IFPS had a dream of creating software that would dominate the market for a computerized, plain-language tool for financial planning by executives. In the meantime, Microsoft Excel came to dominate the market for financial planning software. The combination of Excel, Crystal Ball, and OptQuest provides a powerful way for you to enhance your deterministic models by adding stochastic assumptions and finding optimal solutions to complex real-world problems. Building such models will give you greater insight into the problems you face, and may cause you to view your business in a new light.

ORGANIZATION OF THIS BOOK

This book is intended for analysts who wish to construct stochastic financial models, and anyone else interested in learning how to use Crystal Ball. Instructors with a practical bent may also find it useful as a supplement for courses in finance, management science, or industrial engineering.

The first six chapters of this book cover the features of Crystal Ball and OptQuest. Several examples are used to illustrate how these programs can be used to enhance deterministic Excel models for stochastic financial analysis and planning. The remaining seven chapters provide more detailed examples of how Crystal Ball and OptQuest can be used in financial risk analysis of investments in securities, derivatives, and real options. The technical appendices provide details about the methods used by Crystal Ball in its algorithms, and a description of some methods of variance reduction that can be employed to increase the precision of your simulation estimates. All of the models described in the book are available on the accompanying CD-ROM, as is a link to a Web site from which a trial version of Crystal Ball may be downloaded. The contents of each chapter and appendix are listed below:

Chapter 1 provides an overview of financial modeling and risk analysis through Monte Carlo simulation. It also contains a discussion of risk management and the benefits and limitations of Crystal Ball.

Chapter 2 describes how to specify and interpret Crystal Ball forecasts, the graphical and numerical summaries of the output measures generated during simulation. A retirement portfolio is used for an example.

Chapter 3 takes a helicopter view of building a Crystal Ball model. It starts out with a simple, deterministic business planning Excel model, and then shows you how to add stochastic assumptions to it with Crystal Ball. The chapter also contains a discussion of possible sources of error in your models and how they can be controlled.

Chapter 4 contains a deeper look at specifying Crystal Ball assumptions. It describes Crystal Ball's basic distributions and shows you how to select distributions using historical data and/or your best expert judgment. The chapter also describes how to use, estimate, and specify correlations between assumptions in a Crystal Ball model.

Chapter 5 covers the use of decision variables in detail. A decision variable is an input whose value can be chosen by a decision maker. Decision variables enable you to harness the power of Crystal Ball and OptQuest to find optimal solutions. A first look at real options is included in this chapter.

Chapter 6 lists and explains the runtime options available in Crystal Ball as well as how and when to use them.

Chapter 7 discusses the relative merits of using the concepts of net present value and internal rate of return in deterministic and stochastic models. Examples include capital budgeting in finance and customer lifetime value in marketing.

Chapter 8 describes how to add stochastic assumptions to pro forma financial statements, then perform sensitivity analyses using tornado charts and Crystal Ball sensitivity charts.

Chapter 9 presents examples of using Crystall Ball to construct single- and multiperiod portfolio models. It also compares the Crystal Ball results for a single-period model to the analytic solution in a special case where an analytic solution can be found.

Chapter 10 discusses Value at Risk (VaR) and its more sophisticated cousin, Conditional Value at Risk (CVaR), the relative merits of VaR and CVaR, and how they are used in risk management.

Chapter 11 describes how to simulate financial time series with Crystal Ball. It covers random walks, geometric Brownian motion, and mean-reverting models, as well as a discussion of autocorrelation and how to detect it in empirical data.

Chapter 12 shows how to create Crystal Ball models for financial option pricing, covering European, American, and exotic options. It includes a model to demonstrate how to simulate returns from option strategies, using a bull spread as an example. It also shows how to use Crystal Ball to evaluate a relatively new derivative security, a principal-protected instrument.

Chapter 13 concludes the main body of the text with a discussion of how Crystal Ball and OptQuest are used to value real options. It also contains a brief review of the literature and some applications of real options analysis.

Appendix A contains short descriptions of each available Crystal Ball assumption. Each description includes the assumption's parameters, probability mass or density function, cumulative distribution function, mean, standard deviation, and notes about the distribution and/or its usage.

Appendix B provides a brief description of how Crystal Ball generates the random numbers and variates during the simulation process.

Appendix C describes some variance reduction techniques, methods by which an analyst changes a model to get more precise estimates from a fixed number of trials during a simulation.

Appendix D provides information on downloading the Crystal Ball software and Excel files that are used in this book.

Appendix E contains citations for the references in the text to academic and practitioner literature relating to financial modeling and risk analysis. A glossary is also included.

Acknowledgments

For their conversations and help (unwitting, by some) in writing this book I would like to thank: Chris Anderson, Bill Beedles, George Bittlingmayer, David Blankinship, Eric Butz, Sarah Charnes, Barry Cobb, Tom Cowherd Jr., Riza Demirer, Amy Dougan, Bill Falloon, Dave Fredericks, Larry Goldman, Douglas Hague, Emilie Herman, Steve Hillmer, Mark Hirschey, Joe B. Jones, David Kellogg, Paul Koch, Mike Krieger, Chad Lander, Michael Lisk, Howard Marmorstein, Samik Raychaudhuri, Catherine Shenoy, Prakash Shenoy, Steve Terbovich, Michael Tognetti, Lucie Trepanier, Eric Wainwright, Bruce Wallace, and Laura Walsh. Special thanks go to Suzanne Swain Charnes for help with editing and time taken to indulge my interest in Crystal Ball over the years.

I enjoyed writing this book, and hope that it helps you learn how to build stochastic models of realistic situations important to you. I will appreciate any feedback that you send to jcharnes@ku.edu.

John Charnes
Lawrence, Kansas 2006

About the Author

Dr. John Charnes is professor and Scupin Faculty Fellow in the finance, economics, and decision sciences area at the University of Kansas School of Business, where he has received both teaching and research awards. Professor Charnes has taught courses in risk analysis, computer simulation, statistics, operations, quality management, and finance in the business schools of the University of Miami (Florida), University of Washington (Seattle), University of Minnesota (Minneapolis), and Hamline University (St. Paul).

He has published papers on financial risk analysis, statistics, and other topics in *Financial Analysts Journal, The American Statistician, Management Science, Decision Sciences, Computers and Operation Research, Journal of the Operational Research Society, Journal of Business Logistics*, and *Proceedings of the Winter Simulation Conference*. Professor Charnes has performed research, consulting, and executive education for more than 50 corporations and other organizations in Kansas, Missouri, Washington, Minnesota, Florida and Ontario, Canada.

Professor Charnes holds PhD (1989), MBA (1983), and Bachelor of Civil Engineering (1980) degrees from the University of Minnesota. Before earning his doctorate, he worked as a surveyor, draftsman, field engineer, and quality-control engineer on numerous construction projects in Minnesota, Iowa, and Maryland. He has served as president of the Institute for Operations Research and the Management Sciences (INFORMS) College on Simulation, and proceedings coeditor (1996) and program chair (2002) for the Winter Simulation Confererences.

CHAPTER 1

Introduction

L ife is stochastic. Although proponents of determinism might state otherwise, anyone who works in business or finance today knows quite well that future events are highly unpredictable. We often proceed by planning for the worst outcome while hoping for the best, but most of us are painfully aware from experience that there are many risks and uncertainties associated with any business endeavor.

Many analysts start creating financial models of risky situations with a base case constructed by making their best guess at the most likely value for each of the important inputs and building a spreadsheet model to calculate the output values that interest them. Then they account for uncertainty by thinking of how each input in turn might deviate from the best guess and letting the spreadsheet calculate the consequences for the outputs. Such a "what-if" analysis provides insight into the sensitivity of the outputs to one-at-a-time changes in the inputs.

Another common procedure is to calculate three scenarios: best case, worst case and most likely. This is done by inserting the best possible, worst possible, and most likely values for each key input, then calculating the best-case outputs when each input is at its best possible value; the worst-case outputs when each input is at its worst possible value; and using the base case as the most likely scenario. Scenario analysis shows the ranges of possibilities for the outputs, but gives no idea of the likelihood of output values falling between the extremes.

What-if and scenario analysis are good ways to get started, but there are more sophisticated techniques for analyzing and managing risk and uncertainty. This book is designed to help you use the software programs Crystal Ball and Excel to develop financial models for risk analysis. The spreadsheet program Excel has dramatically changed financial analysis in the past 30 years, and Crystal Ball extends the capability of Excel by allowing you to add stochastic assumptions to your spreadsheets. Adding stochastic assumptions provides a clearer picture of the possibilities for each of the outputs of interest. Reading this book and following the examples will help you use Crystal Ball to enhance your risk analysis capabilities.

Throughout the book, I use the word *stochastic* as a synonym for *random* or *probabilistic*, and as an antonym for *deterministic*. The majority of spreadsheet models in use today are deterministic, but every spreadsheet user knows at some level that there is a degree of uncertainty about each of the inputs to his or her models.

Crystal Ball enables you to use a systematic approach to account for uncertainty in your spreadsheet models.

The first six chapters of this book demonstrate how to use Crystal Ball. The remainder of the text provides examples of using Crystal Ball models to help solve problems in corporate finance, investments, and financial risk management. The appendices provide technical details about what goes on under the hood of the Crystal Ball engine.

This chapter is an overview of financial modeling and risk analysis. Some example applications are listed below where these tools provide insights that might not otherwise come to light, and you get a glimpse of how straightforward it is to assess financial risk using Crystal Ball and Excel. For a simple model that is already built and ready to run, we will interpret the output and analyze the model's sensitivity to changes in its inputs. The chapter concludes with a discussion of the benefits and limitations of risk analysis with Crystal Ball and Excel.

FINANCIAL MODELING

For the purposes of this book, *financial modeling* is the construction and use of a spreadsheet depiction of a company's or an individual's past, present, or future business operations. To learn more about deterministic financial modeling, see Proctor (2004), Sengupta (2004), or Koller, Goedhart, and Wessels (2005). For each situation where we wish to use a stochastic model, we begin with a deterministic Excel model, then add stochastic assumptions with Crystal Ball to generate stochastic forecasts. By analyzing the stochastic forecasts statistically, we can make inferences about the riskiness of the business operations described by the model. The risk analysis process became much easier and more widely available with the introduction of Crystal Ball to the marketplace in 1987.

RISK ANALYSIS

The first recorded instances of risk analysis are the practices of the Asipu people of the Tigris-Euphrates valley about 3200 B.C. (Covello and Mumpower 1985). The Asipu would serve as consultants for difficult decisions such as a proposed marriage arrangement, or the location of a suitable building site. They would list the alternative actions under consideration and collect data on the likely outcomes of each alternative. The priest-like Asipu would interpret signs from the gods, then compare the alternatives systematically. Upon completion of their analysis, they would etch a final report to the client on a clay tablet, complete with a recommendation of the most favorable alternative (Oppenheim 1977).

According to the *Oxford English Dictionary* (Brown 2002), the term *risk analysis* means the "systematic investigation and forecasting of risks in business and commerce." The word *risk* comes through French, Latin, and Italian from the Greek word *rhiza*, in reference to sailors navigating among cliffs. Note that although some authorities believe that *risk* is derived from the Arabian word *rizq*, meaning "subsistence" it is difficult to explain how this meaning developed into that of "danger" (Klein 1967). If you bought this book to help you analyze business problems, I will bet that you have no trouble seeing the connection between the risks of managing a business and the perils of navigating a sailing vessel around cliffs and barely submerged rocks that can damage the hull and sink the ship.

Imagine an ancient Greek mariner piloting a ship as it approaches a cliff or point of rocks in uncharted waters. Another sailor is on lookout in the crow's nest at the top of the mast to give the earliest possible warning about how far down into the water an outcrop from the cliff might be. A navigator nearby with sextant and compass is keeping track of where the ship has been and the direction in which it's headed. His lookout warns him at the first sign of trouble ahead, but it is up to the pilot to decide how wide to take the turn around the cliff. Cutting the corner too close can save time but might sink the ship. Veering far from the edge is safer, but adds costly travel time.

In navigating a strait between two cliffs, the pilot's decision is even more difficult. Being too far from one cliff can mean being too close to the opposing cliff. The pilot must weigh the risks, use judgment and instinct to carefully choose a course, and then hope for the best as vessel and crew proceed through the strait.

It is the pilot's job to take all of the available information into account and decide how best to sail the ship in uncharted waters. The pilot wants a clear analysis of all the dangers and opportunities that lie ahead, in order to decide whether the potential time savings of the ship's chosen course outweigh the disastrous consequences of hull damage. Even though the ship may have been through many different straits in the past, the pilot needs a systematic investigation and forecasting of the risks associated with the planned course through each new strait encountered during the voyage.

If you are running a business (or are an analyst helping to run a business), you are often in situations conceptually similar to those facing the pilot of a sailing vessel in uncharted waters. You know where your business has been, and you are always on the lookout for dangers and opportunities on the horizon. You operate in an environment fraught with uncertainty. You know that future circumstances can affect you and your business greatly, and you want to be prepared for what might happen. In many situations, you need to weigh the favorable and unfavorable consequences of some decision and then choose a course of action. Similar to a ship pilot, it is your job to decide how best to navigate the straits of your business environment. What do you do?

Fortunately, mathematicians such as Simon LaPlace and Blaise Pascal developed the fundamental underpinnings of risk analysis in the seventeenth century by devising the mathematical methods now used in probability theory (Ore 1960). From these precepts came the science of statistics. "What?" you ask, "I studied probability and statistics in college and hated every minute of them. I thought I was done with that stuff. How can it help me?"

In short, probability and statistics help you weigh the potential rewards and punishments associated with the decisions you face. This book shows you how to use Crystal Ball to add probabilistic assumptions and statistical forecasts to spreadsheet models of a wide variety of financial problems. In the end, you still must make decisions based on your best judgment and instincts, but judicious use of the methods of probability and statistics that we go through in this book will help you in several ways.

The modeling process described here enables you to investigate many different possibilities, hone your intuition, and use state-of-the-art software tools that are extremely beneficial for managing risk in dynamic business environments. The risk analysis process forces you to think through the possible consequences of your decisions. This helps you gain comfort that the course of action you select is the best one to take based on the information available at the time you make the decision. Risk analysis is the quantification of the consequences of uncertainty in a situation of interest, and Crystal Ball is the tool for carrying it out.

MONTE CARLO SIMULATION

Risk analysis using Crystal Ball relies on developing a mathematical model in Excel that represents a situation of interest. After you develop the deterministic model, you replace point estimates with probability distribution assumptions and forecast the distribution of the output. The forecasted output distribution is used to assess the riskiness of the situation.

For simple models, the output distribution can be found mathematically to give an analytic solution. For example, consider the simple cost equation

$$(\text{Total Cost}) = \$100 + \$15 \times (\text{Quantity Produced}),$$

where (Quantity Produced) is modelled as a normal probability distribution with mean, $\mu = 50$, and standard deviation, $\sigma = 10$, and we want to know the probability that (Total Cost) is greater than \$900. We don't need Crystal Ball for this situation because we can easily obtain an analytic solution.

A result in probability theory holds that if a random variable X follows the normal distribution with mean, μ, and standard deviation, σ, then the random variable $Y = a + bX$ will also be normally distributed with mean, $a + b\mu$, and standard deviation, $b\sigma$. Therefore, we can easily determine that (Total Cost) is normally distributed with mean, $100 + (15 \times 50) = \$850$, and standard deviation, $15 \times 10 = \$150$. Using a table of cumulative probabilities for the standard normal distribution, or using the Excel function = 1-NORMDIST (900,850,150, TRUE), we can find that the probability is 36.94 percent that (Total Cost) is greater than \$900. See the file Analytic.xls for these calculations, along with a Crystal Ball model that validates the solution.

	A	B	C
1	**Profit.xls**		
2			
3			
4	**Assumptions**	**Notation**	**Value**
5	Price	P	$ 50.00
6	Unit Sales	S	10
7	Variable cost percentage	V	60%
8	Fixed cost	F	$ 100.00
9			
10	**Forecast**		
11	Profit	π	$ 100.00
12			
13	**Model**		
14	Revenue	$ 500.00	
15	Variable Cost	$ 300.00	
16	Fixed Cost	$ 100.00	
17	Profit	$ 100.00	

FIGURE 1.1 Simple profit model in Profit.xls. Cells C5:C7 are defined as Crystal Ball assumptions. Cell C11 is a Crystal Ball forecast.

In practice however, it is easy to find situations that are too difficult for most analysts to solve analytically. For example, consider a simple situation where unit sales, S, follow the Poisson distribution with mean 10; price, P, is lognormally distributed with mean $50 and standard deviation $10; variable cost percentage, V, has the beta distribution with parameters minimum = 0%, maximum = 100%, alpha = 2, and beta = 3; and fixed cost, $F = \$100$. Then profit, π, is calculated as

$$\pi = SP(1 - V) - F \qquad (1.1)$$

in the Profit.xls model shown in Figure 1.1. The stochastic assumptions in Profit.xls are shown in Figure 1.2. For this model, it is easy to obtain a forecast distribution for profit with Crystal Ball and find the probability of making a positive profit to be approximately 76 percent (Figure 1.3), but it is not so easy to determine the distribution mathematically and obtain the probability of positive profit by analytic solution.

Further, Crystal Ball enables us do sensitivity analysis very easily. The sensitivity chart in Figure 1.4 shows that most of the variation in profit arises from the Assumption V, the variable cost percentage. If we are able to control this variable, then the model shows that we can reduce the variation of profit by reducing the variation in V. If this variable is beyond our control, the chart indicates that we should work first on V when we are fine-tuning the model by improving our estimates of the assumption variables.

With Crystal Ball, we obtain an approximate solution using Monte Carlo simulation to generate the output distribution. One of the features of Monte Carlo

Assumptions

Worksheet: [Profit.xls]Sheet1

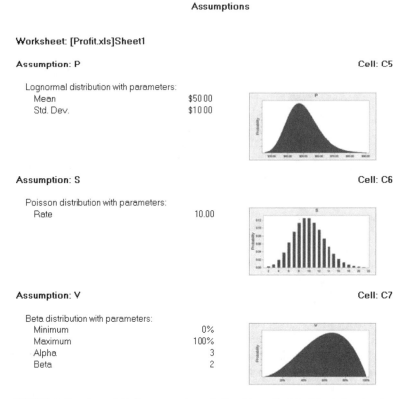

Assumption: P   Cell: C5

    Lognormal distribution with parameters:
      Mean $50 00
      Std. Dev. $10 00

Assumption: S   Cell: C6

    Poisson distribution with parameters:
      Rate   10.00

Assumption: V   Cell: C7

    Beta distribution with parameters:
      Minimum   0%
      Maximum   100%
      Alpha   3
      Beta   2

FIGURE 1.2   Crystal Ball assumptions defined in cells C5:C7 of the simple profit model.

is that the more simulation trials we run, the closer is our approximation to the true distribution. The technique of Monte Carlo simulation has been used for this purpose for many years by scientists and engineers working with large and expensive mainframe computers. In combination with today's small and inexpensive personal computers, Crystal Ball and Excel bring to everyone the ability to run Monte Carlo simulations on a PC.

In statistics, one of the earliest uses of simulation (albeit without a computer), was that by the mathematical statistician William S. Gossett, who used the pen name "Student" to conceal his identity and appease his employers at Guinness brewing company. To verify his mathematical derivations, Gossett repeatedly drew random samples of numbers from a bowl, wrote them down, and painstakingly made his calculations. The results he obtained were within the tolerances expected from an experiment involving random sampling. Gossett's sampling experiments are conceptually similar to what we do on computers today, but Crystal Ball does for us in seconds what must have taken Gossett weeks or months to do by hand in his day.

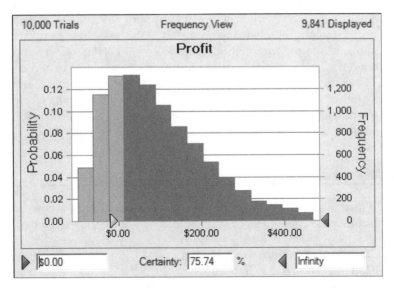

FIGURE 1.3 Forecast distribution for the simple profit model. The certainty of 75.74 percent for the range from 0.00 to infinity is the Crystal Ball estimate of the probability of positive profit, $\Pr(\pi > 0)$ for the model specified by Expression 1.1.

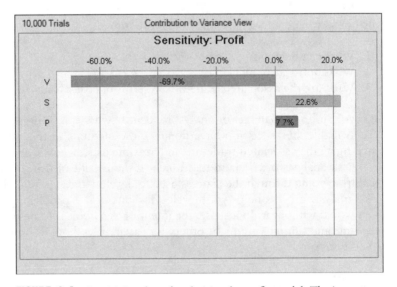

FIGURE 1.4 Sensitivity chart for the simple profit model. The input variables (assumptions) P, S, and V are listed from top to bottom in decreasing order of their impact on the output variable (forecast), profit.

The term *Monte Carlo* originated in a conversation between two mathematicians employed by Los Alamos National Laboratory as a code word for their secret work on the atomic bomb (Macrae 1992). John von Neumann and Stanislaw Ulam applied Monte Carlo methods to problems involving direct simulation of behavior concerned with random neutron diffusion in fissionable material (Rubinstein 1981). The name was motivated by the similarity of the computer-generated results to the action of the gambling devices used at the casinos in the city of Monte Carlo in the principality of Monaco. The term caught on and is now widely used in finance, science, and engineering.

RISK MANAGEMENT

When analyzing risk with the methods presented in this book you will be able to quantify the consequences of uncertainty by answering three main questions:

1. What can happen?
2. How likely is it to happen?
3. Given that it occurs, what are the consequences?

All good managers go through a process by which they consider these questions somehow, even if subconsciously. By taking the time to answer the questions in quantifiable terms, you will develop deeper insight into the problems you face.

Risk analysis is part of a broader set of methods called *risk management*, which also seeks to find answers to three main questions:

1. What can be done?
2. What options are available?
3. What are the associated trade-offs in terms of costs, benefits, and risks?

It is your job as a manager or analyst to identify what can be done and what options are available, but once you have done so, the methods in this book will help you investigate the associated trade-offs in terms of costs, benefits, and risks.

Risk analysts often claim that much of the benefit of using Crystal Ball comes just from going through the process used to develop and fine-tune their models. The risk analysis process helps you develop insights into a problem more quickly than you would without it. In a sense, the intent of this book is to help save you some of the time and tuition you might otherwise pay in the school of hard knocks to reach good decisions.

BENEFITS AND LIMITATIONS OF USING CRYSTAL BALL

This section describes some of the benefits and the limitations of using Crystal Ball and Excel for risk analysis. When it is applicable, diligent use of these tools yields deeper insight and understanding that will lead to better decision making. However, the tools have their limits as described below.

Benefits

- Careful study of the situation being modeled usually reveals the key input factors that lead to success. Sometimes it will become obvious what these factors are during model building. However, Crystal Ball has built-in sensitivity analysis tools to help identify the key input factors.
- As mistakes are costly, it is better to evaluate before implementation. A valid model of a situation can help save much time and expense compared to experimenting with aspects of the actual situation to see what happens. This book is intended to help you build valid models.
- Computer hardware and software make simulation easy. Until recently, the use of Monte Carlo simulation was limited to those who had access to large mainframe computers and the expertise to program them. Today's personal computers have the same computational horsepower as yesterday's mainframes. Crystal Ball has been developed over the years to make the addition of stochastic inputs and the calculation of output statistics as easy as possible.
- Realistic situations can be analyzed with relatively simple models. While many realistic situations have a host of potential complications, most often just a few of these have the greatest effect on the outputs. Crystal Ball's sensitivity analysis features help you identify the effects of the factors having the greatest impact.
- Risk analysis can be a convincing agent for change. For those who understand the modeling process and the output produced by Crystal Ball, experimenting with the model can demonstrate very well the impact of changes to the system. If you have earned the buy-in of key decision makers, the model can be a powerfully persuasive tool.

Limitations

- Validity of the input data is essential. As with any other computer program, the output is only as good as the input. The aphorism "garbage in, garbage out" will always be true for Crystal Ball models as it will be for every computer program.
- If you can't model it, you can't simulate it. Your ability to build Crystal Ball models is subject to the limitations of Excel. If you cannot build an Excel spreadsheet to represent the situation, then you cannot use Crystal Ball for simulation. Fortunately, the hundreds of functions built into Excel make it very versatile, and Crystal Ball allows you to use Excel's VBA capabilities if necessary for specialized purposes.
- Risk analysis requires expert insight to make decisions. Crystal Ball will not make decisions for you. It will help you gain insight into the problem, but you must still reach conclusions and make decisions based on your judgment and intuition about the situation you are analyzing.

- Crystal Ball gives approximate rather than exact solutions. This "limitation" is mostly an academic criticism. Many purists prefer to use only models that avail themselves to analytic solution. When confronted by a realistic complication that precludes analytic solution, they simply assume away the complication. Most practitioners, however, wish to include realistic complications and are happy to accept the trade-off of getting an approximate solution with simulation. The limitation is that they might have to run the model longer to obtain the desired precision. However, most practitioners prefer an approximate solution to a realistic problem over an exact solution to an oversimplified problem that is only a rough approximation to reality.

CHAPTER 2

Analyzing Crystal Ball Forecasts

In this chapter, using an example of accumulating funds for retirement, we see the graphical and numerical summaries of forecasts that Crystal Ball provides automatically. This chapter serves as a review of elementary statistical analysis, focused on the standard output built into Crystal Ball.

SIMULATING A 50–50 PORTFOLIO

Let's say that you want to start saving for your retirement. You are 30 years old and wish to retire at age 60. You plan to put away an inflation-adjusted $10,000 per year, and would like to know how much wealth you will have accumulated after 30 years. At this point, you consider only two types of assets: stocks and bonds.

If you had perfect foresight, you would know exactly what returns each investment would bring over the next 30 years. With that information, you wouldn't need Crystal Ball and could optimize your portfolio by investing in only those assets that you knew would go up. Of course, no one has perfect foresight, so what do you do? In this chapter, we'll consider an oversimplified model for investing retirement funds and use it to illustrate how to analyze Crystal Ball forecasts.

Accumulate.xls

Overview. For this model we assume that returns on stocks and bonds during the next 30 years will resemble (in a statistical sense) the returns that have been observed during the years 1926 to 2004. You have heard that diversification is a good thing to do when investing your money, so you decide initially to split the money you want to set aside for retirement each year by putting one half into stocks and one half into bonds. We call this the 50–50 portfolio, and model it in the Excel file Accumulate.xls.

The model draws returns on stocks and bonds randomly for each year and calculates the wealth you will have accumulated for retirement 30 years from now, assuming a constant 3 percent inflation rate. A segment of this model is shown in Figure 2.1. Note that rows 14 through 40 are hidden to save space.

	A	B	C	D	E	F	G	H
1	Accumulate.xls							
2								
3	Allocations			Year 30 Wealth				
4	Stocks	50%		$ 3,729,307				
5	Bonds	50%						
6	Amount	$ 10,000						
7								
8	Inflation Rate		3%					
9								
10	Accumulated Values							
11	YEAR	Stock Return	Bond Return	Beg Stock	End Stock	Beg Bond	End Bond	Total
12	1	1.1517	1.0585	$ 5,000	$ 5,758	$ 5,000	$ 5,293	$ 11,051
13	2	1.1517	1.0585	$ 10,908	$ 12,563	$ 10,443	$ 11,054	$ 23,617
41	30	1.1517	1.0585	$ 2,741,723	$ 3,157,530	$ 540,160	$ 571,777	$ 3,729,307

FIGURE 2.1 Spreadsheet segment from Accumulate.xls showing accumulated value after 30 years of retirement savings where 50 percent was put into stocks and 50 percent into bonds each year. Note that Rows 14 through 40 are hidden.

Forecast. You want to see the possible distribution of wealth you will have accumulated after 30 years—Year 30 Wealth. Cell D4 has the formula =H41 to get Year 30 Wealth displayed near the top of the spreadsheet.

Stochastic assumptions. Cells B12:B41 represent the total annual return on stocks for years 1 through 30. Each year's return on stocks is lognormal with mean 1.1517 and standard deviation 0.2746. Cells C12:C41 represent the total annual return on bonds for years 1 through 30. Each year's return on bonds is lognormal with mean 1.0585 and standard deviation 0.0735. In this model, all assumptions are statistically independent of each other (that is, all correlations are zero). The parameters of the lognormal distributions were chosen with the help of Crystal Ball's distribution-fitting feature, which is described in Chapter 4.

Decision variable. The sole decision variable in this model is Cell B4, the proportion of each year's investment that is allocated to stocks. The proportion allocated to bonds is calculated in Cell B5 as =1−B4 to ensure that the entire investment is put into either stocks or bonds each year. The initial proportion allocated to stocks is 50 percent.

Summary. Figure 2.2 shows the frequency view of a forecast chart for Year 30 Wealth obtained after running the simulation for 10,000 trials. Note that the distribution is highly skewed to the right because of a few instances of very high returns over the 30-year period.

Frequency Chart

The default graph in the Forecast window is a frequency chart (also known as a histogram) that shows how often a forecast cell had a value falling in each of several possible intervals. In the forecast window for Year 30 Wealth in Figure 2.2, the possible values range from $0 to $15 million, and are broken up into 15 equal

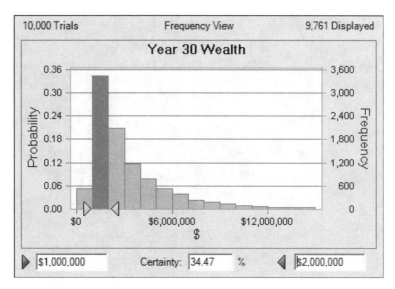

FIGURE 2.2 Frequency chart showing accumulated value after 30 years of retirement savings where 50 percent was put into stocks and 50 percent into bonds each year. The estimated probability of accumulating between $1 million and $2 million is shown in the **Certainty** field.

intervals (of size $1 million). The height of each bar indicates how many simulation trials resulted in a Year 30 Wealth value that fell in the corresponding interval.

For example, the tallest bar in Figure 2.2 indicates that Year 30 Wealth was between $1 million and $2 million in just fewer than 3,600 trials. The right side of the histogram has the frequency scale. Because there were 10,000 trials run, and the estimated probability (certainty) of Year 30 Wealth being between $1 million and $2 million is 34.47 percent, we know that there must have been 3,447 trials that resulted in Year 30 Wealth between $1 million and $2 million. The left side of the histogram has the probability scale. The text "9,761 Displayed" in the upper right corner of the window indicates that Year 30 Wealth was greater than $15 million (literally, "off the chart") on 239 of the 10,000 simulation trials run. We know that all of the undisplayed values must be above $15 million rather than below $0 because the portfolio value can never be negative under the assumptions we used.

Cumulative Frequency Chart

Change the forecast window by clicking on **Preferences, Forecast. . .**, then selecting **Cumulative Frequency** in the **View** field and clicking **OK**. You may also click on View → Cumulative Frequency in the top menu of the forecast window. The cumulative frequency chart in Figure 2.3 shows the frequency with which the simulation trials fell into each interval or below. For example, from the cumulative frequency

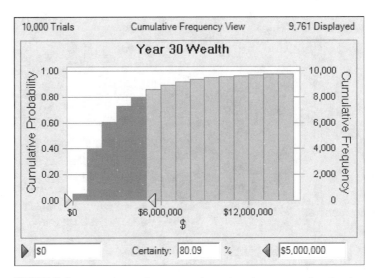

FIGURE 2.3 Cumulative frequency chart showing accumulated value after thirty years of retirement savings where 50% was put into stocks and 50% into bonds each year. The estimated probability of accumulating more than $1 million is shown in the **Certainty** field.

chart you can see that in 80.09 percent of the trials, 30-year wealth had a value below $5 million. Another way to interpret this example is to say that the estimated probability is approximately 80 percent that 30-year wealth will be less than $5 million.

Note that Crystal Ball also provides a reverse cumulative frequency chart (not pictured here) that shows the frequency with which the simulation trials fell into each interval or above. You can cycle through the different views by using the keystroke combination **Ctrl-d** when the forecast window is active. Table 2.1 lists the keystroke combinations (sometimes called "hot keys" or "keyboard shortcuts") that are available to alter your view of the forecast window. Make the Year 30 Wealth forecast window active and experiment with different combinations to see the effects.

Statistics View

The statistics view of the Forecast window in Figure 2.4 provides numerical summaries of the forecast. Descriptions of the statistics computed automatically by Crystal Ball in Figure 2.4 are listed below. The number of each statistic in the list can be used in the Excel formula =CB.GetForeStatFn(Range,Index) as the value of Index. The statistics and their indices are also listed in Table 4.1, and usage of the =CB.GetForeStatFn(Range,Index) is illustrated in Cells D46:E57 in Accumulate.xls.

TABLE 2.1 Keystroke combinations ("hot keys") that can be used to cycle through settings available in the Chart Preferences dialog. These commands work on the primary distribution—the theoretical probability distribution for assumptions, and the generated values for forecasts and overlay charts.

Hot Key	Description
Ctrl-d	Cycles through chart views: Frequency, Cumulative Frequency, Reverse Cumulative Frequency (for assumption and forecast charts)
Ctrl-b or Ctrl-g	Cycles through bins or group interval values to adjust the number of data bins used to create the chart
Ctrl-l	Cycles through gridline settings: None, Horizontal, Vertical, Both
Ctrl-t	Cycles through chart types: Area, Line, Column; for sensitivity charts: Bar (direction), Bar (magnitude), Pie (in Contribution to Variance view)
Ctrl-3	Cycles between two-dimensional and three-dimensional chart display
Ctrl-m	Cycles through central tendency marker lines: None, Base Case, Mean, Median, Mode (except for sensitivity and trend charts)
Ctrl-n	Toggles the legend display on and off
Ctrl-p	Cycles through percentile markers: None, 10%, 20%, ..., 90%
Spacebar	Cycles through window views when Excel is not in Edit mode: Chart, Statistics, Percentiles, Goodness of Fit (if distribution fitting is selected—except for trend charts)

For the mathematical expressions in the list below, we denote the values produced by the simulation in a forecast cell as $y_1, y_2, \ldots, y_n$, where n is the number of iterations run before the simulation stops.

1. **Trials.** The first item listed in the statistics view is **Trials**, which is also called the number of iterations, n. A trial (or iteration) is a three-step process in which Crystal Ball generates a random number for each assumption cell, recalculates the spreadsheet model(s), and collects the result(s) for the forecast window(s). The number of trials is the only descriptive statistic value that is under your direct control. Use the **Run Preferences** dialog box to specify the maximum number of trials.

2. **Mean.** The next item in the Statistics View is **Mean**, which is the same as the arithmetic average. It is calculated as

$$\text{Mean} = \overline{Y} = \frac{1}{n} \sum_{i=1}^{n} y_i.$$

Even though the window indicates that only 9,761 trials are displayed, the value $3,775,824 for the mean in Figure 2.4 is calculated from all 10,000 trials of the simulation.

10,000 Trials	Statistics View	9,761 Displayed

Statistic	Forecast values
▸ Trials	10,000
Mean	$3,775,824
Median	$2,425,951
Mode	---
Standard Deviation	$5,942,930
Variance	$35,318,416,769,8
Skewness	32.20
Kurtosis	1,918.70
Coeff. of Variability	1.57
Minimum	$570,705
Maximum	$392,617,426
Mean Std. Error	$59,429

FIGURE 2.4 Forecast chart statistics for accumulated value after 30 years of retirement savings where 50 percent was put into stocks and 50 percent into bonds each year.

If you wish to calculate statistics for selected values of the forecast, click on **Preferences, Forecast...**, then the **Filter** tab. You will be able to include or exclude any specified range of values from the calculations. This feature will come in handy later for calculating expected tail loss.

The mean is one of three measures of location computed by Crystal Ball. The other two measures of location are the median and the mode. In a highly skewed distribution such as Year 30 Wealth, the mean may not be the best indication of the location of the distribution. Use the certainty range in the forecast chart to see for yourself that the probability of Year 30 Wealth equalling or exceeding the mean is only about 30 percent.

3. **Median.** The median is the value in the middle of the distribution. For example, 6 is the median of the distribution of values 1, 3, 6, 7, and 9. In a distribution with an odd number of values, the median is found by ordering the values from smallest to largest and then selecting the middle value. In a distribution with an even number of values, the median is equal to the mean of the two middle ordered values.

For Year 30 Wealth, the median value in Figure 2.4 is $2,425,951, which means that the probability is about 50 percent that our retirement portfolio will be that large or larger at that time. The median is less sensitive to outliers than the mean. For that reason, it is sometimes preferred to the mean as a measure of location, as it is here because the Year 30 Wealth forecast frequency distribution is highly skewed.

4. **Mode.** The mode is the single value that occurs most frequently in a set of values. For a forecast that can take on continuous values, it is likely that no single value will occur more than once, so the mode is often listed as dashes (−−) in the statistics view, as it is in Figure 2.4.

5. **Standard Deviation.** The standard deviation is a measure of dispersion, or spread, of a distribution. Think of it as roughly equal to the average distance of each value from the mean, although as you can see in the formula below, it is not exactly equal to that:

$$\text{Standard Deviation} = s = \sqrt{\frac{1}{n-1} \sum_{i=1}^{n} (y_i - \bar{y})^2}. \tag{2.1}$$

The standard deviation is one of two equivalent measures of spread computed by Crystal Ball. The other measure of spread is the variance. In many applications, the standard deviation is preferred because it is measured in the same units as the forecast variable.

6. **Variance.** The variance is another measure of dispersion that is equivalent to the standard deviation. Because the variance is equal to the standard deviation squared, it sometimes appears in the statistics view as a very large number. The variance is calculated as:

$$\text{Variance} = s^2 = \frac{1}{n-1} \sum_{i=1}^{n} (y_i - \bar{y})^2.$$

7. **Skewness.** Skewness is a measure of asymmetry of a frequency distribution. The distributions pictured in Figure 2.5 display negative, positive, and near-zero skewness. The formula for skewness used by Crystal Ball is

$$\text{Skewness} = \frac{1}{n} \sum_{i=1}^{n} \left(\frac{y_i - \bar{y}}{s} \right)^3.$$

The large positive skewness of Year 30 Wealth can be seen in Figure 2.2, and is measured as 32.20 in Figure 2.4. The fact that the mean of \$3.776 million is so much larger than the median of \$2.426 million is also evidence of large positive skewness. Alternative measures of skewness are

$$\frac{3(\text{Mean} - \text{Mode})}{\text{Standard Deviation}} \quad \text{and} \quad \frac{3(\text{Mean} - \text{Median})}{\text{Standard Deviation}},$$

either of which you can calculate easily from the Crystal Ball output.

With all else equal, positive skewness in accumulated wealth is desirable; however, note that here the large positive skewness makes it misleading to expect to earn the mean wealth. As calculated above, there is less than a 30 percent chance that you will actually accumulate the mean wealth or more.

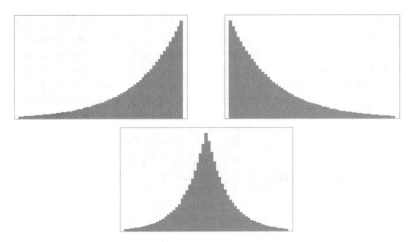

FIGURE 2.5 Frequency distributions depicting negative (Skewness = −2), positive (+2), and near-zero (0.02) skewness at top left, top right, and bottom center, respectively.

8. Kurtosis. Kurtosis is a measure of peakedness, which is equivalent to measuring tail thickness. The formula for kurtosis used by Crystal Ball is

$$\text{Kurtosis} = \frac{1}{n} \sum_{i=1}^{n} \left(\frac{y_i - \bar{y}}{S} \right)^4.$$

If two distributions have the same standard deviation, the one with the higher kurtosis will have a higher peak and heavier tails. All normal distributions have a kurtosis of 3.0, and frequency distributions with a kurtosis near 3.0 are called *mesokurtic*. Distributions that have significantly higher kurtosis are called *leptokurtic* and those with significantly lower kurtosis are called *platykurtic*.

Some computer programs and authors subtract 3.0 from the definition above used by Crystal Ball. The technical name for this is then *excess kurtosis*, but you may see it too called kurtosis by some authors, so beware. In fact, the statistic calculated by Excel's **=KURT(ref)** command and its Data Analysis tool is actually excess kurtosis—calculated by a slightly different formula than Crystal Ball—but is labelled simply as kurtosis.

Figure 2.6 shows an overlay chart for two distributions that have mean zero and standard deviation one. The distributions with the lower peak is the standard normal distribution, which has kurtosis = 3.0, as does every normal distribution. The distribution labeled Mixture has kurtosis = 12.1. It could have come from a market in which 5% of the time returns have high variability and 95 percent of the time they have low variability (see the file **Kurtosis.xls** for details).

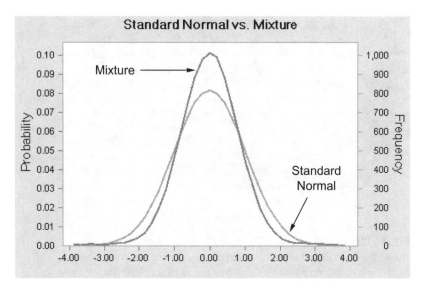

FIGURE 2.6 Overlay chart depicting a mesokurtic standard normal distribution (kurtosis = 3) and a leptokurtic mixture distribution (kurtosis = 11.7). See the file Kurtosis.xls for details.

9. Coefficient of Variability. The coefficient of variability, also known as the coefficient of variation, is a relative measure of dispersion found as

$$\text{Coefficient of Variability} = \frac{s}{\bar{y}}.$$

It might be more useful than standard deviation for some purposes. For example, a standard deviation of 10 may be insignificant if the mean is 10,000 (giving a coefficient of variability = .001) but may be substantial if the mean is 100 (coefficient of variability = .1). Because the mean $\bar{y}$ and standard deviation s have the same units, the coefficient of variability is dimensionless.

Crystal Ball calculates it routinely as part of the standard output, but the coefficient of variability is best used only when all simulated values are positive. When the values can be both positive or negative, the mean can be zero or negative. When the mean value is near zero, the coefficient of variability is sensitive to small changes in the standard deviation, which can limit its usefulness. When the mean value is negative, use the absolute value of the coefficient of variability to get a more meaningful relative measure of dispersion.

10. Minimum. The minimum is the smallest value of all the observed forecast values. Note for models using unbounded-on-the-left stochastic assumptions such as the normal distribution, the more trials that are run, the smaller the minimum is likely to be simply because there are more opportunities for Crystal Ball to generate extreme observations.

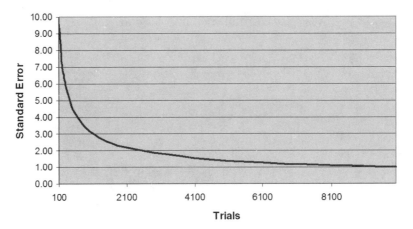

FIGURE 2.7   Plot of $100/\sqrt{n}$ for n in the interval $[100, 10000]$. This plot shows how the standard error of the mean decreases as a function of the number of trials in the simulation. Much of the decrease in standard error is gained after only 2,000 trials.

11. Maximum. The maximum is the largest value of all the observed forecast values. For assumptions that are unbounded on the right such as the normal or lognormal distributions, the more trials that are run, the larger the maximum is likely to be simply because there are more opportunities for Crystal Ball to generate extreme observations.

12. The Range is the difference between the minimum and the maximum. In versions of Crystal Ball before 7.2, the Range was listed in the statistics view of the forecast window. For backward compatibility, the command =CB.GetForeStatFN(range,12) will return the Range statistic, which is simply the Minimum subtracted from the Maximum. Do not confuse the CB.GetForeStatFN argument range, which represents the address of a forecast cell, with the Range statistic described here.

13. Mean Standard Error. The mean standard error is a measure of precision of the estimate of the mean. The smaller the mean standard error, the greater the precision. Figure 2.7 shows how the mean standard error decreases in a nonlinear manner as the number of trials increases for a forecast distribution having a standard deviation of 100. Most of the precision in the estimate is gained by 2,000 trials.

Forecast Window Percentiles View

The percentiles view in Figure 2.8 gives the forecast values that are just larger than the corresponding percent of all the values. For example, the 80th percentile for Year 30 Wealth is $4,985,234. This means that 80 percent of the forecast values were less than that amount, while 20 percent were greater than that amount. Note

10,000 Trials	Percentiles View	9,761 Displayed

Percentile	Forecast values
▶ 0%	$570,705
10%	$1,136,465
20%	$1,415,528
30%	$1,686,409
40%	$2,019,034
50%	$2,425,951
60%	$2,966,009
70%	$3,762,445
80%	$4,985,234
90%	$7,298,984
100%	$392,617,426

FIGURE 2.8 Forecast chart percentiles for accumulated value after 30 years of retirement savings where 50 percent was put into stocks and 50 percent into bonds each year.

that the 50th percentile of $2,425,951 is the same as the value of the median in Figure 2.4.

VARYING THE ALLOCATIONS

We started with a simple example of allocating 50 percent to each type of fund, which we call the 50–50 portfolio. Now we will compare forecasts for different allocations of stocks and bonds to the portfolio.

Decision Table Tool

In file Accumulate.xls, select cell B4, then click on Define > Define Decision.... Fill in the fields in the Define Decision Variable dialog as shown in Figure 2.9. Click OK and watch cell B4 turn yellow to indicate that a Crystal Ball decision variable is defined there. After this definition, you can use the Decision Table tool to vary the allocation into stocks from 10% to 90% in steps of 10%.

Click on Run > Tools > Decision Table.... In the Specify target (step 1 of 3) dialog, Year 30 Wealth will be the only forecast listed (Figure 2.10), so click Next >. In the Select one or two decisions (step 2 of 3) dialog, Stocks will be the only available decision variable. Move this rightward to the Chosen Decision Variables window by clicking >> (Figure 2.11), then click Next >.

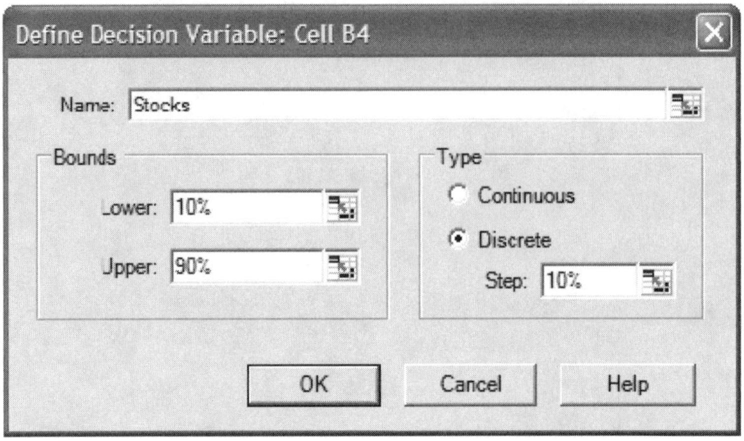

FIGURE 2.9 Dialog window showing settings to specify nine different allocations into stocks each year. The allocation to stocks varies from 10 percent to 90 percent in steps of 10 percent.

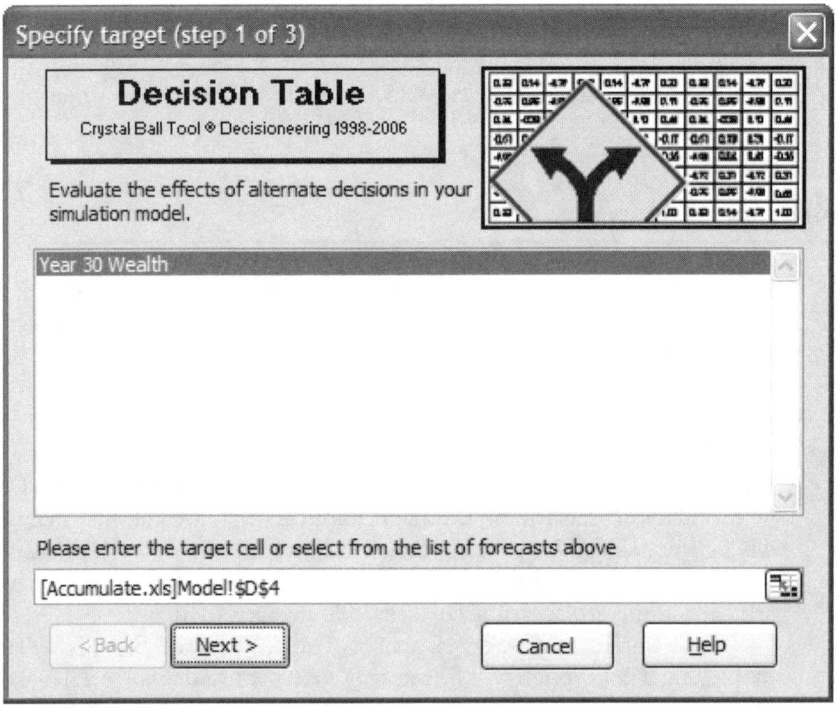

FIGURE 2.10 Step 1 in using the Decision Table tool.

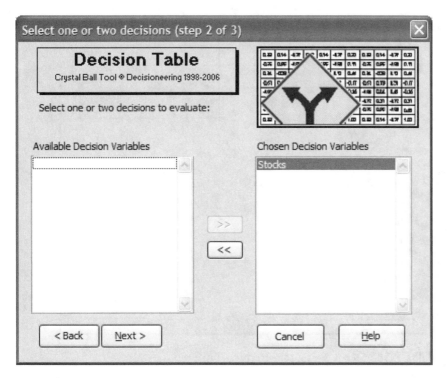

FIGURE 2.11 Step 2 in using the decision table tool.

The Specify options (step 3 of 3) dialog should look like Figure 2.12. Specify 2000 trials as shown in Figure 2.12 and click Start. Crystal Ball will run 2,000 trials for each of the nine allocations.

When Crystal Ball finishes its decision table analysis, you should see a new worksheet with nine Crystal Ball forecasts in cells B2:J2. The value in each cell is the mean of the forecast for Year 30 Wealth for the corresponding allocation to stocks that appears in Row 1 of the worksheet.

Trend Chart

Select cells B2:J2, then click Trend Chart. Your trend chart should look like that depicted in Figure 2.13, which clearly shows how the risk and expected reward increases as you increase your allocation to stocks.

The certainty bands in Figure 2.13 are centered on the median, so for each of the nine allocations listed on the horizontal axis, the 10 percent band extends from the 45th to 55th percentile, the 25 percent band extends from the 37.5th percentile to the 62.5th percentile, the 50 percent band extends from the 25th percentile to the 75th percentile, and the 90 percent band extends from the 5th to the 95th

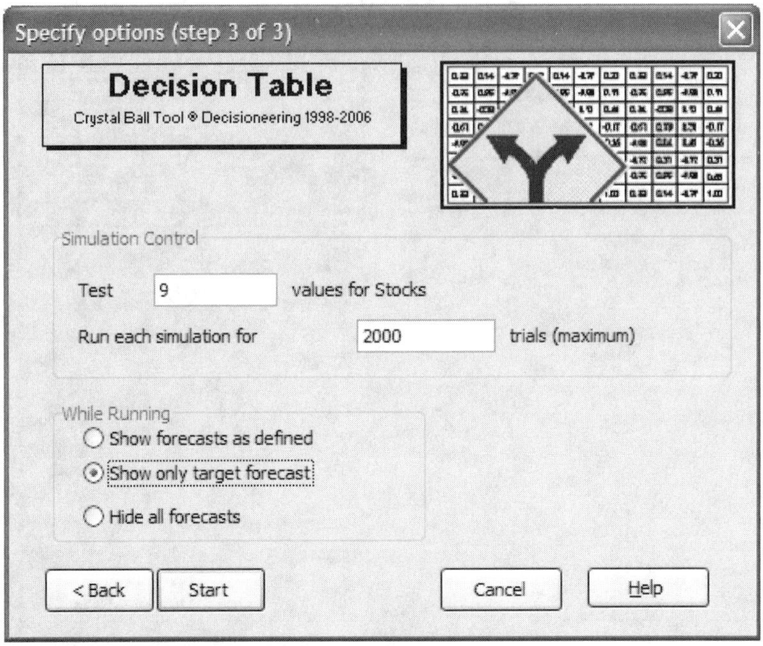

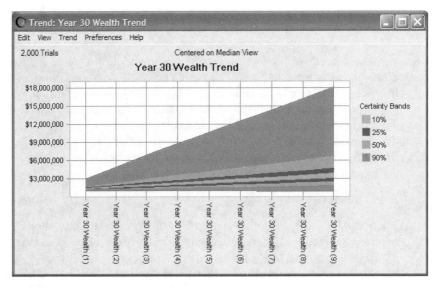

FIGURE 2.12 Step 3 in using the Decision Table tool.

FIGURE 2.13 Trend chart comparing accumulated values after 30 years of retirement savings for nine different allocations into stocks and bonds each year. Year 30 Wealth (1) represents a 10 percent allocation to stocks—the 10–90 portfolio, Year 30 Wealth (2) represents a 20 percent allocation to stocks—the 20–80 portfolio, . . . , and Year 30 Wealth (9) represents a 90 percent allocation to stocks—the 90–10 portfolio.

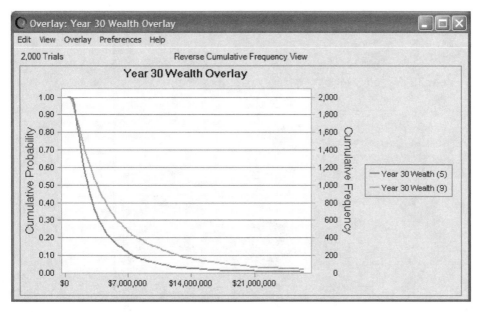

FIGURE 2.14 Overlay chart comparing accumulated value after 30 years of retirement savings for two different allocations into stocks and bonds each year. **Year 30 Wealth (5)** represents a 50 percent allocation to stocks and 50 percent allocation to bonds, and **Year 30 Wealth (9)** represents a 90 percent allocation to stocks and 10 percent allocation to bonds.

percentile of each forecast distribution. The slopes of the lines connecting each of these percentiles provide insight into the behavior of the wealth distribution as we vary the portfolio allocations to stocks and bonds.

The facts that the spread of the lines increases and that seven of the eight lines (all but the 5th percentile line) are sloped upwards indicate that greater allocation to stocks provides greater upside potential for Year 30 Wealth. The negative slope of the 5th percentile line indicates slightly greater downside risk as more of the portfolio is allocated to stocks, but for many investors this downside risk is outweighed by the much greater upside potential.

Overlay Chart

In the worksheet created by Crystal Ball's decision table analysis, select cell **F2**, then hold down the **Ctrl Key** and click on cell **J2**. Next, click on **Overlay Chart**. Use the hot keys **Ctrl-t** and **Ctrl-d** to make your chart look like that in Figure 2.14, which compares the risk profiles of a 50–50 portfolio to a 90–10 portfolio. The risk profiles are line graphs depicting the probability on the vertical axis that each portfolio yields a Year 30 Wealth greater than the corresponding monetary value on the horizontal axis.

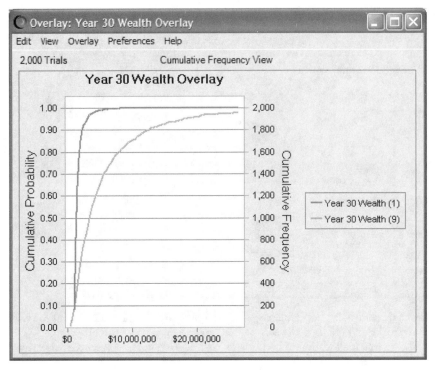

FIGURE 2.15 Overlay chart comparing accumulated value after 30 years of retirement savings for two different allocations into stocks and bonds each year. Year 30 Wealth (1) represents a 10 percent allocation to stocks and 90 percent allocation to bonds, and Year 30 Wealth (9) represents a 90 percent allocation to stocks and 10 percent allocation to bonds.

The 90–10 portfolio almost completely dominates the 50–50 portfolio in the sense that the line representing the 90–10 portfolio is above and to the right of the 50–50 line almost everywhere. For Year 30 Wealth values below about $1 million, the lines are virtually indistinguishable. While very risk-averse investors might prefer the 50–50 portfolio because it dominates the 90–10 portfolio slightly in the worst 10 percent of the cases, most investors would prefer the 90–10 portfolio's wealth distribution because of its near equivalence in the lowest 10 percent and dominance in the upper 90 percent of the potential returns.

Figure 2.15 presents information comparing the 90–10 portfolio to the 10–90 portfolio that is similar to that provided by Figure 2.14 for comparing the 50–50 portfolio to the 90–10 portfolio. However, because Figure 2.15 is a cumulative frequency chart, the near dominance of the 90–10 portfolio is manifested by the 90–10 line lying to the right and below the line for the 10–90 portfolio for Year 30 Wealth values above $1 million.

PRESENTING THE RESULTS

The example in this chapter illustrates both positive and negative aspects of simulation analysis.

On the positive side, Crystal Ball provides a clear picture of the entire distribution of results with views that can be easily selected to suit the tastes of your audience. For example, some people prefer frequency distributions, while others prefer cumulative or reverse cumulative distributions. The statistics window automatically displays most of the descriptive statistics that decision makers might be interested in seeing. The percentiles window and trend chart present views that can also be helpful for interpreting and comparing output distributions. This lets decision makers compare forecasts on a wide variety of dimensions.

A negative aspect is that output distributions can be compared on so many dimensions. Until you become accustomed to thinking about distributions of results rather than single measures such as the mean or median, trying to interpret the output can be somewhat overwhelming.

Crystal Ball gives you the ability to present the output in a wide variety of ways. Selecting the best way to communicate your results is a skill that requires some effort on your part to acquire. This book provides many examples of using Crystal Ball as a decision tool. Working through the examples and generating the output on your computer as you read will help you decide what is best for you and your clients.

CHAPTER 3

Building a Crystal Ball Model

Monte Carlo simulation is a tool for modeling uncertainty. Typically, we begin with a deterministic spreadsheet model of the situation we are analyzing, then use Crystal Ball to add stochastic assumptions to represent the most important sources of uncertainty. In the past, stochastic modeling was an endeavor best undertaken only by highly trained scientists and engineers working on mainframe computers. Crystal Ball has been developed over the years to make Monte Carlo simulation accessible to financial analysts and others using Excel on personal computer workstations rather than coding in a programming language such as C++ or FORTRAN. This chapter goes through the process of starting with a simple financial model and adding stochastic assumptions to a deterministic model in order to illustrate the basics of building Crystal Ball models.

SIMULATION MODELING PROCESS

Most analysts facing a business problem follow the typical process for stochastic modeling:

1. Develop a model that "behaves like" the real problem, with a special consideration of the assumptions—the random or probabilistic input variables.
2. Run a set of trials to learn about the behavior of the simulation model.
3. Continually modify the model until it has credibility with the decision makers.
4. Analyze the forecast (output) statistics and graphics to help make decisions about the real problem.

The analysis and decisions in step 4 often will lead you to think about new problems or variants of the old problem, in which case you should go to step 1 to develop a new model or modify the old model to reflect the variant of the old problem.

Example: AKGolf.xls

For the upcoming golf season, Alaskan Golf (AG) wishes to order a shipment of golf clubs to offer for sale in its retail stores and affiliated pro shops. It plans to

	A	B	C
1	**AKGolf.xls**		
2			
3	Variable	Name	Value
4	Clubs ordered	O	1000
5	Unit cost per club	C	$300
6	Demand during golf season	D	800
7	Sales during golf season	S_1	800
8	Initial price	P_1	$395
9	Sales at end of season	S_2	200
10	Sale Price	P_2	$195
11	Profit	Profit	$55,000

FIGURE 3.1 Deterministic spreadsheet model for Alaskan Golf purchase decision.

purchase 1,000 HeMan Stick drivers—a helium-filled club that the manufacturer promises will elevate any player's game. AG can purchase the drivers at a cost of $300 each, and plans to sell them during the golf season for $395 each. At the end of the season, all remaining HeMan Sticks will be sold for $195 to clear the shelves. AG has asked you to compute their profit if the demand for HeMan Sticks is 800 units during the season. The file AKGolf.xls shown in Figure 3.1 has a deterministic spreadsheet model for this situation. Cell C11 shows that the profit will be $55,000 from purchasing 1,000 HeMan Sticks at the beginning of the golf season, selling 800 at $395 each during the season, and selling the remaining 200 at $195 each during the end-of-year sale to clear the shelves.

This spreadsheet can be used to do a "what-if" analysis, where the demand for drivers in C6 is changed to various values to see the effects on profit in C11. This is informative but cumbersome, as the analyst must keep track of the input values for C6 and the corresponding output values in C11, then somehow analyze the results for a rudimentary form of sensitivity analysis. Monte Carlo simulation with Crystal Ball can be regarded as a sophisticated form of "what-if" analysis, as the program will keep track of all these changes during its run. Further, with Crystal Ball it is easy to change more than one input at a time, as we will see in the next section.

DEFINING CRYSTAL BALL ASSUMPTIONS

A stochastic input cell in Crystal Ball is called an *assumption*, while an output cell is called a *forecast*. In this section, we will add assumptions and a forecast to the deterministic model in AKGolf.xls to create a stochastic model.

TABLE 3.1 Stochastic assumptions to be added to AKGolf.xls.

Assumption	Cell	Distribution
Demand during Golf Season	C6	Triangular(500,800,1500)
Initial Price	C8	Uniform(355,395)
Sale Price	C10	Uniform(175,195)

Defining Assumptions

Now let's take into account two sources of uncertainty: (1) the demand for drivers is stochastic, and (2) the retail clerks and golf professionals who sell the clubs at retail are allowed to give consumers slight discounts on the listed prices.

For the demand distribution, we assume that the lowest possible demand during the season is 500 drivers, the largest possible demand is 1,500 drivers, and the most likely demand is 800 drivers. These three parameters are used to define a triangular probability distribution in the manner shown below. To keep things simple, we will assume that all drivers left unsold at the end of the season will be sold during the end-of-year sale at the sale price in Cell C10.

The golf professionals are allowed to give their customers discounts of up to 10 percent on both the initial prices and the sales prices, which reduce their commissions proportionately. To model this discounting, we assume that the average initial price of drivers sold during the season is uniform with a minimum of $355, and a maximum of $395. The average end-of-season sales price is uniform with a minimum of $175, and a maximum of $195. Table 3.1 summarizes the Crystal Ball assumptions to be added to the model in file AKGolf.xls.

Follow the steps below to define the assumptions in Cell C6:

1. Select cell C6, then click on Cell→Define Assumption.
2. Choose the triangular distribution from the distribution gallery (Figure 3.2).
3. Enter the parameter values and a name for the assumption. By default, CB will look first for an Excel-defined named, then in the cells at immediate left and just above for an assumption name. Figure 3.3 shows where to enter the parameter values.
4. Click Enter to see a depiction of the defined distribution. Your distribution should look like that shown in Figure 3.3. Press OK to return to the spreadsheet. It is OK to press OK without seeing the depiction, but pressing Enter first is good practice to check that the entered distribution is what you intend to use.

Cell C6 will turn green to indicate that an assumption cell is defined there. By following the steps above for cell C6, it should be straightforward for you to define the stochastic assumptions listed for cells C8 and C10 in Table 3.1.

If an error occurs in step 1, try entering an arbitrary numerical value in the cell first—Crystal Ball needs to recognize the location as a number cell. In Crystal Ball 7.2 and higher, when you attempt to define an assumption in an empty cell, a value of 0

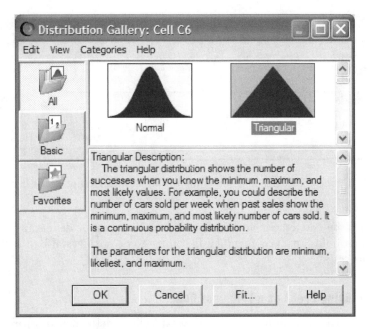

FIGURE 3.2 Distribution gallery showing the triangular and normal distributions. To see all of Crystal Ball's distributions, click on All at upper left and use the upper set of scroll bars to move through the distributions.

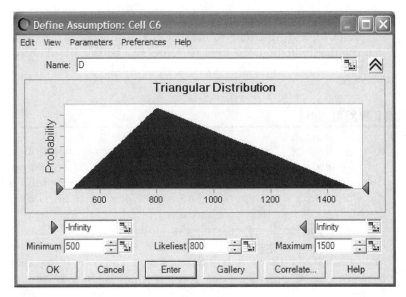

FIGURE 3.3 Defining the demand assumption for the Alaskan Golf purchase decision. Note that both the Name: and the Units: can be specified with a cell reference.

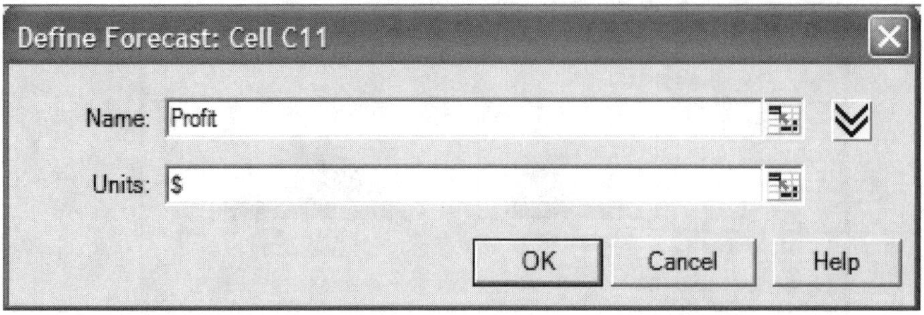

FIGURE 3.4 Defining the demand assumption for the Alaskan Golf purchase decision.

will be entered for you automatically. You cannot define an assumption in a cell that holds an Excel formula. If you try to do so, Crystal Ball will give you an error message.

Defining Profit as a Forecast Cell

A stochastic output cell in a Crystal Ball model is called a *forecast cell*. To define cell C11 as a forecast cell, follow the steps below:

1. Select cell C11, then click on Cell→Define Forecast.
2. Enter the name and units (optional) in the text boxes (Figure 3.4).
3. Click OK.

Cell C11 will turn blue to indicate that a forecast cell is defined there. When you run the simulation, the forecast values will be calculated and collected for each run, then displayed graphically in a forecast window.

RUNNING CRYSTAL BALL

It is usually a good idea at this point to run just one iteration of the simulation to make sure that the calculations appear to be correct. To run one iteration, click Run→Single Step, then make sure that the model correctly reflects the new values showing in the assumption cells. This is good practice to help debug the logic of the model.

When you are ready to run the model, click Run→Run, or just click the Run icon on the Crystal Ball toolbar. The forecast window should appear automatically. When the simulation stops you can use it to analyze the output as shown in Chapter 2. Your forecast chart should resemble that shown in Figure 3.5.

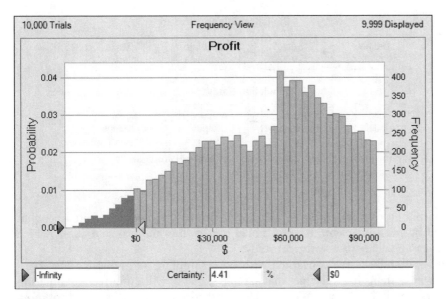

FIGURE 3.5 Profit forecast for the Alaskan Golf purchase decision. Note that the probability of negative profit is less than 5 percent.

SOURCES OF ERROR

Monte Carlo simulation modeling is similar to statistical sampling in many respects, but differs in the type of up-front creativity required by the analyst. To compare and contrast statistical sampling and simulation modeling, Figure 3.6 shows a stylized view of steps taken in conducting a statistical study and a simulation study.

In a statistical study, the analyst defines a population to study, specifies numerical measures to be obtained, and develops a sampling frame—a list of all potential population elements that could potentially be included in a sample. The statistical analyst then randomly selects a sample of elements from the sampling frame and calculates sample statistics such as the mean and standard deviation. These sample statistics are then used to make inferences about the population using procedures such as hypothesis tests or confidence intervals. Virtually every introductory statistics textbook covers these inferential statistical procedures. Note that no matter what the stated population of interest, it is the sampling frame that actually defines the population about which inferences can be made in a statistical study.

In a simulation study, the analyst builds a model to represent the business problem of interest, runs the simulation, analyzes the output, then makes a decision—which can sometimes be simply to improve the model and rerunning several times before making a decision about the business problem. Crystal Ball is designed to run the simulations and provide graphical and numerical summaries

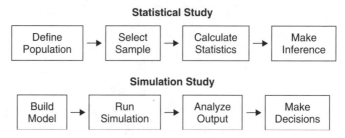

FIGURE 3.6 Stylized depictions of a statistical study and a simulation study.

of the output (forecasts) automatically and flawlessly. However, no matter what the stated business problem, it is the model that defines the problem about which decisions can be made in a statistical study.

Statistical analysts are concerned with both sampling and nonsampling error. *Sampling error* stems from the fact that sample statistics will differ from population parameters simply by chance. Well-established theory tells us all we need to know to control sampling error in a well-executed statistical study. *Nonsampling error* is more insidious, coming about from faulty methods of data collection, incorrect sampling methods, errors in recording data, or erroneous entry of the data into the computer. It is difficult or perhaps even impossible to find and eliminate all sources of nonsampling error, although many professional statistical consulting firms have devised methods to eliminate most sources of nonsampling error based on long experience.

Crystal Ball is well debugged and tested, so there is no worry about the accuracy of its algorithms. By far, the biggest concern in a simulation study is model error. *Model error* is present because any model is an abstraction that cannot take into account every detail and nuance of the real problem. By definition, a model contains only the stochastic relationships that are most germane to the problem. All models are wrong to the extent that they omit minor details. Good models are useful if they include enough of the major details to help a decision maker reach a properly informed decision.

It is easy to create a bad model. *Model risk* is the risk of using the wrong model, implementing the correct model incorrectly, failing to assess the stochastic inputs adequately, or omitting important stochastic inputs that should be included. Good model building is a craft that requires some experience to develop. Fortunately, this craft can be learned by studying the models in this book and those available from other sources, such as the Web site **www.crystalball.com**.

Simulation error is caused by the fact that simulation is a sampling experiment. This is the same as sampling error in a statistical study. Simulation error should not be ignored, but is usually a lesser problem than model error because it is relatively inexpensive to reduce simulation error by simply increasing the number of trials.

It can also be measured and controlled through the variance reduction techniques described in Appendix C.

CONTROLLING MODEL ERROR

Good models have three basic requirements:

1. *Verification.* Ensuring that the values and formulas are entered correctly in Excel.
2. *Validation.* Assuring that your model faithfully mimics the actual situation or system.
3. *Credibility.* Acceptance of your verified and validated model for use by decision makers.

Verification should be done at every step along the way. The Excel auditing tools can be very useful for this purpose, and you should strive to make your models as readable as possible so that you and others can understand the logic of the model when you come back to it after setting it aside for some time.

Validation is done using a verified model. A validated model will give outputs that seem to be reasonable to a subject matter expert. Proper validation of a model is part of the craft of modeling that takes some experience to learn.

A credible model is obtained when a verified and validated model is accepted for use by the decision makers. Credibility is earned over time, and it is usually best to keep decision makers informed about your progress in building the model, and to solicit their input at several points during the model building process. This will help get "buy-in" from them when it comes to put the model to work.

This chapter describes the basic steps involved in building models. As you go through the models in the rest of the book, you will begin to get a feel for how best to go about creating models for your own purposes. The next chapter takes a more in-depth view of selecting and specifying Crystal Ball assumptions.

CHAPTER 4

Selecting Crystal Ball Assumptions

T his chapter reviews basic concepts of probability and statistics using graphics from Crystal Ball's distribution gallery, a portion of which is shown in Figure 4.1. If you have not had a class in basic probability and statistics at some point in your life or you need a refresher on these topics, consult a business statistics textbook such as Mann (2007). This chapter is intended to show the basics of how to specify probability distributions to be used as stochastic assumptions with Crystal Ball.

Version 7.2 of Crystal Ball has 20 distributions from which to choose when defining assumptions. To see them, click the All button at the upper left of the distribution gallery. Six basic distributions are described here along with the binomial distribution.

CRYSTAL BALL'S BASIC DISTRIBUTIONS

Yes-No

Probabilists named the Bernoulli distribution in honor of the mathematician who showed analytically around 1700 the truth of the intuitive notion that when a fair coin is tossed repeatedly, it will come up heads about 50 percent of the time. It is perhaps the simplest of all probability distributions. The random variable Y has the Bernoulli distribution if it can take only one of two possible values, $y = 0$ or $y = 1$. The value $y = 1$ is called a "success," and $y = 0$ is called a "failure" in probability parlance. In Crystal Ball, the Bernoulli distribution is known as the yes-no distribution.

Crystal Ball calls $y = 1$ "yes" and $y = 0$ "no" because these terms often make sense in a modeling context. For example, Figure 4.2 shows Crystal Ball's yes-no distribution for $\Pr(\text{yes}) = 0.5$, where y represents the number of heads obtained in one toss of a fair coin. "Yes" means a head was tossed so $y = 1$, while "no" means a tail was tossed so $y = 0$.

Now consider the type of situation that drew Bernoulli's interest. The spreadsheet segment in Figure 4.3 shows a simple model to be used for finding the number of heads observed when tossing a fair coin five times. Each of the assumptions in cells B3:B7 are yes-no distributions with $\Pr(\text{yes}) = 0.5$, so each assumption cell will

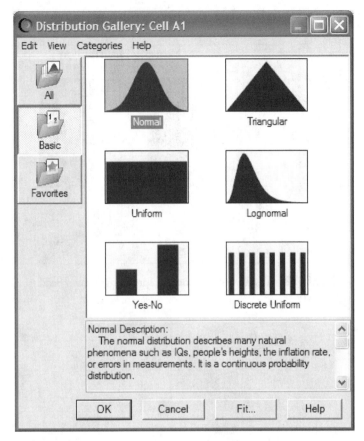

FIGURE 4.1 The basic distributions listed in Crystal Ball's distribution gallery.

contain 1 on approximately 50 percent of the trials and 0 on the remaining trials. Each assumption cell's value is generated independently of the other cells' values. The forecast in cell **B8** has the formula =SUM(B3:B7).

Of course, we need not use simulation to model this situation because it is easy to determine the forecast distribution analytically. However, simulating a situation for which we know the analytical solution can be comforting. If we get results with simulation that are in accord with the analytical results, then we have some assurance that simulation will provide good approximate answers to questions regarding situations where analytical results are difficult or impossible to attain.

For a simple example of finding an analytical result, consider the spreadsheet model **FiveTosses.xls** shown in Figure 4.4, which shows each of the $2^5 = 32$ combinations of 0s and 1s that can occur on five tosses of a fair coin. Each combination is equally likely to occur. The number of heads in each combination is

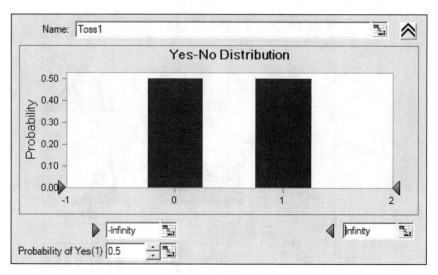

FIGURE 4.2   Yes-no distribution to represent getting a head ($y = 1$) on one toss of a fair coin.

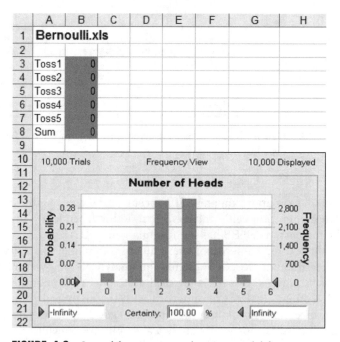

FIGURE 4.3   Spreadsheet segment showing model for determining the distribution of five flips of a fair coin. Cells B3:B7 are yes-no(0.5) assumptions, and their sum in cell B8 is a Crystal Ball forecast.

	A	B	C	D	E	F	G	H	I
1	FiveTosses.xls			Toss1	Toss2	Toss3	Toss4	Toss5	Sum
2				0	0	0	0	0	0
3	Toss1	0		0	0	0	0	1	1
4	Toss2	0		0	0	0	1	0	1
5	Toss3	0		0	0	0	1	1	2
6	Toss4	0		0	0	1	0	0	1
7	Toss5	0		0	0	1	0	1	2
8	Sum	0		0	0	1	1	0	2
9				0	0	1	1	1	3
10	#Heads	Freq.	Prob.	0	1	0	0	0	1
11	0	1	0.03125	0	1	0	0	1	2
12	1	5	0.15625	0	1	0	1	0	2
13	2	10	0.3125	0	1	0	1	1	3
14	3	10	0.3125	0	1	1	0	0	2
15	4	5	0.15625	0	1	1	0	1	3
16	5	1	0.03125	0	1	1	1	0	3
17		32	1.00	0	1	1	1	1	4
18				1	0	0	0	0	1
19				1	0	0	0	1	2
20				1	0	0	1	0	2
21				1	0	0	1	1	3
22				1	0	1	0	0	2
23				1	0	1	0	1	3
24				1	0	1	1	0	3
25				1	0	1	1	1	4
26				1	1	0	0	0	2
27				1	1	0	0	1	3
28				1	1	0	1	0	3
29				1	1	0	1	1	4
30				1	1	1	0	0	3
31				1	1	1	0	1	4
32				1	1	1	1	0	4
33				1	1	1	1	1	5

FIGURE 4.4 Spreadsheet segment showing model for determining the distribution of five flips of a fair coin. Cells **B3:B7** are yes-no(0.5) assumptions, and their sum in cell **B8** is a Crystal Ball forecast.

found by summing across the row for each combination. So to find the probability of each of the possible numbers of heads, we simply divide the frequency of occurrence of {0, 1, 2, 3, 4, 5} by 32, the total number of combinations to get the probabilities listed in cells **C11:C16** in Figure 4.4. These are the probabilities associated with the binomial(0.5,5) distribution used below.

Binomial

While not included in Crystal Ball's distribution gallery list of basic assumptions, the binomial distribution is so closely related to the yes-no distribution that it is included here and used later in the chapter. The binomial(p,n) is the distribution of

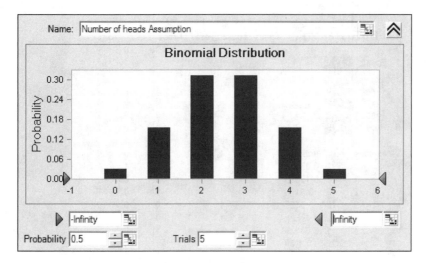

FIGURE 4.5 Binomial(0.5,5) distribution to represent the number of heads on five tosses of a fair coin.

the sum of a fixed number, n, of Bernoulli trials that all have the same probability of success, p. Thus, the problem of determining the distribution of the number of heads in five tosses of a fair coin can be solved by using one Crystal Ball assumption—the binomial(0.5,5) assumption shown in Figure 4.5.

Figure 4.6 depicts a model that gives the same results as that in Figure 4.3 by using Crystal Ball to simply generate the number of heads in five tosses from the distribution in Figure 4.5, and displaying the results in the forecast defined in cell **B4** with the Excel formula =B3. The forecast distribution in Figure 4.6 looks almost identical to the forecast distribution in Figure 4.3, because the differences are due only to sampling error.

Discrete Uniform

The discrete uniform(L,H) distribution assigns equal probability to the set of integers between L and H, inclusive. For $L = 1$ and $H = 6$, it is the probability distribution representing the number of spots showing on the top face of a fair die rolled randomly. To illustrate the use of the discrete uniform, consider a problem with which Sir Isaac Newton dealt in the seventeenth century (Anděl 2001).

The problem can be stated as follows:

- Player A has 6 fair dice and wins if he rolls at least one ace (one spot showing on the top face of a die).
- Player B has 12 fair dice and wins if he rolls at least two aces.
- Player C has 18 fair dice and wins if he rolls at least three aces.

Which player has the greatest chance of winning?

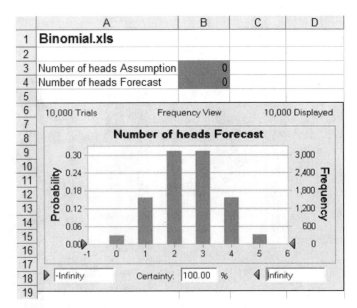

FIGURE 4.6 Simple model to represent the number of heads observed on five tosses of a fair coin. Cell **B3** is a binomial(0.5,5) assumption. Cell **B4** is a forecast cell with the formula =B3.

Most seventeenth-century gamblers felt that because the ratio of rolls to aces (6:1) is the same for each player, the probability of winning should also be the same for each player. Newton's analytical solution to this problem uses the Binomial distribution and is now considered trivial by probabilists. However, we will use simulation to find the approximate values of each player winning and compare the results to Newton's analytical solution. Figure 4.7 shows a spreadsheet model of the situation.

The Newton.xls model uses 6 discrete uniform assumptions in cells **B5:B10**, 12 discrete uniform assumptions in cells **E5:E16**, and 18 discrete uniform assumptions in cells **H5:H22** to simulate the result of rolling each die. All 36 of these assumptions resemble the distribution shown in Figure 4.8 for cell **B5**, which is discrete uniform on the integers {1, 2, 3, 4, 5, 6}. Each of the 36 discrete uniform distributions generates observations independently of the others during the simulation runs.

In the cell to the immediate right of each die's result in Newton.xls is an Excel IF function that checks to see whether the result is a ace or not. For example, cell **C5** contains the command =IF(B5=1,1,0), which puts a 1 in cell **C5** if the assumption in B5 delivers a 1 during any iteration, and a 0 otherwise. This is an example of an indicator variable, which is a useful modeling concept that we use often throughout this book. Cells **C11**, **F17**, and **I23** find the sums of the indicator variables in the cells directly above them, **C5:C10**, **F5:F16**, and **I5:I22**, respectively. The cells

	A	B	C	D	E	F	G	H	I
1	**Newton.xls**								
2									
3		Player A			Player B			Player C	
4	Die	Result	Ace?	Die	Result	Ace?	Die	Result	Ace?
5	1	3	0	1	3	0	1	3	0
6	2	3	0	2	3	0	2	3	0
7	3	3	0	3	3	0	3	3	0
8	4	3	0	4	3	0	4	3	0
9	5	3	0	5	3	0	5	3	0
10	6	3	0	6	3	0	6	3	0
11	Aces for A		0	7	3	0	7	3	0
12	A Wins?		0	8	3	0	8	3	0
13		Mean	0.6628	9	3	0	9	3	0
14				10	3	0	10	3	0
15				11	3	0	11	3	0
16				12	3	0	12	3	0
17				Aces for B		0	13	3	0
18				B Wins?		0	14	3	0
19					Mean	0.6205	15	3	0
20							16	3	0
21							17	3	0
22							18	3	0
23							Aces for C		0
24							C Wins?		0
25								Mean	0.5933

FIGURE 4.7 Spreadsheet segment showing model for Newton's dice problem.

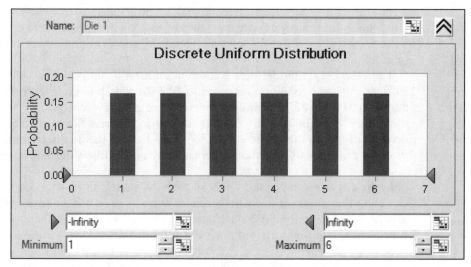

FIGURE 4.8 Discrete uniform distribution used for modeling the roll of one die for Newton's dice problem.

TABLE 4.1 Table of values for Index in the Crystal Ball function =CB.GetForeStatFN(Range,Index) and the corresponding forecast statistic. See Chapter 2 for a definition of each statistic.

Index	Statistic
1	Trials
2	Mean
3	Median
4	Mode
5	Standard deviation
6	Variance
7	Skewness
8	Kurtosis
9	Coefficient of variability
10	Minimum
11	Maximum
12	Range
13	Mean standard error

labeled A Wins? B Wins? and C Wins? are indicator variables to detect when the number of aces for A is greater than or equal to one, the number of aces for B is greater than or equal to two, and the number of aces for C is greater than or equal to three, respectively. These cells, C12, F18, and I24 are defined as Crystal Ball forecast cells.

Finally, cells C13, F19, and I25 use the =CB.GetForeStatFN(Range,Index) command to find the mean of each forecast. The arguments for this command are Range, which is simply a reference to a Crystal Ball forecast cell, and Index, which is an integer between 1 and 13. Specify the integer for Index that corresponds to the desired forecast statistic listed in Table 4.1. For example, we use Index = 2 in Newton.xls because we want the means of the indicator variables in cells C13, F19, and I25.

The resulting means after 10,000 runs are shown in cells C13, F19, and I25 to be 0.6628, 0.6205, and 0.5933. These values can be compared to the known probabilities obtained with the binomial distribution: 0.6651, 0.6187, and 0.5973, respectively. Thus, the solution to the problem is that Player A has the greatest chance of winning, followed by Player B, then by Player C. In a later chapter, we will see how to determine the precision of the estimates from simulation models.

Uniform

The uniform distribution is the simplest of all *continuous* probability distributions. It has only two parameters, the minimum and maximum values. It produces any continuous value between the minimum and maximum with equal likelihood. The

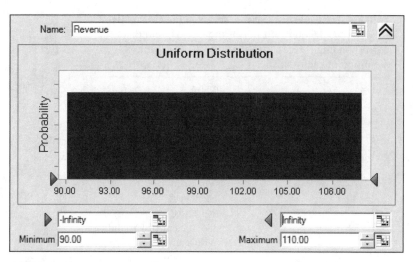

FIGURE 4.9 Continuous uniform distribution used for modeling a firm's revenue, where the minimum possible value is $90, the maximum is $110, and all values in between are equally likely to occur.

uniform distribution depicted in the dialog window shown in Figure 4.9 models a situation where a firm's revenues range from $90 to $110, and all values in between are equally likely to occur.

In dialog windows for its discrete distributions, Crystal Ball displays the possible values of the random variable on the horizontal axis and the associated probabilities on the vertical axis, as in Figure 4.8. For continuous distributions such as the uniform, Crystal Ball does not display values on the vertical axis because probability for continuous random variables is associated with intervals on the horizontal axis and not with single values. Because they represent probabilities for intervals rather than single numbers, the plots for continuous distributions are graphs of probability density functions, or simply PDFs.

Use the uniform distribution when you know the minimum and the maximum values, but not a most likely value. The uniform distribution is completely specified by its two parameters, Minimum and Maximum. Because all values between Minimum and Maximum are equally likely to occur, its PDF has a uniform height over that range.

The uniform is sometimes called the "distribution of maximum ignorance," and should be replaced with a better estimate if one becomes available in later stages of the modeling process. However, there are some situations where the uniform may be the best distribution; for example, to model (1) where a leak might occur on a pipeline, or (2) time to failure of a component after a "burn-in" period, but before the required time to replace it.

The spreadsheet segment in **Uniform.xls** shown in Figure 4.10 models the situation where a firm's revenues follow the uniform(90,110) distribution and

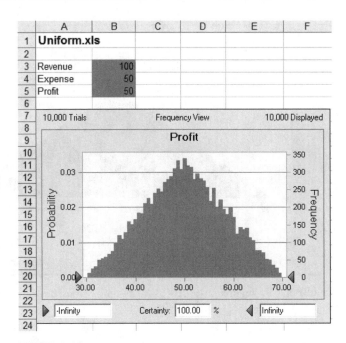

FIGURE 4.10 Spreadsheet model for situation where a firm's revenues are modeled as uniform(90,110), and where expenses are modeled as uniform(40,60). The resulting distribution of profit is triangular(30,50,70).

expenses follow the uniform(40,60) distribution. The difference, profit, is defined as a forecast in cell **B5**, and a forecast chart for it has been copied and pasted onto the spreadsheet. It can be shown with the mathematical method of convolution (e.g., see Vose 2000) that the theoretical distribution of profit in this example is triangular(30,50,70), which is verified by the forecast chart in Figure 4.10.

Triangular

The triangular distribution is appropriate for use when you have little or no data available, but you know the minimum, maximum, and most likely values of a random variable. The triangular distribution is completely specified by its three parameters, **Minimum**, **Likeliest**, and **Maximum**. These three values are sufficient to determine the triangular shape shown in the icon. Of course, **Minimum** must be less than **Maximum**, and **Likeliest** must be in between (or equal to one of) these values. Figure 4.11 depicts a triangular(90,100,110) distribution.

The spreadsheet segment in **Triangular.xls** shown in Figure 4.12 models the situation where a firm's revenues follow the triangular(90,100,110) distribution and expenses follow the triangular(45,50,55) distribution. The difference, profit, is

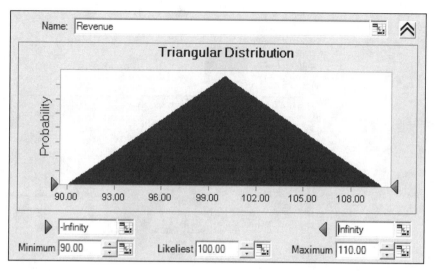

FIGURE 4.11 Triangular(90,100,110) assumption used for modeling revenue in Figure 4.12.

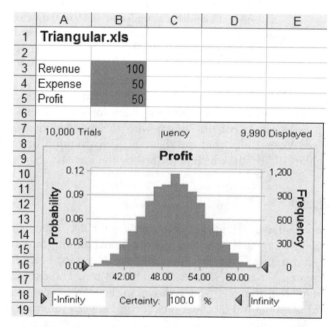

FIGURE 4.12 Spreadsheet model for situation where a firm's revenues are modeled as triangular(90,100,110), and where expenses are modeled as triangular(45,50,55).

defined as a forecast in cell **B5**, and a forecast chart for it has been copied and pasted onto the spreadsheet. Note how the distribution for profit has a bell shape similar to the normal distribution to be discussed next.

Because it is often used as a first estimate of the distribution, the triangular distribution is applicable to many situations. When using it, you may wish to consult with a subject matter expert (e.g., an engineer, cost analyst, or project manager) to determine which values to use for the parameters.

Compared to the normal distribution, the triangular distribution over-emphasizes the tails and underemphasizes the middle values. Always try to replace Triangular distributions with better estimates if they become available in later stages of the modeling process.

Normal

The normal distribution is perhaps the most widely known continuous probability distribution because it describes many natural phenomena. It has the familiar bell shape that Crystal Ball uses for its Define Assumption icon.

The normal distribution is specified by its two parameters, the **Mean** and **Std Dev** (standard deviation). Because it is symmetrical, the mean is equal to the median (50th percentile). The mode (point on the horizontal axis at which the PDF is highest) is also equal to the mean and median. Values simulated from the normal distribution are more likely to be close to the mean than far away. Figure 4.13 shows a normal distribution with mean 10 percent and standard deviation 5 percent.

Some examples of what might be modeled by a normal distribution include (1) the rate of return on stocks, (2) the rate of inflation, (3) sales revenue, (4) heights of

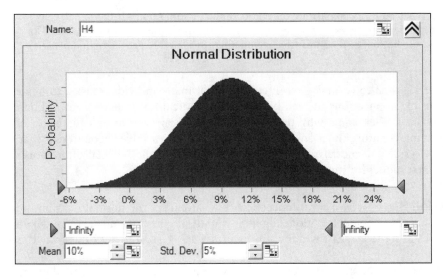

FIGURE 4.13 Normal(10%, 5%) distribution.

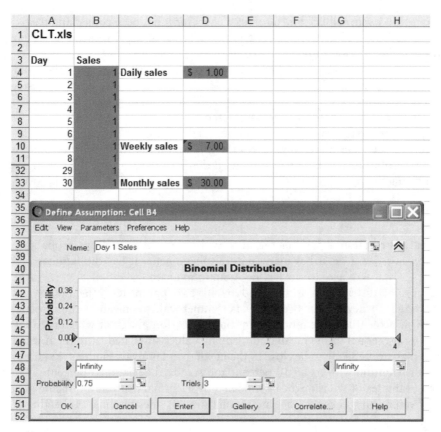

FIGURE 4.14 File CLT.xls built to demonstrate the effects of the Central Limit Theorem. Each day's sales is generated independently from one of the binomial(0.75,3) assumptions in Cells **B4:B33**. This assumption appears at the bottom of the spreadsheet. Note that rows 12 through 31 are hidden.

people, or (5) time to complete work composed of many individual tasks, to name a few possible applications. A well-known mathematical result—the Central Limit Theorem (CLT)—explains why the normal distribution does an adequate job of describing many natural phenomena. Not every random variable encountered when building Crystal Ball models is normally distributed, but the Normal often works well as a first model for many stochastic assumptions.

Central Limit Effect The central limit effect is what causes the normal distribution to be a suitable choice for modeling many natural phenomena. The model in Figure 4.14 and the forecast windows in Figures 4.15, 4.16, and 4.17 illustrate this effect.

The file **CLT.xls** generates daily sales with a binomial(0.75,3) distribution, a skewed distribution that is far from normally distributed, as can be seen in

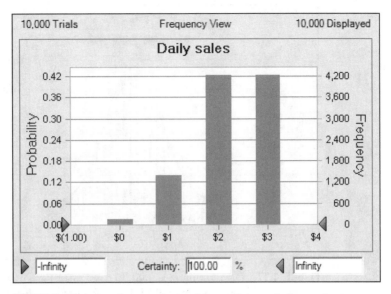

FIGURE 4.15 Distribution of sales for one day. Each day's sales is generated from the binomial(0.75,3) distribution, and this forecast chart depicts that distribution.

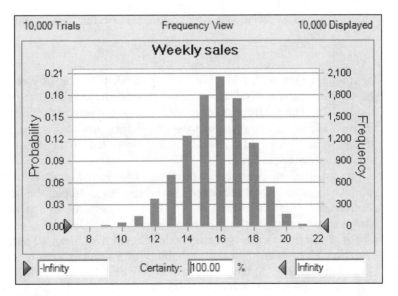

FIGURE 4.16 Distribution of sum of seven days' sales. Each day's sales is generated from the binomial(0.75,3) distribution. This forecast chart shows how the distribution of weekly sales is bell-shaped, but not quite a normal distribution.

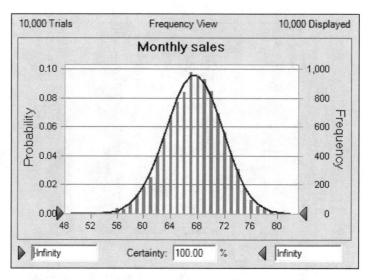

FIGURE 4.17 Distribution of sum of 30 days' sales. Each day's sales is generated from the binomial(0.75,3) distribution. This forecast chart shows how the distribution of monthly sales is close to normal because of the central limit effect. The curve superimposed on the histogram is the PDF for the normal distribution with mean and standard deviation parameters that are equal to the sample mean and standard deviation statistics calculated from the 10,000 simulated values.

Figure 4.15. However, when we look at the distribution of weekly sales, which is the sum of seven days' sales, we see the mound-shaped distribution that is shown in Figure 4.16. The distribution of monthly sales, the sum of 30 days' sales depicted in Figure 4.17, very much resembles the bell-shaped probability density function (PDF) of the normal distribution, which is superimposed on the frequency chart of the forecast values for comparison.

In financial modeling, the random variables of interest often are measures produced as sums of other random variables. For example, the normal distribution is often used to model rates of return. This makes it easy to analyze risks associated with a single period without using Crystal Ball. For example, if we know that the rate of return on Stock A is normally distributed with mean 10 percent and standard deviation 15 percent, then the probability of a negative return is 0.2525. This can be seen in Figure 4.18, where the probability of a negative return is found in cell **B5** with the command =NORMDIST(0,B3,B4,TRUE). The file also uses Crystal Ball with 10,000 iterations find an approximate value of 25.23 percent for this probability.

Mixture of Normals   Sometimes you may be interested in modeling a situation where a stochastic input is a mixture of two distributions. For example, suppose you

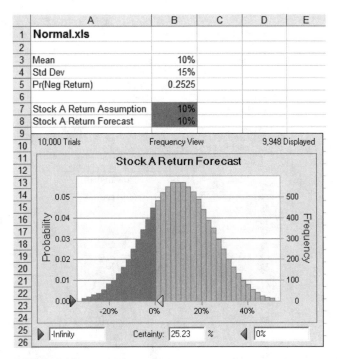

FIGURE 4.18 This file uses Excel's NORMDIST distribution function and Crystal Ball to find the probability that the rate of return is negative for a stock with mean return of 10 percent and standard deviation of 15 percent.

are interested in simulating stock rates of return for a market in which one of two regimes will prevail: Regime 1, where monthly rates of returns are normally distributed with mean $\mu = 1$ percent and standard deviation $\sigma = 1$ percent, and Regime 2, where monthly rates of returns are normally distributed with mean $\mu = 1$ percent and standard deviation $\sigma = 3$ percent. The market is in Regime 1 on 80 percent of the months and in Regime 2 on 20 percent of the months. See Figure 4.19 and the file **Mixture Model.xls**.

In the mixture model simulation depicted in Figure 4.19, a yes-no assumption is used in cell **A9** to generate values of either 0 or 1. The prevailing regime is determined from the yes-no assumption with the formula =2-A9. Thus, when the yes-no assumption cell is 1, cell **B9** will indicate Regime 1, and when the yes-no assumption is 0, cell **B9** will indicate Regime 2. Because a value of 1 is generated on about 80 percent of the trials as shown in cell **B4**, Regime 1 prevails about 80 percent of the time and Regime 2 prevails on the rest of the trials. The normally distributed rate of return is generated in cell **E9** from an assumption whose parameters depend on the prevailing regime. The total return in cell **A11** is mound-shaped but has heavier tails than a normal distribution.

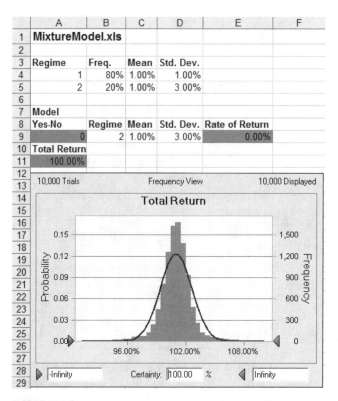

FIGURE 4.19 Mixture model for generating rates of return on a stock under two different regimes. The forecast window pasted at the bottom of the spreadsheet has the PDF of a normal distribution superimposed on it to show how the mixture of two normal distributions is mound-shaped but has a higher peak and heavier tails than a single normal distribution with mean and standard deviation parameters that are equal to the sample mean and standard deviation statistics calculated from the 10,000 simulated values.

Lognormal

Unlike the normal distribution, the lognormal distribution is bounded on the left by zero; however, it is unbounded on the right just as the normal distribution. This makes it useful for situations where values are positively skewed and cannot be negative, such as the total return on stock when the stockholder's potential loss is limited to the amount he or she has invested, or for sales of a product, which cannot be negative.

The lognormal distribution takes its name from the fact that it represents a random variable whose natural logarithm follows the normal distribution. Like the

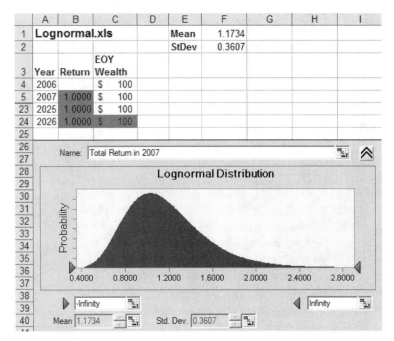

FIGURE 4.20 Model of cumulative effect of growth of $100 over a 20-year period where each year's return is a lognormally distributed random variable with mean 1.1734 and standard deviation 0.3607 in cells E1 and E2, respectively. Note that rows 6 through 22 are hidden.

normal distribution, it has two parameters, **Mean** and **Std. Dev.** File **Lognormal.xls** in Figure 4.20 has a model where each year's return is a lognormally distributed random variable with mean 1.1734 and standard deviation 0.3607 in cells **F1** and **F2**, respectively. (Notice that if you click in the **Mean** field you will see that the mean is defined as an absolute reference **$F$1**. This facilitates copying and pasting Crystal Ball data from one assumption cell to another. The **Std. Dev.** is defined in the same way, which you can verify by clicking in that field.) The model generates annual total returns independently each year from the same lognormal distribution, and the forecast in cell **C24** shows the potential distribution of wealth at the end of Year 2026. This distribution appears in Figure 4.21.

Many variables in financial modeling are suitable for use of the lognormal distribution; for example, stock or real estate prices, critical pharmaceutical doses, salaries in a company, amount of oil in a reservoir, or incubation time for an infectious disease. This comes about from the central limit effect where random variables arise as products of other variables. Products can be found as sums of logarithms, so the CLT implies that the sum of the logarithms will be normal. If the logarithm of a random variable is normally distributed, then the variable is lognormally distributed.

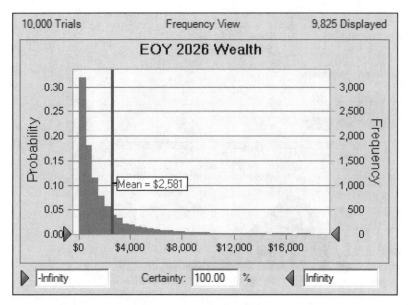

FIGURE 4.21   Forecast window from model shown in Figure 4.20 of cumulative effect of growth of $100 over a 20-year period where each year's return is a lognormally distributed random variable with mean 1.1734 and standard deviation 0.3607 in cells **F1** and **F2**, respectively.

USING HISTORICAL DATA TO CHOOSE DISTRIBUTIONS

In the Lognormal.xls model, we used historical data to estimate the mean and standard deviation for future returns. These data are located on the **Data** worksheet of the Lognormal.xls file. If you have historical data on an input variable, there are at least two different methods for using them in a Crystal Ball model: (1) direct sampling, and (2) sampling from a fitted distribution.

Direct Sampling

This method uses the data values directly in the simulation. For example, we can calculate the historical annual returns on a stock and use them for projecting future returns. This is illustrated in the file DirectSampling.xls shown in Figure 4.22, which has historical total returns for small cap stocks for each year between 1926 and 2002 inclusive.

The assumptions in cells **B5:B23** are identical, but generate independent observations from a Discrete Uniform distribution on the integers {1926, 1927, ... , 2002}. These integers correspond to the rows of the array in cells **A2:B80** on the **Data** worksheet, which are used with Excel lookup commands in Cells **C5:C23** on

	A	B	C	D
1	**Direct Sampling.xls**			
2				
3	Year	Sampled Year	Total Return	EOY Wealth
4	2006			$ 100
5	2007	1940	0.915	$ 92
6	2008	1933	2.653	$ 243
7	2009	1938	1.287	$ 313
8	2010	1976	1.561	$ 488
9	2011	1948	0.959	$ 468
10	2012	2002	0.826	$ 386
11	2013	1941	0.890	$ 344
12	2014	1932	1.028	$ 353
13	2015	1968	1.433	$ 506
14	2016	1962	0.859	$ 434
15	2017	1968	1.433	$ 623
16	2018	1937	0.446	$ 278
17	2019	1955	1.211	$ 337
18	2020	1937	0.446	$ 150
19	2021	1970	0.830	$ 125
20	2022	1946	0.878	$ 110
21	2023	1929	0.489	$ 54
22	2024	1954	1.629	$ 87
23	2025	1979	1.437	$ 125

FIGURE 4.22 Crystal Ball model to demonstrate how to use direct sampling of historical data for predicting future returns. Each of cells **B5:B23** has a discrete uniform(1926,2002) distribution representing the years of the return data in a separate worksheet. Each time a year is selected randomly in column **B**, the corresponding return is placed in the same row of column **C**.

the **Model** worksheet. For instance, cell **C5** has the command

=VLOOKUP(B5,Data!$A$2:$B$78,2,FALSE)

which takes the randomly generated year from cell **B5** and finds the corresponding return to put in cell **C5**. This method is equivalent to writing each return on a slip of paper and placing in a bowl, then sampling with replacement from the bowl to determine the return for each year.

The downsides to the direct sampling approach are that

- The simulation can only reproduce what has already happened, and
- The number of trials usually exceeds the number of data values available, so that you will be using the same values many times over.

Thus, using direct sampling can lead to a false sense of precision and is not generally recommended.

Sampling from a Fitted Distribution

In this method, Crystal Ball uses standard techniques of statistical inference to fit a theoretical distribution to your data using one of the distribution gallery's continuous distributions. The fitting and selection is nearly automatic, although it does require some judgment and subject matter knowledge to use most effectively.

If a suitable theoretical distribution can be found, sampling from a fitted distribution is preferred over direct sampling or sampling from an empirical distribution because:

- Historical datasets typically contain relatively few observations. Fewer than 100 is not uncommon in some finance applications (as in the example we use here), and so are "rough." A fitted distribution will typically be "smooth" and might well better represent the underlying stochastic process generating the data than does the direct sample from a limited number of past observations.
- Unless extra tail information is appended to the historical data, it cannot generate values less than the minimum nor greater than the maximum. In many models, the tails of the distribution produce values that lead to some of the model's most interesting results and thus provide useful information. For example, in "stress-testing" a portfolio, analysts evaluate the impact of potential future occurrences of events that could cause problems in a portfolio. Such stress scenarios often come from the tails of the input distributions affecting the portfolio.
- There is often good reason to expect that a theoretical distribution is applicable in many financial applications. For example, many researchers have found that annual stock returns often appear to be normally distributed, and stock prices generally follow lognormal distributions.
- Fitted distributions are efficient. Direct sampling requires storing all *n* observations for reuse. Sampling from a fitted distribution is accomplished for all of Crystal Ball's continuous distributions with algorithms that its authors have embedded in the program code.
- Fitted distributions are easier to change. For example, if the historical volatility of a stock is 20 percent, but you think it is likely to double, all you have to do is change the standard deviations of the assumptions you are using to generate returns.

In situations for which we know that there is a limit on how large or small a generated value can be, we can set a limit on our generated values for any distribution with a truncation limit in Crystal Ball.

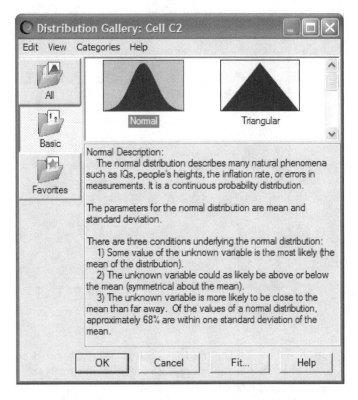

FIGURE 4.23 Dialog for step 1 of fitting a distribution to data.

Fitting Distributions to Data

Crystal Ball provides the button Fit... in the distribution gallery window to fit a single distribution to a source of data, and Run→Tools→Batch Fit... to fit more than one distribution to multiple sources of data.

Follow these steps for an example of how to fit a distribution to empirical data with Fit...

1. Open the file Lognormal.xls. Select the Data worksheet, then click on cell C2. Choose Define→Define Assumption... from the top menu or click on the define assumption icon on the Crystal Ball toolbar. You should see a dialog box like that shown in Figure 4.23.
2. Click on the Fit... button at the bottom right center of the dialog box in Figure 4.23. Enter the range B2:B78 into the Range: field of the dialog box as shown in Figure 4.24. For this example, choose the radio buttons to select All continuous distributions and the Anderson-Darling ranking method as shown in the Fit Distribution dialog in Figure 4.24. Then click the OK

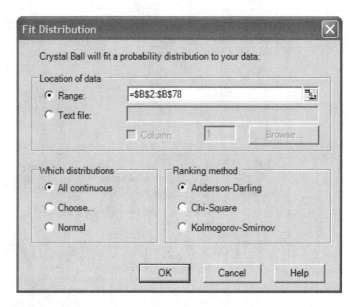

FIGURE 4.24   Dialog for step 2 of fitting a distribution to data.

button on the **Fit Distribution** dialog. You will get a comparison chart similar to that shown in Figure 4.25. By clicking on **Next >>** and **<< Previous**,
you can see plots of the histogram of the data and the theoretical distribution functions for the various fitted distributions. The **Cumulative Frequency**
or **Reverse Cumulative Frequency** views provide better comparisons of the
histogram to the theoretical distribution than does the **Frequency** view.

3. Click **<< Previous** or **Next >>** until you see **Fit #7: Lognormal**. Then click
   Accept and you will see the dialog shown in Figure 4.26. This assumption
   can be copied and pasted to other cells in the model such as Cells **B5:B24** on
   the **Model** worksheet in **Lognormal.xls** using the Crystal Ball **Copy Data** and
   Paste Data commands.

Goodness-of-Fit Testing   Crystal Ball has built into its distribution-fitting procedure
the algorithms to estimate parameters and assess the goodness of fit between the
empirical distribution function (EDF) of your dataset and the cumulative distribution
function (CDF) of each applicable continuous distribution in its distribution gallery.
Not all of the distributions in the gallery are applicable to all datasets. For example,
a lognormal distribution will not be fit to a dataset containing negative values
because the support of the lognormal distribution is bounded from below by zero.
Depending on your data, you may see a message from Crystal Ball warning you of
this fact.

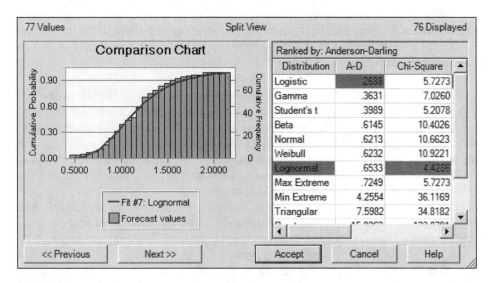

FIGURE 4.25 Comparison chart for fitting a distribution to data.

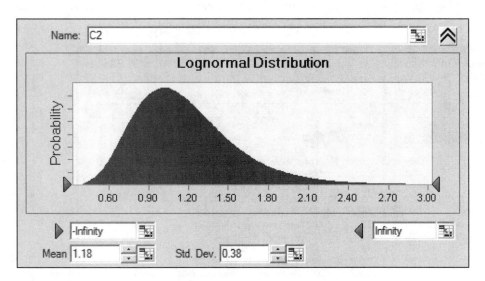

FIGURE 4.26 Lognormal distribution fit to data in file Lognormal.xls.

This section gives a brief description of the procedures used by Crystal Ball for fitting distributions. Suppose a random sample of size n is generated by a stochastic process governed by a cumulative distribution function $F(x)$ (the CDF). Intuitively, the goodness of fit can be tested by measuring the "closeness" of the EDF, $F_n(x)$, to the theoretical CDF, $F(x)$.

Eyeball Test One of the best ways to assess goodness of fit is simply to use the "eyeball test," by comparing the plots of the EDF and each candidate CDF. Crystal Ball helps you do this with frequency charts and cumulative frequency charts as part of its fitting procedure. By specifying the **Cumulative Frequency** view and clicking on **Next >>** and **<< Previous** as described above for the data in **Lognormal.xls**, you can use the eyeball test to assess the fit between the EDF of your data and the CDF of each of Crystal Ball's applicable distributions.

For those who prefer a quantitative measure of goodness of fit, Crystal Ball also calculates the values of three test statistics under the hypothesis that the data were generated from its applicable theoretical, continuous distributions. Figure 4.27 shows the goodness-of-fit statistics calculated for the data in **Lognormal.xls**. In Crystal Ball Version 7, the p-values for these test statistics are not provided, but they may be found or estimated using a reference book such as D'Agostino and Stephens (1986) or an advanced textbook on statistical analysis. These statistics are used for ordering the distributions according to the ranking method you specify in the dialog window shown in Figure 4.24. For example, we chose to rank with the

Comparison Chart

Edit   View   Preferences   Help

77 Values			Goodness of Fit View		76 Displayed

Ranked by: Anderson-Darling

	Distribution	A-D	Chi-Square	K-S	Parameters
▶	Logistic	.2688	5.7273	.0511	Mean=1.1563,Scale=0.1935
	Gamma	.3631	7.0260	.0637	Location=-0.1936,Scale=0.0913,Shape=14.97271
	Student's t	.3989	5.2078	.0744	Midpoint=1.1747,Scale=0.2980,Deg. Freedom=5.21981
	Beta	.6145	10.4026	.0899	Minimum=-3.9065,Maximum=6.2533,Alpha=100,Beta=100
	Normal	.6213	10.6623	.0903	Mean=1.1734,Std. Dev.=0.3607
	Weibull	.6232	10.9221	.0815	Location=0.2592,Scale=1.0276,Shape=2.73769
	Lognormal	.6533	4.4286	.0887	Mean=1.1766,Std. Dev.=0.3800
	Max Extreme	.7249	5.7273	.0859	Likeliest=1.0063,Scale=0.3129
	Min Extreme	4.2554	36.1169	.1657	Likeliest=1.3664,Scale=0.4670
	Triangular	7.5982	34.8182	.2568	Minimum=0.3226,Likeliest=0.9568,Maximum=2.8790
	Pareto	15.8362	122.8701	.3860	Location=0.4410,Shape=1.07341
	Uniform	17.7097	80.0130	.3891	Minimum=0.4174,Maximum=2.6824
	Exponential	17.8069	137.4156	.3968	Rate=0.8411

<< Previous   Next >>   Accept   Cancel   Help

FIGURE 4.27 Goodness-of-fit statistics for data in file **Lognormal.xls**.

Anderson-Darling statistic and the lognormal distribution appears as the seventh entry in the table shown in Figure 4.27.

Do not assume that the highest ranking distributions in the table necessarily correspond to the best distributions for use in your model. The choice of the best distribution depends on its use in your model and the judgement of a subject matter expert (SME). For example, while the logistic distribution is ranked highest in Figure 4.27, the lognormal distribution is a better choice for total return in this case because of the product version of the central limit effect described above.

Caveats Things to keep in mind when using historical data include:

- Empirical data are usually not available, at least not immediately. For new offerings of products or services, there may well be no historical data at all, and for improved offerings of products or services, the historical data may not be indicative of what is to come in the future. In situations like these, you will need to specify assumptions based on subject matter expert input. Of course, once the new offering is in place, you should have processes in place to record data on the stochastic variables of interest for reparameterizing your model when it is updated.
- Some information may be biased or otherwise inappropriate, simply because the data collector did not anticipate that the data would be used for risk analysis or financial modeling. Thus, sometimes the data may be a mix of observations from two or more stochastic variables, or be collected over a period of time where the parameters (for example, the mean or standard deviation) for a single variable may have changed over time. This may make the historical data invalid for use in fitting distributions.
- As mentioned above, fitting a distribution to data requires judgment to determine whether the "best-fit" distribution is appropriate. The ability to make this judgement is developed with experience. Novices may have to rely on SMEs for their judgement.

The good news is that the results of interest in most models often depend on the mean and the variance of inputs more than on the specific probability distributions used. If you find yourself in a situation where potential users of your model are questioning the appropriateness of the input distributions, you may find it helpful to try different distributions. As long as the different distributions have the same mean and variance, the central limit effect will apply to most realistic models and the forecast distributions will be relatively insensitive to the choices of the distribution families of the assumptions.

Paradoxically, while good empirical data are the best source for helping to determine which assumptions to choose from the distribution gallery, you should not rely on them too much. Subject matter knowledge and good judgment are also necessary ingredients for constructing good models.

What If No Historical Data Are Available?

Financial models are often built to analyze situations that do not yet exist; for example, new products or projects in which the company has little or no historical data to help choose assumptions. In this case, you will have to make your own subjective estimates of which assumptions to use in the model, or solicit the help of a SME. The uniform and triangular distributions are often good first choices.

The uniform distribution is sometimes called the "distribution of maximum ignorance" because it requires only two parameters to specify, the Minimum and the Maximum. By considering every value between the minimum and maximum to be equally likely to occur, we are being very conservative in our approach. Quite often SMEs who know nothing about probability distributions will be able to help you choose the parameters of the uniform distribution simply by your asking for the highest and lowest possible values that they think may occur.

Depending on the distribution, you may define the distribution using different combinations of the mean, standard deviation, minimum, maximum, or selected percentiles. For example, Figure 4.28 shows the alternative ways for defining a lognormal distribution. The possible parameter sets that can be used depend on the distribution to be defined. It is sometimes easier to elicit estimates of percentiles

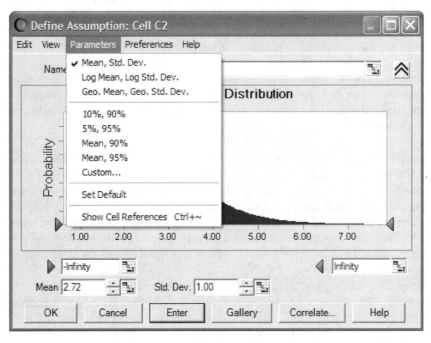

FIGURE 4.28 Parameters drop-down menu for the lognormal distribution.

or other parameters for assumptions from SMEs, and the Parameters menu was developed to make easier the task of defining distributions. Expert opinion is usually more readily available than empirical data, but you should be prepared to justify and/or defend your choices no matter how you selected your assumptions.

If you have a better feel for the situation than maximally ignorant, you may want to consider using the triangular distribution. Like the uniform, it requires a minimum and maximum values, but it also requires a Likeliest value. This is also known as the mode of the distribution and specifies the point on the horizontal axis above which the density is the highest.

Building a model without historical data can provide many valuable insights. However, as soon as possible, you should collect data on the stochastic variables driving your forecasts and parameterize the assumptions. Among other reasons, this will also allow you to estimate any correlations between the assumptions, which can make a huge difference in the forecast results.

SPECIFYING CORRELATIONS

Crystal Ball gives you the ability to specify correlations between assumptions in your models. This is important because quite often several assumptions will be affected by the same factor. For example, returns on stocks all tend to be affected by the same market forces, although to varying degrees. The correlation coefficient measures the degree to which one assumption moves with another.

The type of correlation known to most people from their college statistics courses is the Pearson product-moment correlation coefficient. This is the same correlation coefficient that Excel calculates with its =CORREL(array1,array2) command. However, it turns out that the Pearson coefficient does not generalize easily to all distributions, so Crystal Ball uses the Spearman rank correlation coefficient instead of the Pearson. In this section, we elaborate on the distinction between Pearson and Spearman correlation coefficients.

Pearson Correlation Statistic If we have n observations on a random variable X denoted as $x_1, x_2, \ldots, x_n$, and n observations on another random variable Y denoted as $y_1, y_2, \ldots, y_n$, we can calculate the degree of linear association between them with the Pearson correlation coefficient, r_{xy}. This coefficient ranges from -1 to $+1$. If X tends to be above (below) its mean value whenever Y is above (below) its mean value, then r_{xy} will be close to $+1$. Conversely, if X tends to be below (above) its mean value whenever Y is above (below) its mean value, then r_{xy} will be close to -1. Simply put, the correlation coefficient is a measure of the tendency for one random variable's observations to follow the movement of another variable's observations.

The Pearson correlation coefficient is calculated by first finding the mean of each set of observations as

$$\overline{x} = \frac{\sum_{i=1}^{n} x_i}{n} \text{ and } \overline{y} = \frac{\sum_{i=1}^{n} y_i}{n}.$$

	A	B	C	D	E	F
1	YEAR	Small Cap Stocks	Large Cap Stocks	SC Stocks Rank	LC Stocks Rank	
2	1926	0.9568	1.1191	21	36	
3	1927	1.2716	1.3674	53	70	
4	1928	1.4236	1.4145	62	73	
5	1929	0.4891	0.9196	2	17	
78	2002	0.8257	0.7790	9	5	
79						
80	0.78707	Pearson Correlation for B2:B78 with C2:C78				
81	0.81119	Spearman Correlation for B2:B78 with C2:C78				

FIGURE 4.29 Comparison of correlation coefficients for data in PearsonSpearman.xls. Note that rows 6 through 79 are hidden.

Then the Pearson product-moment correlation statistic is calculated as

$$r_{xy} = \frac{\sum_{i=1}^{n}(x_i - \bar{x})(y_i - \bar{y})}{\sqrt{\sum_{i=1}^{n}(x_i - \bar{x})^2 \sum_{i=1}^{n}(y_i - \bar{y})^2}}.$$

The spreadsheet shown in Figure 4.29 illustrates the calculation of correlations in Excel. If we denote as $x_1, x_2, \ldots, x_{79}$ the total returns on small cap stocks in cells B2:B80, and denote as $y_1, y_2, \ldots, y_{79}$ the total returns on large cap stocks in cells C2:C80, then the Excel formula =AVERAGE(B2:B80) calculates the sample mean $\bar{x}$, =AVERAGE(C2:C80) calculates the sample mean $\bar{y}$, and =CORREL(B2:B80,C2:C80) calculates the Pearson correlation statistic, r_{xy}.

Spearman (Rank) Correlation Statistic The Spearman, or rank, correlation statistic, r_{xy}^S, is a nonparametric estimator of the correlation coefficient that is calculated from the ranks of the observations. Crystal Ball uses Spearman correlations because the Pearson correlation does not work well in simulation algorithms for every one of Crystal Ball's distributions, but the Spearman correlation coefficient does. The Spearman correlation coefficient is the Pearson correlation coefficient calculated for the ranks of the observed values of X and Y.

The rank of an observation is simply its position number in an ordered array when the data are sorted in ascending order. Note that by default, the Excel command =Rank(Number,Ref,Order) will calculate the rank of **Number** in the (ordered or unordered) array **Ref** based on descending order if **Order** = 0 or is blank. The discussion below is applicable whether the data are sorted in ascending or descending order; however, for our purposes, it is easy to change to ascending order by specifying **Order** = 1. Ascending order is used conventionally by most statisticians in assigning ranks. For example, if the observed values of X are

$$1, 7, 3, 1, 0, 1, 5, 2, 7, 3$$

when arrayed in ascending order they are

$$0, 1, 1, 1, 2, 3, 3, 5, 7, 7$$

With ties in ranks, assign the average rank to each tied value. Excel does not assign average ranks by default with its =RANK(Number,Ref,Order) function, but this can be accomplished by using a correction given on an Excel help page:

=[COUNT(Ref) + 1 − RANK(Number,Ref,0)− RANK(Number,Ref,1)]/2.

This is illustrated in the table below:

i	x_i	y_i	rank(x_i)	rank(y_i)
1	1	7	3	9.5
2	7	3	9.5	3.5
3	3	6	6.5	7.5
4	1	7	3	9.5
5	0	6	1	7.5
6	1	5	3	6
7	5	4	8	5
8	2	3	5	3.5
9	7	2	9.5	1.5
10	3	2	6.5	1.5

Let $X' = $ rank(x_i) and $Y' = $ rank(y_i). The Spearman rank correlation statistic is the Pearson product moment correlation calculated from the ranks,

$$r_{xy}^{S} = \frac{\sum_{i=1}^{n}(X_i' - \overline{X'})(Y_i' - \overline{Y_i'})}{\sqrt{\sum_{i=1}^{n}(X_i' - \overline{X'})^2 \sum_{i=1}^{n}(Y_i' - \overline{Y_i'})^2}}$$

The calculations are illustrated in the file **PearsonSpearman.xls**. If there are no ties in the ranks, a shortcut method for calculating Spearman correlation is

$$r_{xy}^{S} = 1 - \frac{6\sum_{i=1}^{n} d_i^2}{n(n^2 - 1)},$$

where $d_i = x_i' - y_i'$.

Using Crystal Ball to Calculate Correlations between Two Assumptions

You can calculate Spearman correlations between two cell ranges using Crystal Ball's **Correlate. . .** button on the Define Assumption dialog window. Using the steps listed below, this was done for the assumptions in cells **H2** and **I2** from the data in cells B2:B78 and C2:C78, respectively, in the spreadsheet **PearsonSpearman.xls**. Cell H2 is lognormal(1.18,0.36), and cell I2 is lognormal(1.13,0.22).

The procedure for calculating the correlation between cells H2 and I2 follows. Once you go through this, you should be able to define correlation between any two pairs of assumptions for which you have data.

1. Select either cell H2 or cell I2, then click on Define→Define Assumption... For this example, I have selected cell H2, SC Stocks, as shown in Figure 4.30.
2. Click on the Correlate... button to get the Define Correlation dialog shown in Figure 4.31, then click on Choose... to get the Choose Assumptions dialog shown in Figure 4.32.
3. Click on the check box next to LC Stocks as shown in Figure 4.32, then click OK. The Define Correlation dialog will appear.
4. Click on the Calc... button to get the Calculate Correlation Coefficient window shown in Figure 4.33. Enter the cell ranges B2:B78 and C2:C78 as shown in Figure 4.33, then click OK. You will see the Spearman correlation coefficient value 0.81119, which is the same as the value shown in cell A81 in Figure 4.29.
5. Click OK to get back to the Define Assumption dialog, which now has (Correlated) added to the label in the dialog window title bar to indicate that the assumption is correlated with at least one other assumption in the spreadsheet.
6. Click OK again to close the dialog.

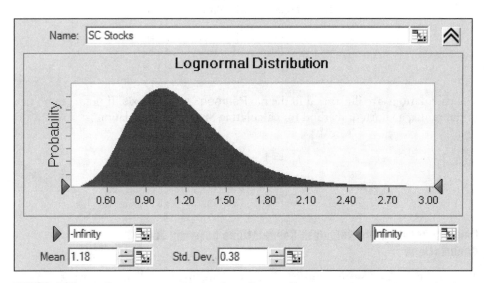

FIGURE 4.30 Define Assumption dialog for cell H2 in file PearsonSpearman.xls. The Correlate... button is second from right at the bottom of the dialog window.

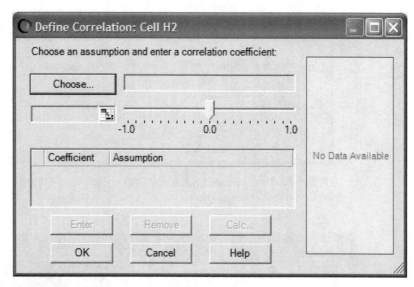

FIGURE 4.31 Define Correlation dialog for cell H2 in file PearsonSpearman.xls.

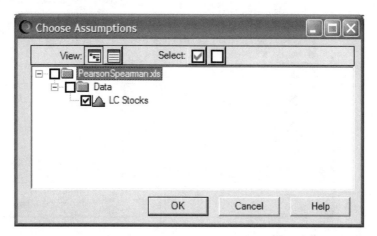

FIGURE 4.32 Choose Assumptions dialog for cell H2 in file PearsonSpearman.xls.

Batch Fit

Crystal Ball's Batch Fit feature enables you to fit distributions to and calculate correlations for several sets of data in one set of steps. In this section we will fit lognormal distributions and find correlations for monthly total returns observed

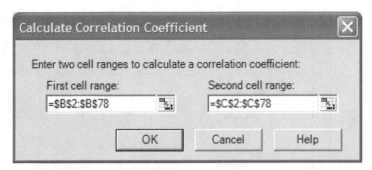

FIGURE 4.33   Calculate Correlation Coefficient dialog for cell H2 in file PearsonSpearman.xls.

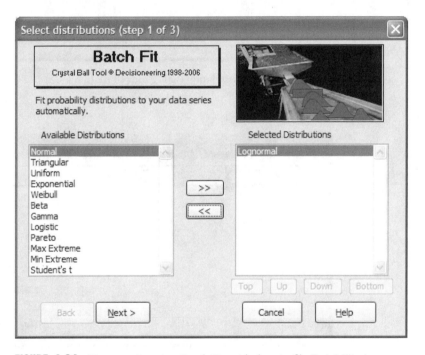

FIGURE 4.34   First step in using Batch Fit with data in file BatchFit.xls.

during the period January 1998 through December 2004. These returns are in the file BatchFit.xls.

Follow these steps to use Batch Fit:

1. Click on Run→Tools→Batch Fit... in the top menu. The Select distributions (step 1 of 3) dialog window will appear.

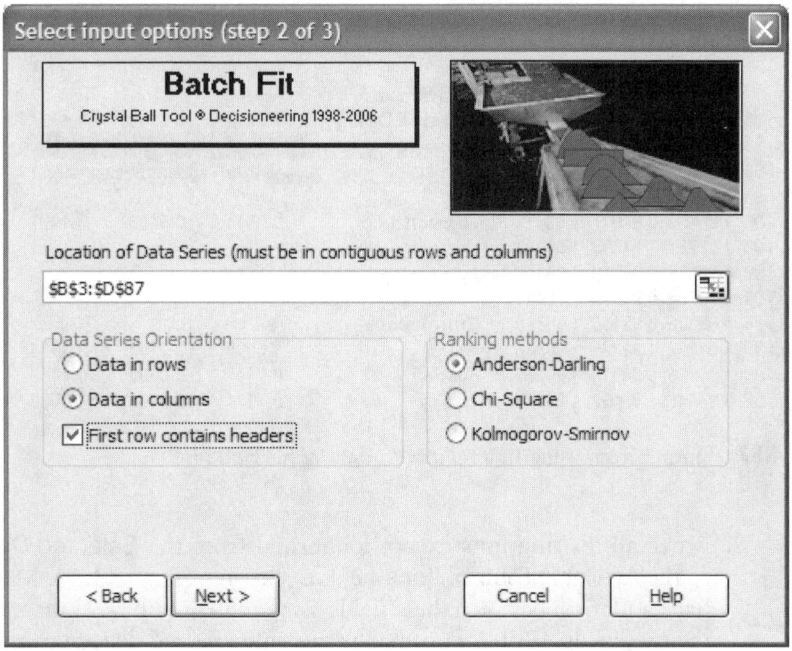

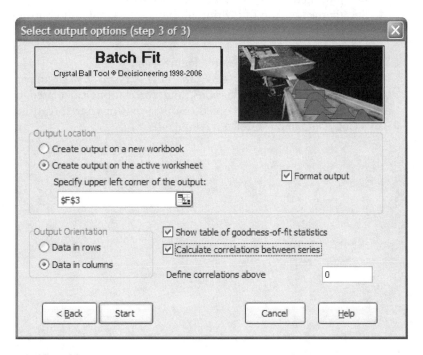

FIGURE 4.35 Second step in using Batch Fit with data in file BatchFit.xls.

FIGURE 4.36 Third step in using Batch Fit with data in file BatchFit.xls.

	A	B	C	D	E	F	G	H	I
1	**BatchFit.xls**								
2									
3	Date	AM	SJM	TBill		Data Series:	AM	SJM	TBill
4	Jan-98	1.10703	1.08466	1.00437		Anderson-Darling:	3.2811	0.5153	3.4927
5	Feb-98	1.05755	1.04410	1.00451		Distribution:	0.00000	0.00000	0.00000
6	Mar-98	1.00822	0.98357	1.00451		Best fit:	Lognormal	Lognormal	Lognormal
7	Apr-98	1.00543	0.93795	1.00450					
8	May-98	1.03092	0.97517	1.00452		Lognormal	3.2811	0.5153	3.4927
9	Jun-98	1.07237	1.04199	1.00448					
10	Jul-98	0.90675	0.95718	1.00448					
11	Aug-98	0.79708	0.91905	1.00413					
12	Sep-98	1.08020	0.99135	1.00368		Correlations	AM	SJM	TBill
13	Oct-98	1.01422	1.02326	1.00348		AM	1.0000	0.2147	-0.1184
14	Nov-98	1.05925	1.06318	1.00378		SJM	0.2147	1.0000	-0.1162
15	Dec-98	0.97046	1.06452	1.00378		TBill	-0.1184	-0.1162	1.0000

FIGURE 4.37   Output from using Batch Fit with data in file BatchFit.xls.

2. Move all distributions except lognormal from the Selected Distributions field to the Available Distributions field as shown in Figure 4.34. Move distributions back and forth between these fields using the << and >> buttons found between the two fields. With lognormal as the only selected distribution, click Next.
3. Specify the location of the data, punch the same radio buttons, and check the box indicated in Figure 4.35, then click Next.
4. Specify the location of the output, punch the same radio buttons, and check the boxes indicated in Figure 4.36, then click Start.

Your spreadsheet should resemble Figure 4.37.

Cells G5:I5 in Figure 4.37 are now Crystal Ball lognormal assumptions having means, standard deviations, and correlations calculated from the data in cells B4:D87. They can be copied to other cells in your spreadsheet using Crystal Ball's CopyData and PasteData commands.

CHAPTER 5

Using Decision Variables

T he first four chapters covered the basics of specifying Crystal Ball assumptions and analyzing Crystal Ball forecasts. This chapter covers the basics of defining and using Crystal Ball decision variables and its decision support tools, Decision Table and OptQuest.

DEFINING DECISION VARIABLES

Decision variables are spreadsheet cells in which the values are varied systematically rather than sampled randomly, as are assumptions. They can be cells that hold values dictated by actual decisions or cells for which we just want to see the effect of one or two variables on selected forecasts in a form of sensitivity analysis.

As an example of the latter, consider the model depicted in Figure 5.1, TwoCorrelatedAssets.xls, where we have two correlated assets and we wish to vary the correlation coefficient to see the effect on the rate of return of a portfolio composed of the two assets. To keep things simple we will simulate a model for which we know the true answer so that we can compare the simulation results to the truth.

Consider a portfolio composed of two assets, A and B. Asset A has a normally distributed rate of return with mean, $\mu_A = 10$ percent, and standard deviation, $\sigma_A = 20$ percent. Asset B has a normally distributed rate of return with mean, $\mu_A = 15$ percent, and standard deviation, $\sigma_B = 30$ percent. We will invest half of our available funds in Asset A and half in Asset B, and we are interested in seeing how the distribution of the rate of return of our portfolio varies as a function of the correlation coefficient, ρ, between the rates of return on Assets A and B. In Two Correlated Assets.xls, cells A9 and A10 are assumptions, and cell A13 is a forecast.

The assumptions in cells A9 and A10 of the file TwoCorrelatedAssets.xls are defined as normal distributions as described in Chapter 4. However, to reflect the limited liability of stock ownership, the rates of return on both assets are truncated

	A	B	C	D	E
1	**Two Correlated Assets.xls**				
2					
3	Parameters				
4	Asset	Mean	Std. Dev.	Correlation	
5	A	10%	20%	0.50	
6	B	15%	30%		
7					
8	**Model**				
9	10.000%	Rate of return on A			
10	15.000%	Rate of return on B			
11	50.000%	Proportion invested in A			
12	50.000%	Proportion invested in B			
13	12.500%	Portfolio ROR			
14					
15					
16	12.500%	True mean rate of return on portfolio			
17	21.794%	True Std. Dev. of rate of return on portfolio			

FIGURE 5.1 Spreadsheet model in file TwoCorrelatedAssets.xls, which models rate of return on portfolio as the correlation coefficient, ρ, varies from -1.00 to $+1.00$ in steps of 0.25. Cell **D5** is a decision variable, cells **A9** and **A10** are assumptions, and cell **A13** is a forecast.

on the left at -100 percent. This is accomplished by entering this value in the field directly above the **Mean** field as shown in Figure 5.2 for the rate of return assumption for Asset B. With a mean of 15 percent and a standard deviation of 30 percent, the normal distribution will rarely produce any values below -100% (which is more than 3.8 standard deviations below the mean), but truncating the distribution ensures that on those rare occasions when a value less than -100% is generated from a nontruncated normal distribution for Asset B, Crystal Ball will discard it and generate another random value in its place. Asset A's rate of return is also bounded from below by -100%.

Note that the title bar of the dialog in Figure 5.2 for cell **A10** indicates that it is correlated with another assumption, in this case the assumption in cell **A9**. During any simulation run, the correlation coefficient is the value in cell **D5**, which is what we will vary with the Decision Table tool.

To make Cell **D5** into a decision variable, first click on it. Then select Define→Define Decision... from the top menu or click on the **Define Decision** icon on the Crystal Ball toolbar. Fill in the fields as shown in Figure 5.3. This tells Crystal Ball that you wish to vary the value in cell **D5** from -1.00 to $+1.00$ in discrete steps of 0.25. Click **OK** and cell **D5**'s background will turn yellow to indicate that a decision variable is defined in that cell. You are now ready to use the Decision Table tool or OptQuest with the model.

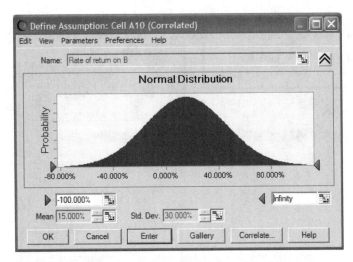

FIGURE 5.2 Define assumption dialog for cell A10 in file TwoCorrelatedAssets.xls.

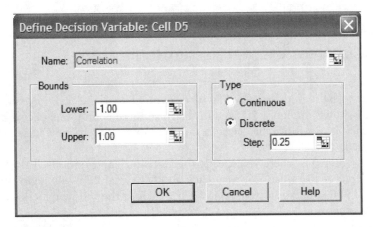

FIGURE 5.3 Define Decision Variable dialog window.

DECISION TABLE WITH ONE DECISION VARIABLE

Select Run→Tools→Decision Table... from the top menu. You will get a dialog window for step 1 like that shown in Figure 5.4. For models with more than one forecast defined, you would first highlight the forecast for which you wish to analyze the sensitivity to the decision variable. As there is only one forecast in this model, there is no choice to be made here, so click Next > to select the forecast Portfolio ROR.

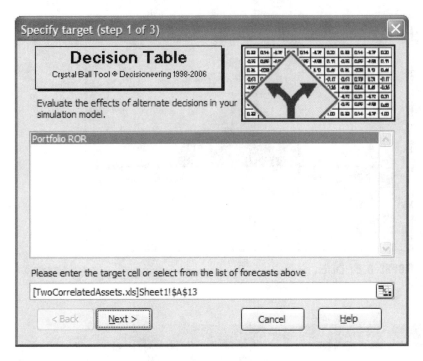

FIGURE 5.4 Dialog window for step 1 of using Decision Table.

The dialog for step 2 is where you choose the decision variables to evaluate, as shown in Figure 5.5. Again, because there is only one decision variable defined, click >> to move the decision variable **Correlation** to the Chosen Decision Variables field, then click **Next>**.

Step 3 is where you specify the Decision Table options. Take the default options depicted in Figure 5.6, then click **Start**. Crystal Ball will begin running nine sets of 10,000 simulation trials, one set for each of the following values of the correlation coefficient:

$$\{-1.00, -0.75, -0.50, -0.25, 0.00, 0.25, 0.50, 0.75, 1.00\}$$

After it has finished running 90,000 simulation trials, Crystal Ball will create a separate workbook like that in Figure 5.7 holding nine forecasts and three buttons: Trend Chart, Overlay Chart, and Forecast Charts.

Trend Chart

To see the trend chart, select the forecasts in cells B2:J2, then click Trend Chart to get a graphical display similar that shown in Figure 5.8. A trend chart displays the certainty bands for several forecasts on one plot. The chart in Figure 5.8 clearly

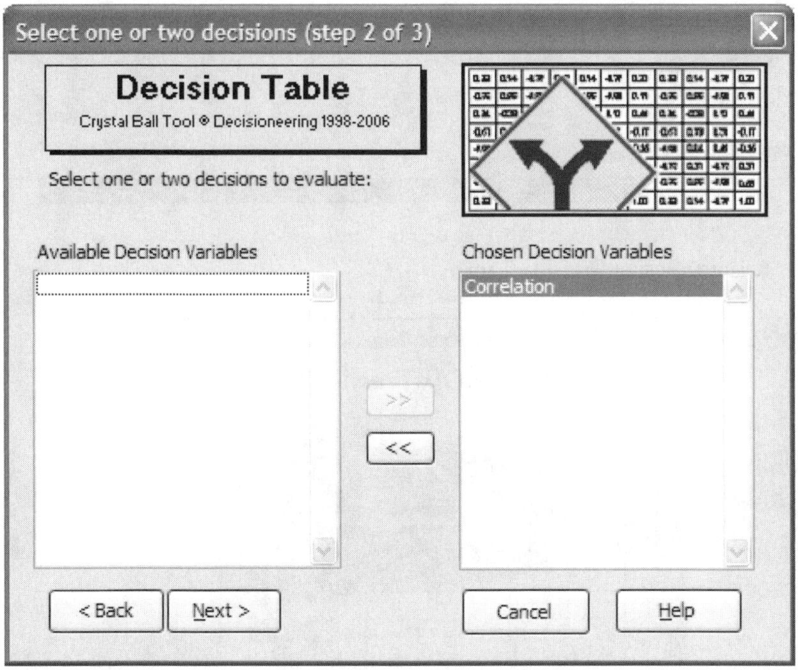

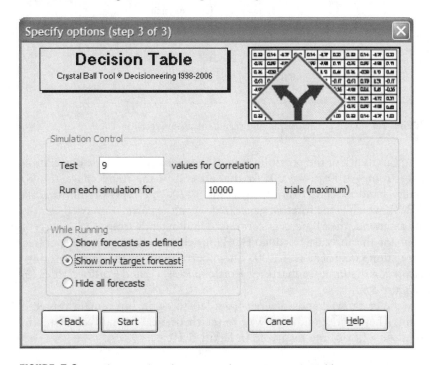

FIGURE 5.5 Dialog window for step 2 of using Decision Table.

FIGURE 5.6 Dialog window for step 3 of using Decision Table.

	A	B	C	D	E	F	G	H	I	J
	Trend Chart / Overlay Chart / Forecast Charts	Correlation (-1.00)	Correlation (-0.75)	Correlation (-0.50)	Correlation (-0.25)	Correlation (0.00)	Correlation (0.25)	Correlation (0.50)	Correlation (0.75)	Correlation (1.00)
2		12.50%	12.51%	12.51%	12.51%	12.51%	12.51%	12.51%	12.51%	12.50%
3		1	2	3	4	5	6	7	8	9

FIGURE 5.7   Results of using Decision Table.

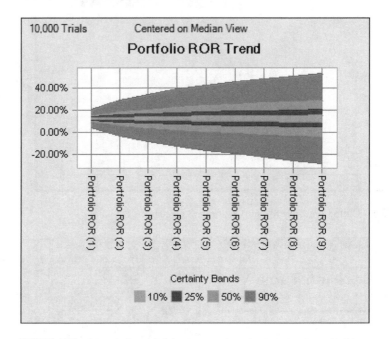

FIGURE 5.8   Trend chart displaying results of using Decision Table.

shows how the variability of the portfolio rate of return increases as the correlation coefficient goes from -1.00 to $+1.00$. At the left end of the trend chart, the 90 percent certainty band extends from 4.3 percent to 20.7 percent for the forecast **Portfolio ROR (1)**, which is the forecast generated when the correlation coefficient is -1.00. At the right end, the 90 percent certainty band extends from -28.6 percent to 53.6 percent for the forecast **Portfolio ROR (9)**, which is the forecast generated when the correlation coefficient is $+1.00$. These correspond to the same certainty intervals indicated in the forecast charts for **Portfolio ROR (1)** and **Portfolio ROR (9)** displayed in Figure 5.9.

Note how the certainty bands diverge from left to right, but remain centered on 12.5 percent. They correspond very well to the theoretical bounds calculated in **Two Correlated Assets.xls**, and displayed in Figure 5.10.

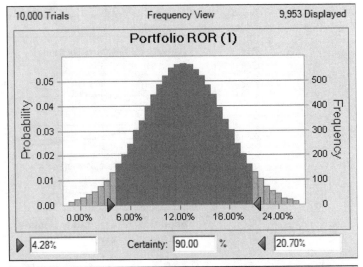

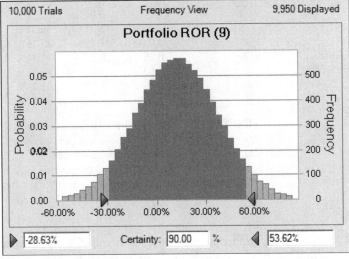

FIGURE 5.9 Frequency charts for Portfolio ROR (1) and (9) from Decision Table results.

These charts conform well to theory, which holds that the rate of return on the portfolio will be normally distributed with mean $\mu_P = w\mu_A + (1 - w)\sigma_B$, and standard deviation

$$\sigma_P = \sqrt{w^2\sigma_A^2 + (1 - w)^2\sigma_B^2 + 2w(1 - w)\rho\sigma_A\sigma_B}, \qquad (5.1)$$

where w is the weight $(0 \le w \le 1)$ of Asset A in the portfolio. For this example, $w = 0.5$.

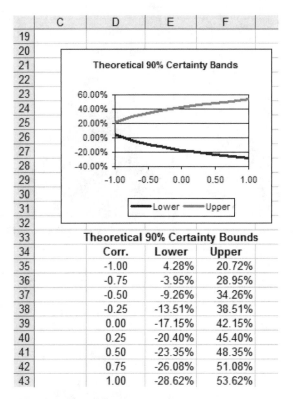

	Corr.	Lower	Upper
	-1.00	4.28%	20.72%
	-0.75	-3.95%	28.95%
	-0.50	-9.26%	34.26%
	-0.25	-13.51%	38.51%
	0.00	-17.15%	42.15%
	0.25	-20.40%	45.40%
	0.50	-23.35%	48.35%
	0.75	-26.08%	51.08%
	1.00	-28.62%	53.62%

FIGURE 5.10 Theoretical 90 percent certainty bounds for trend chart displaying results of using Decision Table. Bounds are calculated as $\mu_P + \Phi^{-1}(y)\sigma_P$, where $\Phi^{-1}(y)$ is the inverse CDF for the standard normal distribution, $y = 0.05$ for the lower bound, and $y = 0.95$ for the upper bound.

It is worth noting that our model differed slightly in at least two ways from the theoretical model underlying Expression (5.1). First, Crystal Ball uses Spearman correlation, ρ^S, for sampling instead of the Pearson correlation, ρ, used in Expression (5.1); however, for normally distributed rates of return this makes little difference. Second, we truncated the rate of return assumptions on the left, which has the effect of changing the standard deviations slightly, but this also made little difference.

Overlay Chart

The forecast charts in Figure 5.9 look similar, but the scales of their horizontal axes are much different. To make it easier to compare forecasts, use an overlay chart. Click on cell **B2**, then hold down the **Ctrl** key and click on cell **J2** to select the forecasts

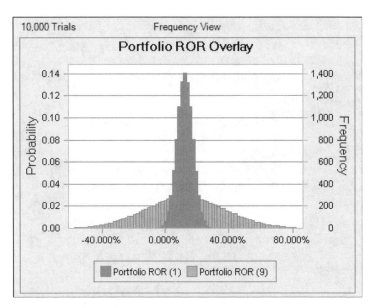

FIGURE 5.11   Overlay chart displaying results of using Decision Table.

for **Portfolio ROR (1)** and **Portfolio ROR (9)**. Then click the **Overlay Chart** button to get a chart like that displayed in Figure 5.11, which clearly shows the difference in dispersion between the forecasts for **Portfolio ROR (1)** and **Portfolio ROR (9)**. You can create an overlay chart for more than two forecasts at a time, but do so with care as they become hard to read when too many forecasts are included.

DECISION TABLE WITH TWO DECISION VARIABLES

You can also use the Decision Table tool with two decision variables. The output is similar to the output with one decision variable, except that Crystal Ball will produce an array containing a forecast for every possible combination of the values specified for each decision. This section contains an example of using Decision Table with a model built as an illustration of how to estimate a value for managerial flexibility.

Model

For an example of a situation with two decision variables, suppose that a firm can invest in a project having a three-year life and a terminal value that depends on the cash flow in the final quarter of the third year. Suppose further that there are only two sources of uncertainty: (1) the average quarterly growth rate of revenue, and (2) variable cost as a percentage of revenue. We assume that average quarterly revenue growth is random and follows a normal distribution with mean = 5 percent, and standard deviation = 5 percent. Variable cost as a percentage of revenue is also

	A	B	C	D	L	M	N
1	**Project.xls**						
2	**Inputs**						
3	**Decision Variables**		**Notes**				
4	Abandon Point	0	Threshold value of cash flow for abandoning project				
5	Expansion Point	10	Threshold value of cash flow for expanding project				
6	**Assumptions**						
7	Avg Q'ly Rev Growth	5%	Average percent growth in quarterly revenue				
8	Var Cost Percentage	50%	Variable cost as a percent of revenue				
9	**Outputs**						
10	**Forecasts**						
11	NPV 1	-$72.66	Net present value with no flexibility				
12	NPV 2	-$72.66	Net present value with option to abandon				
13	NPV 3	-$24.44	Net present value with option to abandon or expand				
14							
15			**NO FLEXIBILITY**				
16							
17			**Year 1**			**Year 3**	
18		Q1	Q2	Q3	Q3	Q4	
19	Revenue	$ 100.00	$ 105.00	$ 110.25	$ 162.89	$ 171.03	
20	Avg. quarterly revenue growth		5.00%	5.00%	5.00%	5.00%	
21							
22	Variable Cost	50.00	52.50	55.13	81.44	85.52	
23		50%	50%	50%	50%	50%	
24	Fixed Cost	60	60	60	60	60	
25							
26	Investment	$ 300.00					
27							**Terminal Value**
28	Cash Flow	(310.00)	(7.50)	(4.88)	21.44	25.52	204.14
29	Discount Factor	0.89	0.89	0.89	0.70	0.70	0.70
30	Discounted Cash Flow	-$275.56	-$6.67	-$4.33	$15.06	$17.92	$143.37
31							
32	NPV	-$72.66					

FIGURE 5.12 Spreadsheet segment from Project.xls. Note that columns E through K are hidden.

normally distributed with a mean of 50 percent, and a standard deviation of 5 percent. The discount rate is assumed to be 12.5 percent. Figure 5.12 shows a spreadsheet segment from Project.xls that is used to value this project with net present value (NPV). For the purposes of this example, we will use the **Mean** of the NPV forecast, ENPV, as the value of the project.

By looking at this project from different perspectives, we can estimate the value of the project manager's flexibility over time to affect the course of the project. To estimate the value of this flexibility, we consider two scenarios to find:

ENPV 1 = The value of the project without managerial flexibility; and
ENPV 2 = The value of the project with managerial flexibility.

The value of the managerial flexibility is then determined as the difference between ENPV 1 and ENPV 2.

With a standard NPV analysis, we assume that the project manager has no flexibility to make decisions during the life of the project. That is, once the project is begun it is run to the end of three years with no expansion if successful, and no abandonment if unsuccessful.

Open the file **Project.xls** and run the simulation model. When the simulation stops, look at the Crystal Ball forecast window for NPV 1, which is also shown in Figure 5.13. The mean net present value is $18.61, which is the value of the project with no flexibility. Note that the output in Figure 5.13 also shows the probability is only about 40 percent that the project will add value to the firm, because the value in the certainty field at the bottom center of the forecast window is 42.92 percent.

Now suppose that we are faced with a similar situation, but this time we have the option to abandon the project if unfavorable circumstances occur. For now, let's use the following decision rule for abandonment. Begin checking in the second quarter of Year 2, and abandon the project if three consecutive quarters of negative cash flow occur. This decision rule is built into rows 50 and 51 of **Project.xls** with indicator variables, as shown in Figure 5.14. Cells **G50:M50** check whether or not to abandon each quarter, and cells **G51:M51** ensure that once abandoned, the project contributes no positive cash flows in future quarters.

The Crystal Ball output in Figure 5.15 shows that the option to abandon has increased the project's value. Because the mean NPV with abandonment possible is $50.62, the value of the abandonment option is estimated to be $50.62 − $18.61 = $32.01. Note that the flexibility to abandon the project does not change the inherent risk structure of the project itself, so in Figure 5.15 the probability that the project adds value to the firm remains the same, that is, Pr(NPV > 0) ≈ 40 percent.

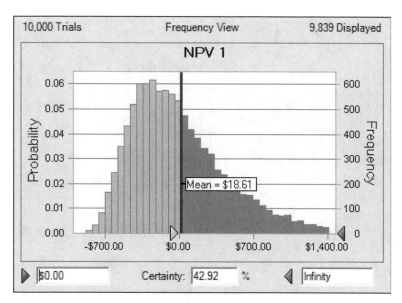

FIGURE 5.13 Crystal Ball forecast for NPV1 for the case of no flexibility in the **Project.xls** model.

	A	B	C	D	L	M	N
34	Abandon Point	0					
35							
36		PROJECT WITH ABANDONMENT OPTION					
37							
38			Year 1			Year 3	
39		Q1	Q2	Q3	Q3	Q4	
40	Revenue	100.00	105.00	110.25	162.89	171.03	
41	Avg. quarterly revenue growth		5.00%	5.00%	5.00%	5.00%	
42							
43	Variable Cost	50.00	52.50	55.13	81.44	85.52	
44		50%	50%	50%	50%	50%	
45	Fixed Cost	60	60	60	60	60	
46							
47	Investment	$ 300.00					
48							Terminal Value
49	Cash Flow	(310.00)	(7.50)	(4.88)	21.44	25.52	204.14
50	Check for abandonment				1.00	1.00	
51	Continue abandonment				1.00	1.00	1.00
52	Realized Cash Flows	(310.00)	(7.50)	(4.88)	21.44	25.52	204.14
53							
54	Discount Factor	0.89	0.89	0.89	0.70	0.70	0.70
55	Discounted Cash Flow	($275.56)	($6.67)	($4.33)	$15.06	$17.92	$143.37
56							
57	NPV	($72.66)					

FIGURE 5.14   Spreadsheet segment from Project.xls model showing the possibility of abandonment. Note that columns E through K are hidden.

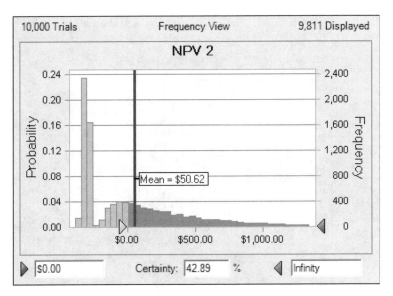

FIGURE 5.15   CB forecast window from Project.xls model showing the possibility of abandonment.

However, by allowing for abandonment, we limit the losses incurred by the firm, just as an active and astute project manager would do in a real-world situation. Because of the ability to limit losses in the left tail of the distribution, the manager's flexibility increases the ENPV of the project.

Now consider another option the manager has with this project, the option to expand if favorable conditions occur. To value the expansion option, we use the following decision rule. Begin checking in the second quarter of Year 2, and expand if we see three consecutive quarters of cash flow greater than $15. The investment in the expansion project will cost $200, and we assume that expansion will double the quarterly revenue and expenses. This decision rule is built into rows 77 and 78 of the spreadsheet model in **Project.xls** shown in Figure 5.16.

	A	B	C	D	L	M	N
60	PROJECT WITH ABANDONMENT AND EXPANSION OPTIONS						
61	Expansion Point	10					
62			Year 1		Year 3		
63		Q1	Q2	Q3	Q3	Q4	
64	Revenue	100.00	105.00	110.25	162.89	171.03	
65	Avg. quarterly revenue growth		5.00%	5.00%	5.00%	5.00%	
66							
67	Variable Cost	50.00	52.50	55.13	81.44	85.52	
68		50%	50%	50%	50%	50%	
69	Fixed Cost	60	60	60	60	60	
70							
71	Investment	$ 300.00					
72							Terminal Value
73	Cash Flow	(310.00)	(7.50)	(4.88)	21.44	25.52	204.14
74	Check for abandonment				1.00	1.00	
75					1.00	1.00	1.00
76							
77	Check for Expansion				1.00	1.00	
78					1.00	1.00	
79	Expansion Cash Flow						
80	Revenue				162.89	171.03	
81	Variable Cost				81.44	85.52	
82	Fixed Cost				60.00	60.00	
83	Investment				-	-	
84	Cash Flow of Expansion				21.44	25.52	204.14
85							
86							
87	Realized Cash Flows	(310.00)	(7.50)	(4.88)	42.89	51.03	408.27
88							
89	Discount Factor	0.89	0.89	0.89	0.70	0.70	0.70
90	Discounted Cash Flow	-$275.56	-$6.67	-$4.33	$30.12	$35.84	$286.74
91							
92	NPV	-$24.44					

FIGURE 5.16 Spreadsheet segment from **Project.xls** model showing the possibilities of abandonment and expansion. Note that columns E through K are hidden.

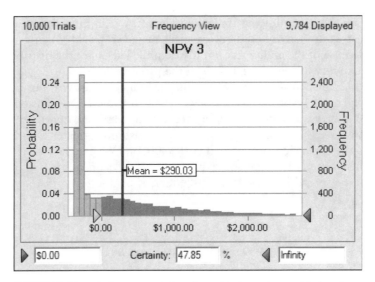

FIGURE 5.17   CB forecast window from Project.xls model showing the possibility of expansion.

The Crystal Ball output in Figure 5.17 shows that the option to expand the project has vastly increased its value. Because the mean NPV with both expansion and abandonment possible is $290.03, the value of the expansion option is $290.03 − $50.62 = $239.41. Note that the flexibility to expand the project did change its inherent risk structure slightly, in that the the probability that the project adds value to the firm increased a bit, that is Pr(NPV > 0) ≈ 48 percent. If you extract the data, you will see that on about 500 trials, the value of NPV 3 was positive while NPV 2 was negative. In this situation we model the realistic behavior of an active decision maker who will capitalize on fortuitous conditions that promote expansion. By expanding when times are good, the decision maker increases the ENPV of the project by adding gains to the right tail of the distribution of possible results.

Threshold Values

In the previous example we arbitrarily specified the decision rule for project abandonment as "abandon the project if three consecutive quarters of negative cash flow occur." Likewise, we arbitrarily specified the decision rule for project expansion as "expand if we see three consecutive quarters of cash flow greater than $15." By adding decision variables to the model we can use the Decision Table tool to help determine if the arbitrary threshold dollar amounts of $0 for abandonment and $15 for expansion are the optimal values to use. That is to say, it is possible that some other threshold values, such as −$5 and $20 might yield higher option values and if so we would like to find the threshold values that yield the highest option values. Note that we could also use decision variables to determine whether using

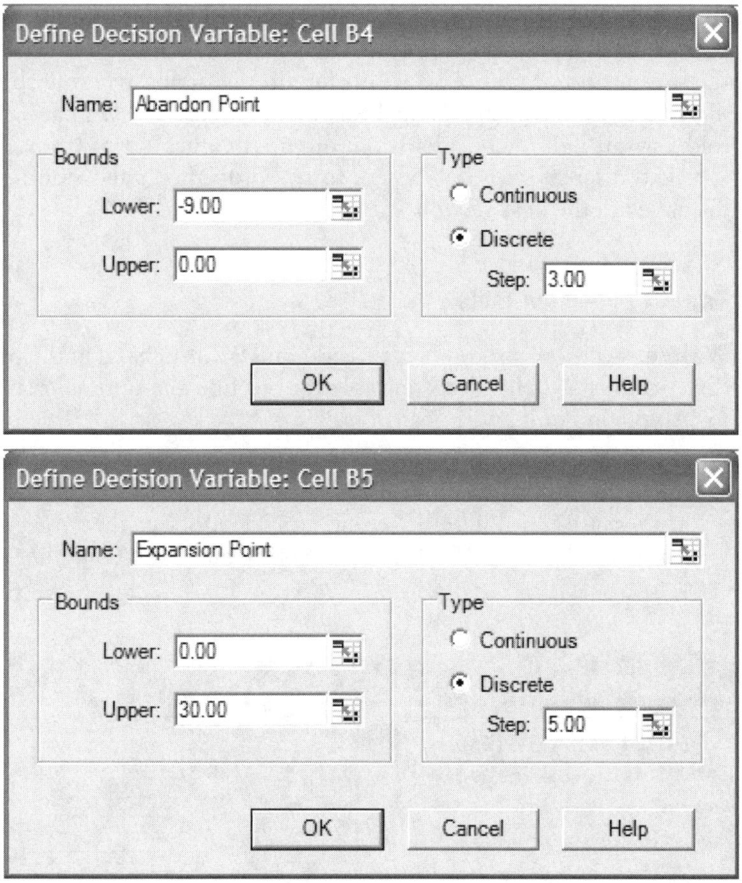

FIGURE 5.18 Decision variables for the threshold value at which to abandon and expand in the Project.xls model.

two or four (or some other number) of consecutive quarters is optimal; however, for illustrative purposes here we will stick to threshold dollar amounts of cash flow.

To see the decision variable for the threshold value of cash flow for abandoning the project, click on cell **B4** in **Project.xls**. Then click on **Define→Define Decision...** on the top menu in Excel. This will bring up the dialog window shown at the top of Figure 5.18. Cell **B4** is named "Abandon Point," and Crystal Ball will consider four different values, $\{0, -3, -6, -9\}$. Note that we specified discrete steps of \$3, but by clicking the Continuous button in the Variable Type section of the dialog window, we could have had Crystal Ball investigate the potentially infinite number of values between virtually any specified lower and upper bounds. Using a discrete variable type limits the number of values that Crystal Ball checks and thus speeds up the analysis.

To see the decision variable for threshold value of cash flow for expanding the project, click on cell **B5** in **Project.xls**. Then click on **Define→Define Decision...** on the top menu in Excel. This will bring up the dialog window shown at the bottom of Figure 5.18. We have named this decision variable "Expansion Point" and have told Crystal Ball to consider seven different values, {0, 5, 10, ..., 30}. Note that we specified discrete steps of $5 here to speed up the analysis and simplify the results displayed in the next section.

Two-Way Decision Table

With the decision variables for cells **B4** and **B5** as defined in the previous section, we can use Crystal Ball's decision table tool to find the optimal combination of values for Abandon Point and Expansion Point.

1. In the top menu, click on **Run→Tools→Decision Table** to bring up Step 1 of the Decision Table tool (see Figure 5.19). Select the target forecast NPV 3 as shown in Figure 5.19). Click the **Next>** button to continue.

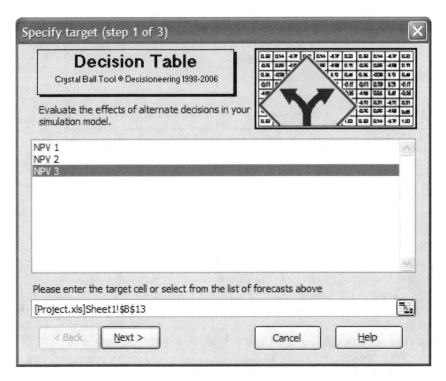

FIGURE 5.19 Step 1 in using the Decision Table tool with the **Project.xls** model.

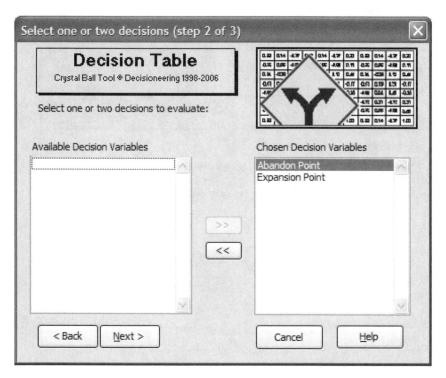

FIGURE 5.20 Step 2 in using the Decision Table tool with the **Project.xls** model.

2. Use the >> button to move the decision variables Abandon Point and Expansion Point into the Chosen Decision Variables box on the right side of the dialog box as shown in Figure 5.20. Click the **Next**> button to continue.

3. Take the default values for the fields in the step 3 dialog box as shown in Figure 5.21. Click the **Start** button to tell Crystal Ball to use the decision table tool to evaluate all possible combinations of the specified values of Abandon Point and Expansion Point.

You have just instructed Crystal Ball to run 10,000 trials for each of $4 \times 7 = 28$ different combinations of decision variable values. The amount of time it takes Crystal Ball to run these 280,000 iterations depends on the speed of your computer.

Interpreting the Results

Figure 5.22 shows the results of using the decision table tool. Cell C3 contains the maximum expected NPV of $299.78, which results from using the following decision rules: (1) Begin checking in the second quarter of year, and abandon the project if three consecutive quarters of cash flow below −$6 occur; and (2) expand if

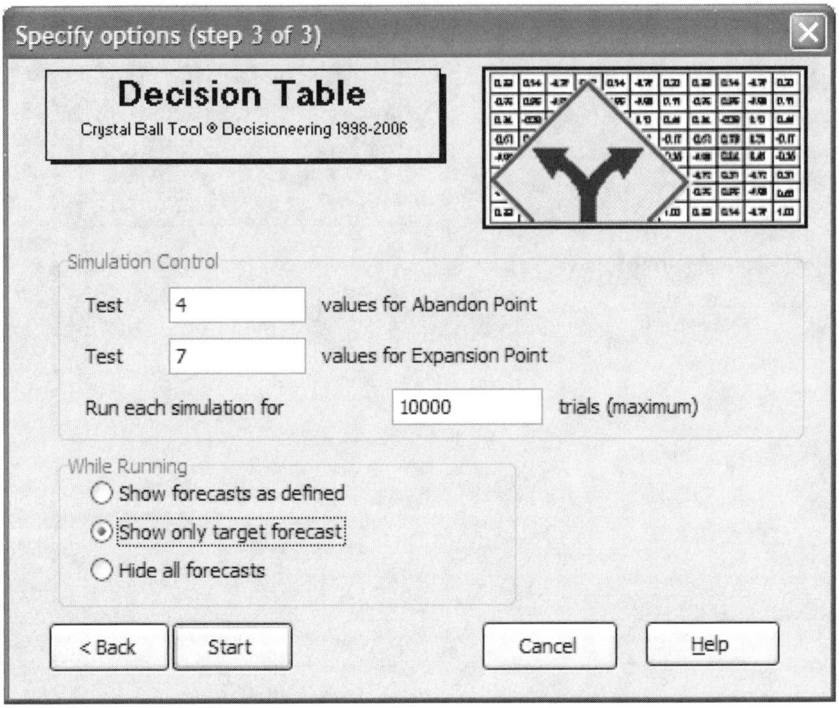

FIGURE 5.21 Step 3 in using the Decision Table tool with the Project.xls model.

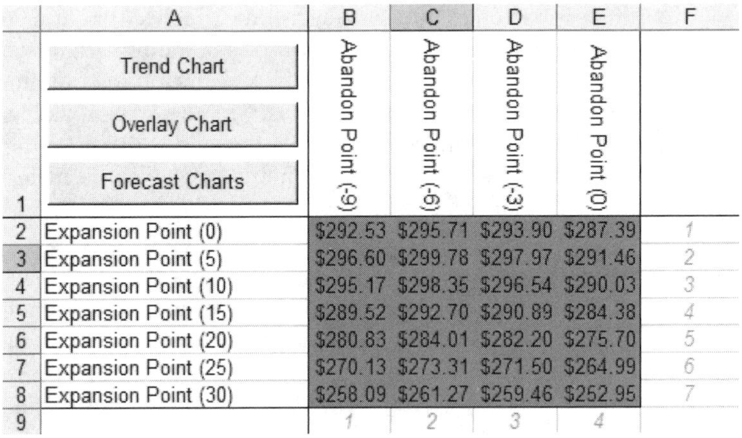

	A	B	C	D	E	F
	Trend Chart	Abandon Point (-9)	Abandon Point (-6)	Abandon Point (-3)	Abandon Point (0)	
	Overlay Chart					
	Forecast Charts					
1						
2	Expansion Point (0)	$292.53	$295.71	$293.90	$287.39	1
3	Expansion Point (5)	$296.60	$299.78	$297.97	$291.46	2
4	Expansion Point (10)	$295.17	$298.35	$296.54	$290.03	3
5	Expansion Point (15)	$289.52	$292.70	$290.89	$284.38	4
6	Expansion Point (20)	$280.83	$284.01	$282.20	$275.70	5
7	Expansion Point (25)	$270.13	$273.31	$271.50	$264.99	6
8	Expansion Point (30)	$258.09	$261.27	$259.46	$252.95	7
9		1	2	3	4	

FIGURE 5.22 Results from using the Decision Table tool with the Project.xls model.

three consecutive quarters of cash flow greater than $5 occur. These new threshold values of −6 and 5 are shown in the labels occupying cells C1 and A3, respectively, in Figure 5.22. Note that the maximum value of $299.78 identified in the Decision Table tool output is $9.75 greater than the $290.03 identified in Figure 5.17. Keep in mind, though, that these figures are just estimates based on 10,000 runs of the simulation. More runs would result in higher precision of the estimates.

At its heart, Monte Carlo simulation is just a computer-based sampling system. Thus, specifying more runs of the simulation will yield more precise results just as including more items in a random sample yields more precise estimates in a statistical study designed to make inferences about a population. Crystal Ball allows you to specify the level of precision that you desire. See Chapter 6 for information on how to specify the precision level.

In this example, we varied the Abandon Point in steps of $3, and the expansion Point in steps of $5. We might be able to identify even higher levels of expected NPV by using smaller steps.

The Decision Table tool works well to find the optimal solution for problems involving one or two decision variables. It also serves to introduce the notion of simulation optimization, which is the process of finding the best values of decision variables that we just completed for abandon point and expansion point. When more than two decision variables are involved, as is typical for more realistic problems, the add-in OptQuest is a more powerful tool for finding an optimal solution. This is the topic of the next section.

USING OPTQUEST

We saw in the last section how a decision table could be set up to find the value of a designated output for selected combinations of two decision variable values. Once that was accomplished, we found the best solution by looking at the values in the table to locate the combination that gave the maximum value of the output. Decision tables work very well for one or two decision variables. However, if there are more than two decision variables, decision tables are cumbersome. This section describes how to use the Crystal Ball tool OptQuest to help find the best decisions to make in situations involving more than two decisions.

Terminology

In order to understand better how OptQuest works, some background knowledge of the terminology is required. This subsection gives definitions for some of the terms that will be used throughout the rest of this section.

> **Constraint.** A *constraint* is a relationship among decision variables that restricts the values of the decision variables. When you define a decision variable, you constrain it individually by specifying the bounds. However,

TABLE 5.1 Forecast statistics available for optimizing or using in a requirement with OptQuest.

Mean	Percentile	Mean standard error
Median	Skewness	Certainty
Mode	Kurtosis	Final value
Standard deviation	Coefficient of variability	
Variance	Range	

with an OptQuest constraint, you can restrict the values of linear combinations of decision variables. For example, an OptQuest constraint might be used to ensure that the sum of weights in a portfolio of assets is equal to 1.0.

Objective. An *objective* gives a mathematical representation of the criterion by which it will be determined what is best or optimal. For the Project.xls model, the objective is the maximization of mean net present value (ENPV) because NPV is a direct measure of the value added to the firm by actions undertaken by a decision maker. However, other objectives could also be chosen, such as minimizing the cost or the riskiness of a decision.

Forecast statistic. A *forecast statistic* is a summary value of a forecast distribution, such as the mean, standard deviation, or variance. The optimization is controlled by maximizing, minimizing, or restricting a selected forecast statistic. For example, in the Project.xls model, we chose to maximize the mean NPV because doing so will, on average, give the best results. Thus, maximizing the mean of a forecast is a good strategy for a firm that makes many decisions on a periodic basis. An individual or a firm that is more risk-averse, however, might choose to minimize the standard deviation, or maximize the 5th percentile of the forecast distribution, for example. Table 5.1 lists the forecast statistics available for optimizing or using in a requirement.

Requirement. A *requirement* is a restriction on a forecast statistic that you can set while trying to optimize on some other statistic. For example, you might be interested in maximizing the mean return on a retirement portfolio while at the same time requiring that the risk as measured by the standard deviation does not exceed some specified value. You can use requirements to set upper and lower limits for any statistic of a forecast distribution.

Example

Open Project.xls, then go to the top menu and select Run→OptQuest. In OptQuest, select File→New. This will start a wizard that will lead you through the dialog windows to set up the tool. The Decision Variable Selection window appears first,

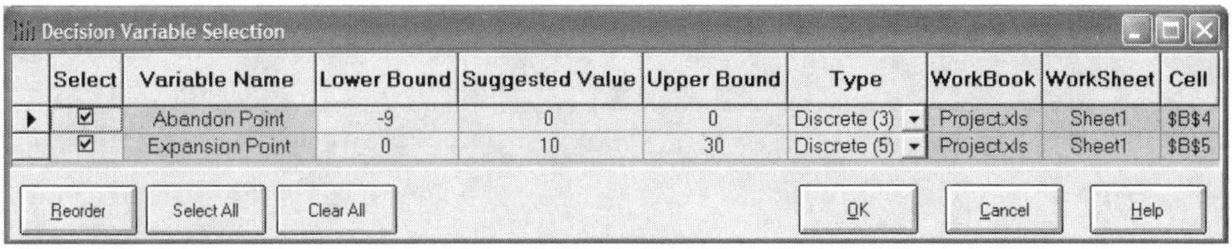

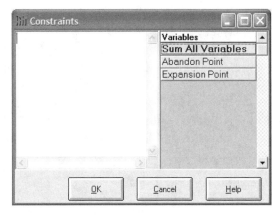

FIGURE 5.23 Decision Variable Selection window for the Project.xls model.

FIGURE 5.24 Constraints window for the Project.xls model.

listing every decision variable defined in the Crystal Ball model. Your window should look like the one shown in Figure 5.23.

The window in Figure 5.23 lets you select which defined decision variables to optimize. The columns and buttons are mostly self-explanatory, although it might not be immediately apparent that Suggested Value is simply the value that is in the decision variable cell when OptQuest is started. To follow this example, you need only to use the default values, so click OK to continue.

The next window that appears is the Constraints window, which is shown in Figure 5.24.

In OptQuest, constraints limit the possible solutions to a model in terms of relationships among the decision variables. In Version 2.3 of OptQuest, you can use the Constraints window to specify only *linear* constraints. In the Project.xls model, we have no constraints on the decision variables (except for the bounds, which we specify when defining the decision variables), so click on OK to continue.

After you exit the Constraints window, the Forecast Selection window appears next, listing all the forecasts defined in the model as shown in Figure 5.25. In the forecast row for NPV 3, click in the Select column. From the drop-down menu, select Maximize Objective, which by default will maximize the mean of the NPV 3

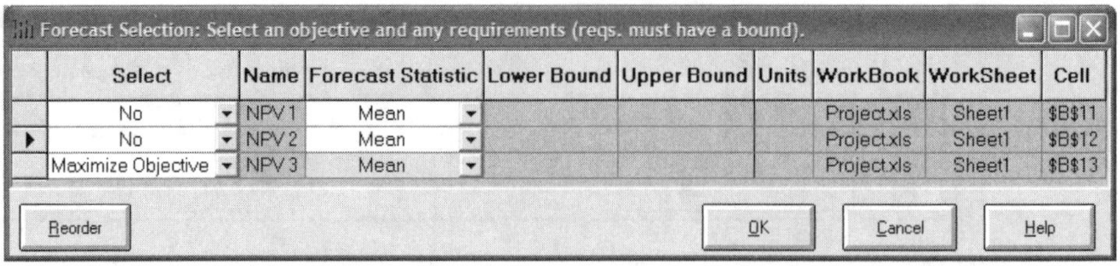

FIGURE 5.25 Forecast Selection window for the Project.xls model.

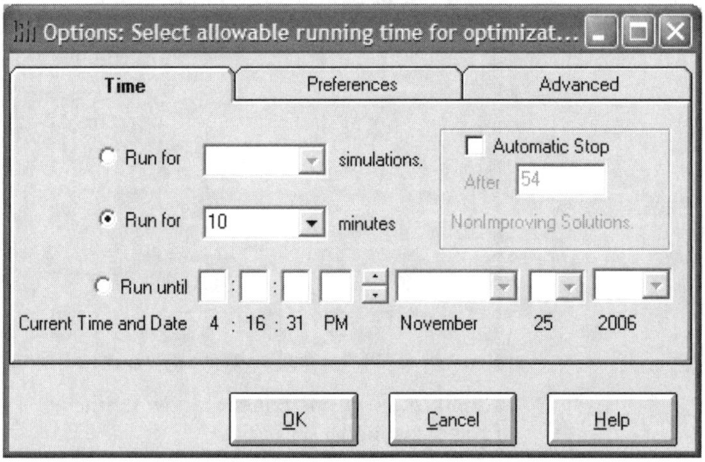

FIGURE 5.26 Options window for the Project.xls model.

forecast. Note that you can choose any of the forecast statistics in Table 5.1 to optimize. Click on OK to continue.

The Options window lets you set options for controlling the optimization process, as shown in Figure 5.26. See the *OptQuest User Manual*, pages 76--81, for a discussion of the choices available in this window. For now, we'll accept all the defaults, so click on OK to continue. Then click on Yes to indicate that you want to run the optimization now.

While the optimization is running, a Status and Solutions window and Performance Graph should appear, as shown in Figures 5.27 and 5.28, respectively.

When running an optimization, you can stop, pause, continue, or restart at any time. You cannot work in Crystal Ball or Excel or make changes in OptQuest when running an optimization, but you can work in other programs. Do not close Excel, Crystal Ball, or OptQuest while running an optimization.

After solving an optimization problem with OptQuest, you can

■ Run a solution analysis to determine the robustness of the results;

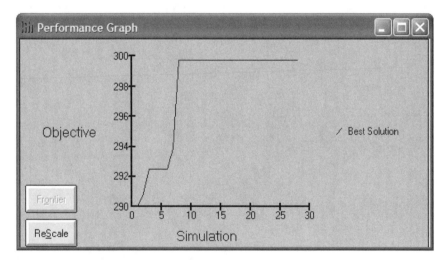

FIGURE 5.27 Status and Solutions window for the Project.xls model.

	Simulation	Maximize Objective NPV 3 Mean	Abandon Point	Expansion Point
	1	290.032	0	10
	2	290.893	-3	15
	3	292.529	-9	0
	7	293.902	-3	0
▶	Best: 8	299.782	-6	5

FIGURE 5.28 Performance Graph for the Project.xls model.

- Run a longer Crystal Ball simulation using the optimal values of the decision variables to assess with more precision the risks of the recommended solution; or
- Use Crystal Ball's analysis features to evaluate the optimal solution further.

For now, notice that the best solution identified in Figure 5.27 is the same as that identified in Figure 5.22 using Decision Table, namely an Abandon Point of −6 and an Expansion Point of 5. For both Figures 5.27 and 5.22, we used four different values for Abandon Point and seven different values for Expansion Point. If we used more values with Decision Table, the Decision Table results would take up more cells than shown in Figure 5.22, and would also have taken longer to generate. However, with OptQuest we could have easily specified an essentially infinite number of values by specifying "continuous" with the pulldown menu in the Type column of Figure 5.23. This would increase the time taken by OptQuest to search for an optimal solution, but it would result in values of Abandon Point and Expansion Point that are closer to the overall optimal values. This is one reason why OptQuest searches for optimality are usually preferred over Decision Table searches.

CHAPTER 6

Selecting Run Preferences

N ow that we have covered the basics of setting up a Crystal Ball model and using its forecasts to help you make decisions, we will take a closer look at the options available to you through the Run Preferences menu to control the execution of your simulation models.

TRIALS

Figure 6.1 shows the Trials tab of the Run Preferences dialog. A Crystal Ball *trial* is the process of generating random variates from the stochastic assumptions you have defined for your model, evaluating the formulas that depend on these values, then calculating and storing the forecast values.

When you click the Run button, Crystal Ball begins executing the steps depicted in Figure 6.2. The actions taken by Crystal Ball at each step are described as follows:

Start is where Crystal Ball prepares itself to run a simulation by looking for the assumption and forecast cells in your spreadsheet, and getting ready to store forecast values in your computer's memory.

Set Values is where each trial begins by Crystal Ball generating a random value for each stochastic assumption and placing it in the corresponding assumption cell.

Recalculate is where Crystal Ball instructs Excel to use the values that were just placed in the assumption cells to update each cell in the spreadsheet that depends on the assumptions.

Get Results is where Crystal Ball takes the updated value from each of the forecast cells and stores it in memory. If you have enabled sensitivity analysis, Crystal Ball also stores the current value of each assumption cell during this step for possible analysis later with sensitivity charts.

Stop marks the completion of each simulation trial. If none of the stopping criteria described below have been satisfied, Crystal Ball returns to the Set Values step as indicated in Figure 6.2.

End is where Crystal Ball returns control to Excel after one of the stopping criteria is met, or after you have clicked on the Stop button in the Crystal Ball toolbar.

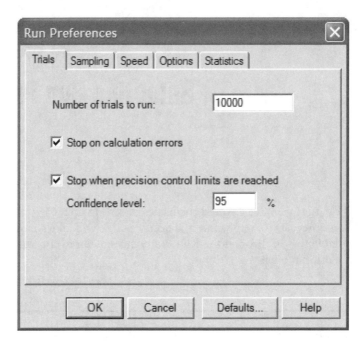

FIGURE 6.1 Run Preferences Trials tab.

Crystal Ball executes the simulation cycle automatically, but it also gives you some control over selected aspects of the execution. This section describes those aspects.

Number of Trials to Run

This is the *maximum* number of trials you want Crystal Ball to run before it stops the simulation. There are other stopping criteria, so sometimes the simulation will stop before the maximum number of trials is reached. In general, the more trials you run, the better (more precise) will be your solution in a statistical sense. A rule of thumb is to use no fewer than 2,000 trials (see Figure 2.7). With Crystal Ball's Extreme Speed feature, 10,000 trials will execute quickly for moderately complex models, so that is the number of trials specified in most of the examples shown in this book.

Stop on Calculation Errors

When this box is checked, Crystal Ball will stop the simulation when a numerical error occurs in an Excel calculation. Numerical errors are often caused by dividing by some zero somewhere. For example, for arrays of values that have different algebraic signs, using Excel's =IRR(values,guess) formula in a forecast cell can sometimes cause a numerical error.

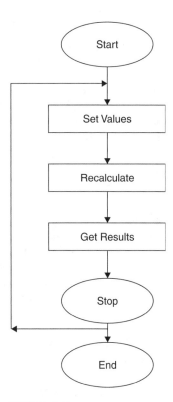

FIGURE 6.2 Simulation cycle.

It is good practice always to have this box checked, as numerical errors are usually the result of errors in model logic and this feature of Crystal Ball will alert you if any such errors are present. However, if you are using =IRR(values,guess) in your model and have difficulty getting Crystal Ball to run to completion, try unchecking this box.

Stop When Precision Control Limits Are Reached

Checking this box enables Crystal Ball's statistical precision-checking feature. The precision of an estimate is determined by the half-width of a $(1 - \alpha)100\%$ confidence interval, which is computed by Crystal Ball for the mean as $z_{\alpha/2}s/\sqrt{n}$, where $z_{\alpha/2}$ is the $(1 - \alpha/2)100$ percentile of the standard normal distribution, s is the Standard Deviation, and n is the number of trials from which the standard error is computed. As discussed in Chapter 2, the value of $s/\sqrt{n}$ is reported in the Statistics View of the Forecast window as Mean Standard Error. Smaller values of s yield smaller half-widths, which yields more precise estimates. Each of the three terms in the half-width calculation ($z_{\alpha/2}$, s, and n) can be used to increase the precision of the estimate of the mean.

The value of $z_{\alpha/2}$ is affected by the number you enter in the **Confidence level** field in Figure 6.1, which is your specification of $1 - \alpha$. For example, when you specify a 95 percent confidence level, then $z_{\alpha/2} = z_{.975} = 1.96$, which means that the precision is measured as roughly two standard errors of the mean. While there may sometimes be good reason to change the value of $1 - \alpha$ in particular situations, leaving the confidence level at 95% will suffice for most financial models.

Crystal Ball calculates the standard deviation of the forecast values, s, using Expression 2.1 as the simulation progresses. While s cannot be affected by options specified in the dialog shown in Figure 6.1, it is possible to increase precision by reducing s (or equivalently, the variance, s^2) through so-called variance reduction techniques, which require structural changes to the model and are described in Appendix C.

The precision of the estimate increases at a rate inversely proportional to the square root of the number of trials. During the simulation, Crystal Ball recalculates the half-width periodically, then stops the simulation when either the maximum number of trials or specified precision is reached, whichever comes first.

As an example of how to use the precision control feature, open the file Accumulate.xls, and click on the Forecast cell **D4**. Then select **Define**→**Define Forecast...** to get the Define Forecast dialog shown in Figure 6.3. Select the **Precision** tab. Note that you might have to click on the More icon—two arrowheads pointing down ($\lor$) in the upper right portion of the dialog to see the tabs. Check the two check boxes and punch the radio button indicated in Figure 6.3, and specify 50000 as the absolute units of precision as shown. Click **OK**.

In Run Preferences, change the **Number of trials to run** to one million (enter 1000000 with no commas), and make sure that **Stop when precision control limits are reached** is checked. Then click **OK**. Press the Run button on the Crystal Ball toolbar. Your simulation model should stop running well before 1 million trials have run, and you should see a Statistics View for **Year 30 Wealth** that looks like that shown in Figure 6.4.

It is also possible to specify precision for the median, the standard deviation, or a selected percentile. This is done by following steps similar to those above for specifying the precision of the mean. See the *Crystal Ball User Manual* for specific details.

SAMPLING

Figure 6.5 shows the **Sampling** tab of the Run Preferences dialog, which has options related to the algorithms for generating the random numbers Crystal Ball uses to drive the simulation. This section gives a high-level overview of these options. For a more technical discussion, see Appendix B.

Random Number Generation

Random numbers are values between 0 and 1 that Crystal Ball generates to drive all the randomness in your models. The algorithm that Crystal Ball uses to generate

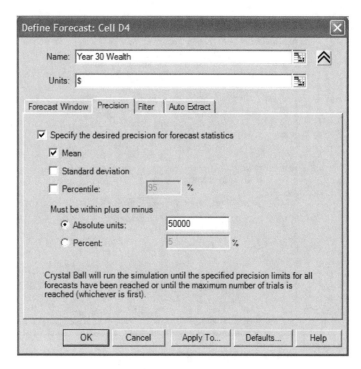

FIGURE 6.3 Define Forecast dialog showing the Precision tab.

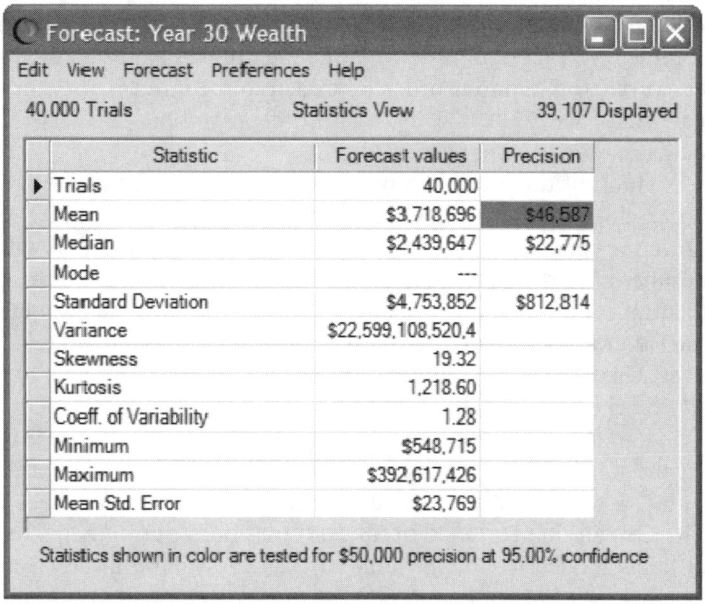

FIGURE 6.4 Statistics View for Year 30 Wealth forecast showing that a precision of $46,587 was reached in 40,000 trials.

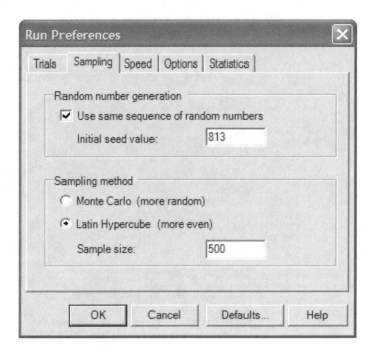

FIGURE 6.5 Run Preferences Sampling tab.

these random numbers has the capability to produce over two billion different values in such a way they appear to have the Uniform(0,1) distribution and be in a completely "random" order, that is, the numbers appear to be serially independent. However, this random order is predetermined and is the same every time Crystal Ball runs. See Appendix B for more details about the algorithm used by Crystal Ball's random number generator.

Think of these random numbers as being placed in the predetermined random order clockwise on the perimeter of a circle with a spinner arrow in the middle. Once the spinner arrow is at its starting point, Crystal Ball will select each random number it needs sequentially in a clockwise direction from the circle beginning with the number at the spinner's starting point. With this image in mind, you can think of the Random number generation options on the Sampling tab as giving you control over where to set the spinner to designate the starting point.

By checking the Use same sequence of random numbers check box and specifying an Initial seed value as indicated in Figure 6.5, you are telling Crystal Ball to set the starting point for its random numbers at the same place each time you run a simulation. The Initial seed value must be an integer between 1 and 2147483647. The Use same sequence of random numbers option helps to compare results for different models having the same stochastic assumptions. By using the same sequence of random numbers in two models, any differences in performance are due to differences in the models rather than sampling error.

If you do not specify an initial seed value, Crystal Ball will determine a seed from the number of milliseconds that have elapsed since Windows began running on your computer. This of course will be different each time you run the simulation, so you can expect Crystal Ball to produce different forecast values on each run.

Sampling Method

Appendix B also provides some technical details and references on the differences between Monte Carlo sampling (MCS) and Latin Hypercube sampling (LHS). As the statistical theory behind MCS is well known, it should be used for applications where your intended audience is most critical, such as in academic research. LHS is a form of stratified sampling where all portions of the tails of a distribution are sure to be sampled. The statistical properties of LHS samples are the subject of current academic research, and no widely accepted methods of assessing precision with LHS are available yet. Nevertheless, LHS is probably the best choice for most practical applications. LHS uses slightly more computer memory than MCS, but this should not pose a problem for most users.

SPEED

Figure 6.6 shows the dialog containing options that let you control how quickly your simulation model executes. Once it is built and debugged, you will ordinarily want it to run as fast as possible. However, there are sometimes reasons for not doing so, such as when you are demonstrating the model to a potential user of its results.

Run Mode

I suggest that you use Extreme Speed (ES) mode whenever you can, but you must realize that it imposes a few constraints on how you build your model because it uses vectorization to speed up the calculations. Essentially, this means that ES mode will perform hundreds of simulation trials at a time in RAM (random access memory), while normal speed performs them one at a time. Most of Excel's 320 functions are supported, but a few are not. The most commonly used unsupported function is the string function. One common way for strings to be used is when an Excel **IF** command puts "Yes" or "No" in a cell that is referenced by another formula. ES mode will not work with the strings "Yes" or "No," but works fine if you replace these with 1 and 0, or the Excel Boolean values **TRUE** and **FALSE**. Consult the *Crystal Ball User Manual* Appendix C for a complete list of unsupported functions and the Crystal Ball Web site for updates on this feature.

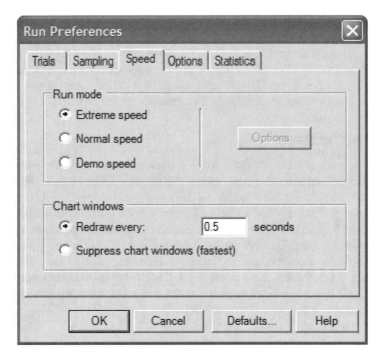

FIGURE 6.6   Run Preferences Speed tab.

Here are some tips for getting the most out of Extreme Speed:

- Make sure that your computer has lots of RAM.
- Build your models so that the UsedRange (upper left rectangle of non-empty cells) is minimized.
- Use Latin Hypercube sampling.
- Avoid references to other worksheets that are not required for your model.
- Avoid using large ranges in function arguments (for example, in the LOOKUP function).

Normal speed should be checked when you use a function not supported by ES mode. Demo speed is useful for demonstrating to others how your model works and animating Excel graphs.

Chart Windows

These two radio buttons let you specify the rate at which Crystal Ball redraws the chart windows. Because this takes time away from doing the calculations during a simulation, suppress the chart windows to get the simulation completed most quickly. This may be most useful when using OptQuest.

OPTIONS

Figure 6.7 shows the Run options, which are mostly self-explanatory. When you are building and refining your model, you should always enable **Store assumption values for sensitivity analysis**, and do sensitivity analyses to help refinement. Once you are satisfied with your model, you can disable storage to help Crystal Ball run the model faster.

It turns out that having highly correlated assumptions can sometimes interfere with sensitivity analysis. For example, assume that you have a model for which the Forecast cell is highly sensitive to Assumption A, but not impacted at all by Assumption B. However, if Assumptions A and B are defined with a high (positive or negative) correlation, the sensitivity analysis could indicate that the forecast is sensitive to both Assumptions A and B just because B tends to follow A. Therefore, when using sensitivity analysis with correlated assumptions, you will want to disable the correlations when you are doing sensitivity analysis. Just remember to turn it back on when you run the model for decision making.

The **Run user-defined macros** option is useful for power users of Crystal Ball and Excel, but for most financial models Excel has built in all the functions that you will need. However, if you are facile with Visual Basic for Applications (VBA)

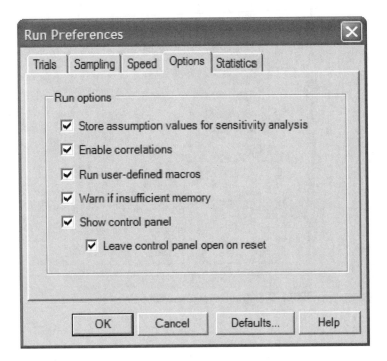

FIGURE 6.7 Run Preferences Options tab.

and wish to do things Excel doesn't already do, or you wish to do extra processing during each trial of the simulation, see the *Crystal Ball User Manual* for how to use macros with a Crystal Ball simulation model.

Enabling **Warn if insufficient memory** will cause Crystal Ball to issue a warning dialog if you don't have enough memory in your computer to run the simulation. The dialog lists several things you can do to help, but the best course of action is to put more RAM in your computer if you see this warning often.

STATISTICS

Figure 6.8 shows the options to change how percentiles are calculated and formatted. Punch the radio buttons to match your taste and that of the decision maker who will use your model's output. The **Calculate capability metrics** check box is used primarily for Six Sigma applications, so is not discussed further here.

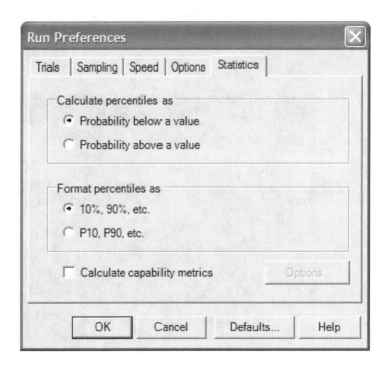

FIGURE 6.8   Run Preferences Statistics tab.

CHAPTER 7

Net Present Value and Internal Rate of Return

N ow that we have completed your introduction to Crystal Ball, we will begin looking at several different types of situations for which Crystal Ball models are useful. We start with net present value (NPV) models, because using Monte Carlo simulation to develop distributions of NPV is a source of controversy among some academics even though it is done routinely by practitioners. In this chapter, we will consider both sides of the controversy and see some models where the distribution of NPV can help the decision maker gain insight into the problem at hand. We will also consider the pros and cons of using internal rate of return (IRR) as a Crystal Ball forecast. It is assumed that you are already familiar with these concepts. For more background information on NPV and IRR, see any introductory finance textbook such as Melicher and Norton (2006).

DETERMINISTIC NPV AND IRR

Suppose that you have the opportunity to purchase an annuity that costs you $100 at Year 0, and is certain to return $30 to you at the end of each Year 1 through 5. These cash flows are depicted in the Excel chart on the spreadsheet segment in Figure 7.1. Denote the cash flow at the end of Year t as C_t, and the relevant annual rate of interest as r. Then the NPV of the annuity is defined as

$$\text{NPV} = \sum_{t=1}^{5} \frac{C_t}{(1+r)^t} + C_0. \tag{7.1}$$

For the cash flows in Figure 7.1, if $r = 10$ percent then NPV = $13.72 as shown in cell **B11**. Therefore, the annuity is a good investment for any individual with a required minimum rate of return of 10 percent because the investment's NPV of $13.72 is greater than zero at that rate.

Be aware that the definition of NPV in Expression 7.1 is slightly different from that used by the Excel **NPV** function. To find the NPV of the annuity in Figure 7.1,

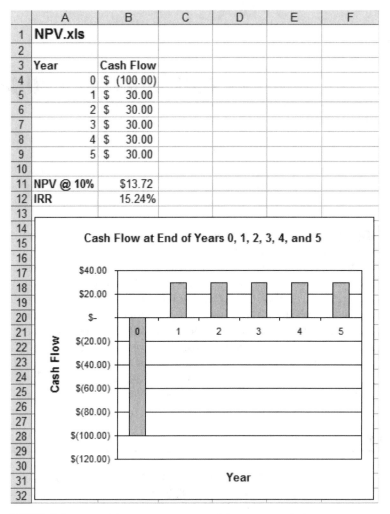

FIGURE 7.1 Spreadsheet segment to model annuity with deterministic cash flows of −$100 at the end of Year 0, and $30 at the end of Years 1 through 5.

we use the Excel formula

$$=NPV(0.1,B5:B9)+B4, \tag{7.2}$$

which is entered in cell **B11** of **NPV.xls**. Most finance textbooks refer to the quantity calculated in this example by Excel's **NPV** function as the present value at end of Year 0 of the cash flows obtained at the ends at Years 1 through 5. To get the *net* present value, we also consider the investment (negative cash flow)

	A	B	C	D
1	**NPV Models.xls**			
2				
3	**Year**	**Z**	**Model 1 Cash Flows**	**Model 2 Cash Flows**
4	0		$ (100.00)	$ (100.00)
5	1	0	$ 30.00	$ 30.00
6	2	0	$ 30.00	$ 30.00
7	3	0	$ 30.00	$ 30.00
8	4	0	$ 30.00	$ 30.00
9	5	0	$ 30.00	$ 30.00
10	**NPV@10%**		$13.72	$13.72
11	**IRR**		15.24%	15.24%

FIGURE 7.2 Spreadsheet segment to model stochastic cash flows at the end of Years 1 through 5. Model 1 cash flows in Years 1 through 5 are IID normal(30,3). Model 2 cash flows follow an additive random walk with normal(0,3) increments.

at Year 0, denoted by C_0 in Expression 7.1. This can be confusing, but the NPV function has been defined this way for so many versions of Excel that Microsoft is understandably loath to change it at this point because so many of their existing customers are accustomed to the nontextbook definition and use it in many of their existing models.

As an alternative to NPV, we can also help decide whether to purchase the annuity by calculating its IRR. The IRR is defined to be the value of r in Expression 7.1 that makes NPV = 0. Because there is no convenient closed-form expression for calculating IRR, we use Excel's IRR function to find it for us. Notice that there is consistency between the financial definition of IRR and Excel's IRR function. Cell B12 in Figure 7.1 shows that the IRR for the annuity is 15.24 percent. You can check this by replacing 0.1 with B12 in Formula 7.2 for cell B11 and seeing that NPV=0.

SIMULATING NPV AND IRR

Now let's assume that we can purchase an investment product for $100 that has stochastic cash flows in Years 1–5. We will use two different stochastic processes for the risky cash flows, and compare the results to the annuity described in the previous section.

Model 1. The cash flows at the end of Years 1–5 are independent and identically distributed (IID) over time. Specifically, each cash flow is calculated as $C_t = 30 + 3Z_t$ for $t = 1, 2, 3, 4$, and 5, where each Z_t is drawn from a normal(0,1) distribution independently of the Z_ts for the other years. The Model 1 cash flows are in cells C5:C9 of file NPVModels.xls shown in Figure 7.2.

Model 2. The cash flows at the end of Years 1–5 are linked over time in an additive random walk model. Year 1 cash flow is computed as $C_1 = 30 + 3Z_1$, so is equal to Model 1's Year 1 cash flow. Years 2–5 cash flows are computed as $C_t = C_{t-1} + 3Z_t$ where the Z_ts for $t = 2, 3, 4,$ and 5 are the same normal(0,1) random variates used to generate Model 1's cash flows. The Model 2 cash flows are in cells D5:D9 of file NPVModels.xls shown in Figure 7.2.

To compare the effect of the IID model to that of the additive random walk model, look at the differences between distributions of NPVs and IRRs in Figure 7.3. Overlay Chart 1 in Figure 7.3 compares the distributions of NPVs for the two models of cash flow. Each distribution has the same true expected value, which is $13.72 as it is for the annuity shown in Figure 7.1. However, a large difference in the variability of the two distributions is evident in the overlay chart. As you can see in Figure 7.4, the standard deviation of the distribution of Model 1 NPV is $5.14, while in Figure 7.5 the standard deviation of the distribution of Model 2 NPV is $16.11. This difference in variability is explained by the difference in the models used to calculate the cash flows. Because the cash flows are linked to each other in the random walk model (Model 2), their variability increases from year to year. For example, in Model 1 the cash flow for Year 5 is calculated as $C_5 = 30 + 3Z_5$, so has a true variance of $3^2 = 9$ and standard deviation of 3. In Model 2, the cash flow for Year 5 is linked to all previous years' cash flows:

$$
\begin{aligned}
C_5 &= C_4 + 3Z_5 \\
&= C_3 + 3Z_4 + 3Z_5 \\
&= C_2 + 3Z_3 + 3Z_4 + 3Z_5 \\
&= C_1 + 3Z_2 + 3Z_3 + 3Z_4 + 3Z_5 \\
&= 30 + 3Z_1 + 3Z_2 + 3Z_3 + 3Z_4 + 3Z_5,
\end{aligned}
$$

so has a true variance of $5(3^2) = 45$ and standard deviation 6.708. The increasing dispersion of cash flow distributions over time in Model 2 reflects the decision maker's increased uncertainty about the cash flows the farther into the future he or she looks. This increased uncertainty in cash flows causes the standard deviation for Model 2 NPV to be larger than the standard deviation for Model 1 NPV in Figure 7.2. Overlay Chart 2 in Figure 7.3 shows similar differences in dispersion for the distributions of IRR.

Using simulation to find a distribution of net present value is heresy to some finance professors, yet many analysts do this routinely without knowing that it is controversial. When the concept of using distributions of NPV to compare investments

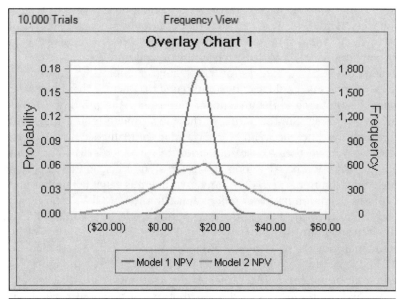

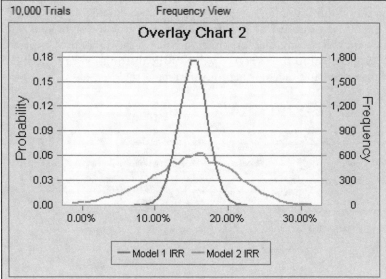

FIGURE 7.3 Overlay charts to compare distributions of NPV (Overlay Chart 1) and IRR (Overlay Chart 2) for Models 1 and 2 in Figure 7.2. In both charts the distribution for Model 1 cash flows has much less dispersion than the distribution for Model 2 cash flows.

was first promoted some 40 years ago by Hertz (1968), computers were not widely available to managers as they are now. At that time, the only practical method of calculating present value available to financial analysts was to estimate the expected value (mean) of potential cash flows for each future period and discount them as we did for each deterministic C_t in Expression 7.1. Doing so ignores the variation in potential future cash flows, and could lead the uninitiated to conclude that there is no difference between the annuity and the investment with stochastic cash flows. However, there is clearly a difference in the nature of these investments, and using simulation to help illustrate the differences can be eye-opening for many decision makers.

The controversy over whether to use simulation to calculate a distribution of NPV stems from the definition of NPV long ago as the sum of discounted expected cash flows. Under this definition, the NPV of any investment is a single number and some adherents of this definition bristle at talk of a distribution of NPV. Proponents of simulation, however, advocate finding the distribution of the sum of discounted potential cash flows from an investment as we did in Figures 7.4 and 7.5, then using the distribution for analyzing the investment's riskiness. When speaking to those who bristle, you may find it helpful to refer to a distribution such as those in Figure 7.4 or 7.5 as a distribution of *potential* NPV rather than a distribution of NPV.

Notice that in this case the means of the distributions of potential net present value are the same (within sampling error) as the NPV calculated as the sum of discounted expected cash flows, $13.72. This will not hold true for all models, and in the next section we will see a model for which the sum of the discounted expected cash flows will not be equal to the expected value of the distribution of the sum of potential cash flows, even after accounting for sampling error.

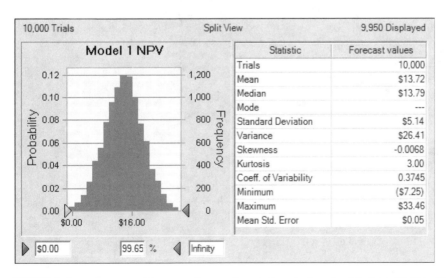

FIGURE 7.4   Split view of forecast chart and statistics window for Model 1 NPV in Figure 7.2.

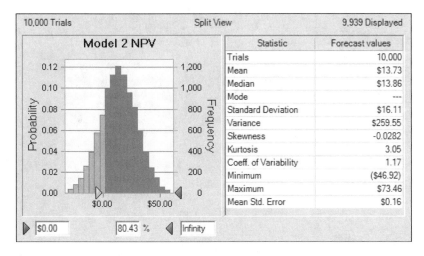

	Split View		
10,000 Trials			9,939 Displayed

Statistic	Forecast values
Trials	10,000
Mean	$13.73
Median	$13.86
Mode	---
Standard Deviation	$16.11
Variance	$259.55
Skewness	-0.0282
Kurtosis	3.05
Coeff. of Variability	1.17
Minimum	($46.92)
Maximum	$73.46
Mean Std. Error	$0.16

FIGURE 7.5 Split view of forecast chart and statistics window for Model 2 NPV in Figure 7.2.

CAPITAL BUDGETING

For an illustration of using simulation for capital budgeting decisions, consider an example from Chapter 10 of the excellent and popular finance textbook by Brealey, Meyers, and Allen (2006). I have tried to make the description below and the Excel models self-complete, but for a fuller discussion of this project see BMA 2006.

Figure 7.6 shows a spreadsheet model in **ScooterNPV.xls** for the Otobai Company, who are considering the introduction of an electrically powered motor scooter for city use. The inputs to be varied and their base-case values are in cells **A4:B8**. The five variable inputs are: market size, market share, unit price (yen), unit variable cost (yen), and fixed cost (billions yen). The model represented in cells **A14:C24** can be stated in the following expressions for Investment in Year 0 and the other variables in Years 1–10:

$$\text{Investment} = 15 \text{ billion yen}$$

$$\text{Revenue} = \text{Market size} \times \text{Market share} \times \text{Unit price}$$

$$\text{Variable cost} = \text{Market size} \times \text{Market share} \times \text{Unit variable cost}$$

$$\text{Depreciation} = \text{Investment} \div 10$$

$$\text{Pretax profit} = \text{Revenue} - \text{Variable cost} - \text{Fixed cost} - \text{Depreciation}$$

$$\text{Tax} = 0.5 \times \text{Pretax profit}$$

$$\text{Net profit} = \text{Pretax profit} - \text{Tax}$$

$$\text{Net cash flow} = \text{Net profit} + \text{Depreciation}$$

	A	B	C	D	E
1	**ScooterNPV.xls**				
2	**Inputs**				
3	**Assumptions**		Minimum	Likeliest	Maximum
4	Market size	1,000,000	900,000	1,000,000	1,100,000
5	Market share	10%	4%	10%	16%
6	Unit price (yen)	375,000	350,000	375,000	380,000
7	Unit variable cost (yen)	300,000	275,000	300,000	360,000
8	Fixed cost (billions yen)	3.000	2.000	3.000	4.000
9					
10	**Output**				
11	**Forecast**				
12	NPV	$3.43			
13					
14	**Cash Flow (billions yen)**	Year 0	Years 1-10		
15	Revenue		37.500		
16	Variable cost		30.000		
17	Fixed cost		3.000		
18	Depreciation		1.500		
19	Pretax profit		3.000		
20	Tax		1.500		
21	Net profit		1.500		
22	Operating cash flow		3.000		
23	Investment	15	-		
24	Net cash flow	(15)	3.000		

FIGURE 7.6 ScooterNPV.xls spreadsheet model.

In the next section, we use this model to demonstrate the use of Crystal Ball's Tornado Chart tool for a deterministic sensitivity analysis of the project's NPV to the model inputs. As is done in BMA 2006, the Tornado Chart tool considers changes in each of the five inputs in turn while the other four are at their base-case values, and keeps track of the corresponding changes in NPV. Note that for each of the five inputs we have defined a Triangular Assumption with parameters shown in cells C4:E8. This was done to facilitate use of the Tornado Chart tool, not to obtain a realistic simulation model for the investment. See Figure 7.14 for a realistic simulation model that *was* created for risk analysis of this project.

Tornado Chart Tool

To use the Tornado Chart tool, select Run→Tools→Tornado Chart... from the top menu. You will see a dialog window like that shown in Figure 7.7. Because NPV is the only Crystal Ball forecast defined in the spreadsheet, click Next > to indicate that you wish to analyze the sensitivity of NPV to the inputs.

Figure 7.8 is the dialog window for Step 2. Click Add Assumptions to cause the inputs to appear in the list as shown in Figure 7.8. Note that we defined the inputs as Crystal Ball assumptions only to make this step easier. After the inputs appear in the list, click Next >.

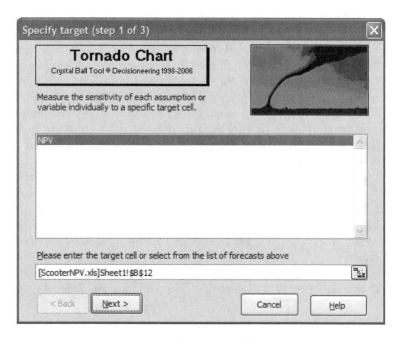

FIGURE 7.7 Step 1 in using the tornado chart tool.

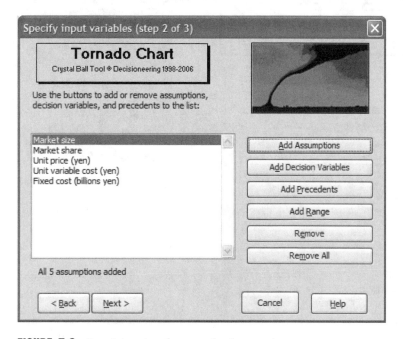

FIGURE 7.8 Step 2 in using the tornado chart tool.

The dialog for Step 3 of using the Tornado Chart tool is shown in Figure 7.9. In this window you can change some options that are self-explanatory. Note that if you take the default values as shown in Figure 7.9, the tool will consider five different levels for each of the five inputs. The levels are determined by the percentiles of the Crystal Ball assumptions that were defined in cells **B4:B8**. Click **Start** to get the results.

A tornado chart like that shown in Figure 7.10 will appear in a new Excel workbook. This chart lists the inputs from top to bottom in decreasing order of the sensitivity of NPV to each input. Thus, Figure 7.10 indicates that NPV is most sensitive to unit variable cost, and least sensitive to market size. The size of any bar corresponds to the magnitude of change in NPV. The color corresponds to the direction of the change in NPV caused by an increase in the input. Because the biggest bars are at the top and the smallest bars are at the bottom, the result is a figure that resembles a tornado. The tornado chart is useful for initial investigation of sensitivities to suggest the order in which we should be concerned with the inputs.

The spider chart in Figure 7.11 depicts the same information as the tornado chart. In this figure, it is the slope of any line that indicates the sensitivity of NPV to

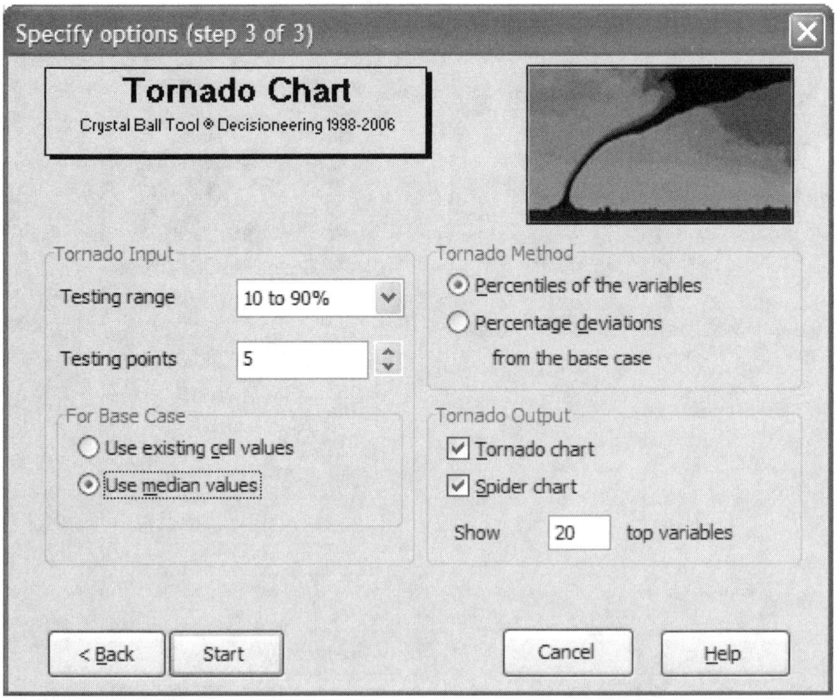

FIGURE 7.9 Step 3 in using the tornado chart tool.

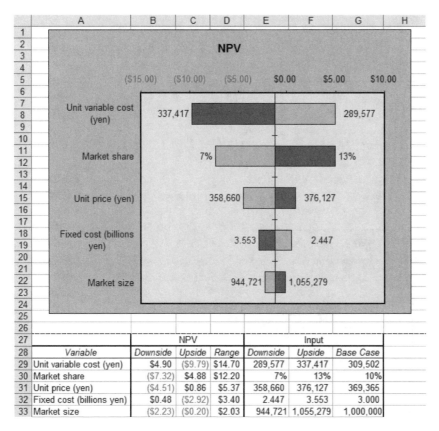

	A	B	C	D	E	F	G	H

FIGURE 7.10   Tornado chart. Darker bars indicate a positive change in the corresponding input.

changes in the corresponding input. For example, Figure 7.11 indicates that NPV is most sensitive to Unit variable cost because the slope of that line is greatest. As the slope of the line is negative, we know that there is an inverse relationship between unit variable cost and NPV. The inputs appear in the same order in the spider chart as they do in the tornado chart.

The Tornado Chart tool is useful for a preliminary, deterministic sensitivity analysis of any spreadsheet cell to its precedents. Although the tool did not require us to do so, it made our job easier here to define NPV as a Crystal Ball forecast and the inputs as Crystal Ball assumptions. When we do so, the output from the Tornado Chart tool will be labelled with the names that we specified when we defined the forecast and assumptions.

A tornado chart resembles the chart provided by Crystal Ball's Sensitivity Analysis feature, but it differs in how it obtains its results. Whereas the Tornado Chart tool obtains results by varying the inputs one at a time deterministically, the Sensitivity Analysis feature of Crystal Ball obtains its results through a statistical

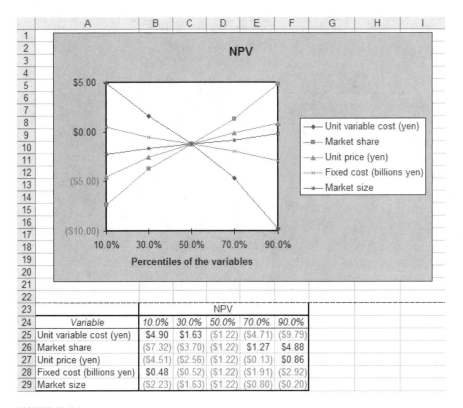

FIGURE 7.11 Spider chart.

analysis of the relationships between the randomly generated inputs and outputs calculated during a set of simulation trials.

Risk Analysis

In this section, we consider a simulation model of Otobai's electric scooter project that follows the suggestions in Chapter 10 of Brealey, Meyers, and Allen (2006). Instead of assuming that the inputs are constant for Years 1–10 as we did above, we will allow them to vary by year. Furthermore, we will link them over time in a multiplicative random walk, and correlate the inputs for each year.

Figure 7.12 shows the five stochastic inputs and their base-case values in cells A4:B8. However, we will introduce randomness through "forecast errors" for each input denoted by $e_{i,t}$ for Inputs $i = 1, 2, 3, 4, 5$ and Years $t = 1, 2, \ldots, 10$. The indexing is as follows:

$$e_{1,t} = \text{Market size forecast error at year } t$$

$$e_{2,t} = \text{Market share forecast error at year } t$$

	A	B	C	D	E
1	**ScooterSimulation.xls**				
2	Inputs			Forecast Errors	
3	Initial Assumptions		Error	Mean	Std. Dev
4	Market size	1,000,000	e_1	0%	5.0%
5	Market share	10%	e_2	0%	5.0%
6	Unit price (yen)	375,000	e_3	0%	1.5%
7	Unit variable cost (yen)	300,000	e_4	0%	5.0%
8	Fixed cost (billions yen)	3.000	e_5	0%	2.5%

FIGURE 7.12   Part 1 of ScooterSimulation.xls.

$$e_{3,t} = \text{Unit price forecast error at year } t$$

$$e_{4,t} = \text{Unit variable cost forecast error at year } t$$

$$e_{5,t} = \text{Fixed cost forecast error at year } t.$$

The simulation uses Crystal Ball's Correlation tool to generate the forecast errors for each year as correlated normal random variates with mean zero and standard deviations shown in cells **E4 : E8** in ScooterSimulation.xls. Figure 7.13 shows the correlation matrix for the forecast errors generated in any given year. The off-diagonal elements on the upper triangular part of the matrix give the value of the correlation between errors during any given year. For example, the correlation

	A	B	C	D	E	F
		Market size Forecast Error (Sheet1)	Market share Forecast Error (Sheet1)	Unit price Forecast Error (Sheet1)	Unit variable cost Forecast Error (Sheet1)	Fixed cost Forecast Error (Sheet1)
41						
42	Market size Forecast Error	1.000	0.800	0.800	-0.800	-0.800
43	Market share Forecast Error		1.000	0.800	-0.800	-0.800
44	Unit price Forecast Error			1.000	-0.800	-0.800
45	Unit variable cost Forecast Error				1.000	0.800
46	Fixed cost Forecast Error					1.000

FIGURE 7.13   Correlation matrix for Crystal Ball assumptions defined for the forecast errors in columns cells C16 : L20 of ScooterSimulation.xls.

between $e_{1,t}$ and $e_{2,t}$ is 0.8, while the correlation between $e_{1,t}$ and $e_{4,t}$ is -0.8. However, the errors are generated independently from year to year. These forecast errors are in cells C16:L20, as shown in the spreadsheet segment in Figure 7.14.

The simulation obtains Year $t = 1$ values for each input by multiplying the base-case value for each input by one plus its forecast error:

$$(\text{Market size})_1 = 1,000,000(1 + e_{1,1})$$

$$(\text{Market share})_1 = 10(1 + e_{2,1})$$

	A	B	C	D	L
10	**Outputs**				
11	**Forecasts**				
12	NPV	$3.43			
13	IRR	15%			
14					
15	**Forecast Errors**	Year 0	Year 1	Year 2	Year 10
16	Market size		0.00%	0.00%	0.00%
17	Market share		0.00%	0.00%	0.00%
18	Unit price		0.00%	0.00%	0.00%
19	Unit variable cost		0.00%	0.00%	0.00%
20	Fixed cost		0.00%	0.00%	0.00%
21					
22	**Dynamic Assumptions**				
23	Market size		1,000,000	1,000,000	1,000,000
24	Market share		10%	10%	10%
25	Unit price (yen)		375,000	375,000	375,000
26	Unit variable cost (yen)		300,000	300,000	300,000
27	Fixed cost (billions yen)		3.000	3.000	3.000
28					
29	**Cash Flow (billions yen)**				
30	Revenue		37.500	37.500	37.500
31	Variable cost		30.000	30.000	30.000
32	Fixed cost		3.000	3.000	3.000
33	Depreciation		1.500	1.500	1.500
34	Pretax profit		3.000	3.000	3.000
35	Tax		1.500	1.500	1.500
36	Net profit		1.500	1.500	1.500
37	Operating cash flow		3.000	3.000	3.000
38	Investment	15	-	-	-
39	Net cash flow	(15)	3.000	3.000	3.000

FIGURE 7.14 Part 2 of ScooterSimulation.xls. Note that columns E through K are hidden.

$$(\text{Unit price})_1 = 375{,}000(1 + e_{3,1})$$

$$(\text{Unit variable cost})_1 = 300{,}000(1 + e_{4,1})$$

$$(\text{Fixed cost})_1 = 3{,}000(1 + e_{5,1})$$

Then the Years $t = 2, 3, \ldots, 10$ values are obtained through the following set of recursive equations:

$$(\text{Market size})_t = (\text{Market size})_{t-1}(1 + e_{1,t})$$

$$(\text{Market share})_t = (\text{Market share})_{t-1}(1 + e_{2,t})$$

$$(\text{Unit price})_t = (\text{Unit price})_{t-1}(1 + e_{3,t})$$

$$(\text{Unit variable cost})_t = (\text{Unit variable cost})_{t-1}(1 + e_{4,t})$$

$$(\text{Fixed cost})_t = (\text{Fixed cost})_{t-1}(1 + e_{5,t}).$$

This set of equations defines a multiplicative random walk for each input. Thus, with a combination of Crystal Ball's Correlation feature and the linking of each year's value to the previous year's values, we are modeling interdependence between inputs and over time. For this example, we have specified some arbitrary values, but in practice a risk analyst will be able to estimate the parameters of the forecast error distributions and the correlations from past projects using company data. Many firms have enterprise resource planning (ERP) systems from which historical data can be retrieved to parameterize the simulation model.

Figure 7.15 shows the distribution of NPV for the scooter project. On average, the project is profitable, but the distribution shows that there is some risk involved as there is nearly a 40% chance that NPV will be negative. Keep in mind that the simulation model described here did not account for any managerial flexibility as did the Project.xls model in Chapter 5. We can easily alter the BMA 2006 model to contain a set of rules similar to those in the Project.xls model. If we build in rules such as those we used to model abandonment or expansion in Project.xls, we would see a similar increase in NPV.

Figure 7.16 shows the distribution of IRR for the scooter project. Because we unchecked the box in Run Preferences for **Stop on calculation errors** as described in Chapter 6, this figure can be somewhat misleading if you look only at the mean of 20%. In the upper left-hand corner we see that only 8,404 trials were completed even though we specified a maximum of 10,000 trials and no other stopping criteria. A mixture of negative and positive cash flows can cause numerical problems with Excel's IRR function, and such instances were simulated in the 1,596 trials not displayed because of error.

Finally, note that cells **B12** and **B13** in Figure 7.14 show values of $3.43 and 15%, respectively, which differ by more than just sampling error from the means of $6.02 and 20% shown in Figures 7.15 and 7.16. This is a manifestation of Jensen's

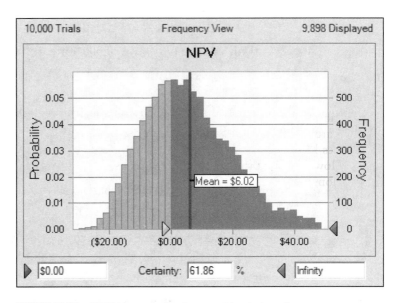

FIGURE 7.15 NPV Forecast for ScooterSimulation.xls.

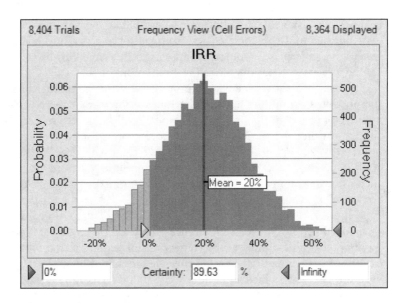

FIGURE 7.16 IRR Forecast for ScooterSimulation.xls.

Inequality, which states that in general,

$$E[f(X)] \neq f(E[X]). \tag{7.3}$$

In words, this means that the values of NPV and IRR shown in Figure 7.14 (denoted by $f(E[X])$ in Expression 7.3) calculated by plugging in the mean values of the stochastic assumptions, are not equal to the expected values of NPV and IRR that we are estimating in Figures 7.15 and 7.16 (denoted by $E[f(X)]$. Historically, academics have professed the use of $f(E[X])$ because of its easiness to calculate by hand. However, the ubiquity of Excel and the availability of Crystal Ball makes calculation of $E[f(X)]$ just as easy nowadays.

Caveats

The use of simulation in capital budgeting has been controversial over the years, but as BMA 2006 point out, it can be a useful tool because the discipline of building a model of a project can in itself lead you to a deeper understanding of the project. Once built and validated, experimenting with the model inputs will also further your understanding.

An institutional advantage of building a simulation model is making explicit and sharing the assumptions that decision makers are using for planning. Oftentimes, different divisions of the same company will make different assumptions about a project on which the divisions are collaborating. Heated discussions sometimes ensue because representatives from the different divisions are operating under different sets of assumptions for the same project, but they are not aware that their assumption sets are different. Having a common simulation model of a project will help to ensure that everyone is operating under the same assumptions.

CUSTOMER NET PRESENT VALUE

The general principle underlying customer lifetime value (CLV) analysis is that customers are financial assets that organizations should manage just like any other asset. Blattberg, Getz, and Thomas (2001), Reichheld (1996), Dwyer (1997), and others have written much about the qualitative and quantitative aspects of managing customers to improve CLV. In this chapter, we will see a simple Crystal Ball model that demonstrates how to calculate distributions of CLV for customer segments with different retention rates.

The model in Figure 7.17 is based on data given for the Buford Electronics case study presented in Blattberg, Getz, and Thomas (2001). In this example, there are two customer segments: the low-volume segment, who are customers from whom the company receives revenues of less than $3,000 per year; and the high-volume segment, who are customers from whom it receives revenues between $25,000 and $100,000 per year.

	A	B	C	D	E	F	G	H	I
1	Lifetime Value.xls								
2									
3	20%	Discount Rate							
4	$ 2,843	NPV for Low-Volume Customers							
5	$ 57,048	NPV for High-Volume Customers							
6									
7	Low-Volume Customers								
8	Year	Retention Rate	Quit This Year	Kept	Retention Cost	Mean Margin	StDev Margin	Actual Margin	Year 0 Value
9	1	75%	0	1	$ 267	$ 360	$ 54	$ 360	$ 78
10	2	80%	0	1	$ 75	$ 595	$ 89	$ 595	$ 361
11	3	85%	0	1	$ 75	$ 805	$ 121	$ 805	$ 422
12	4	85%	0	1	$ 50	$ 1,000	$ 150	$ 1,000	$ 458
13	5	85%	0	1	$ 50	$ 1,000	$ 150	$ 1,000	$ 382
14	6	85%	0	1	$ 50	$ 1,000	$ 150	$ 1,000	$ 318
15	7	85%	0	1	$ 50	$ 1,000	$ 150	$ 1,000	$ 265
16	8	85%	0	1	$ 50	$ 1,000	$ 150	$ 1,000	$ 221
17	9	85%	0	1	$ 50	$ 1,000	$ 150	$ 1,000	$ 184
18	10	85%	0	1	$ 50	$ 1,000	$ 150	$ 1,000	$ 153
19									
20	High-Volume Customers								
21	Year	Retention Rate	Quit This Year	Kept	Retention Cost	Mean Margin	StDev Margin	Actual Margin	Year 0 Value
22	1	40%	0	1	$ 18,000	$ 8,500	$ 1,275	$ 8,500	$ (7,917)
23	2	55%	0	1	$ 1,000	$ 12,480	$ 1,872	$ 12,480	$ 7,972
24	3	65%	0	1	$ 1,000	$ 18,200	$ 2,730	$ 18,200	$ 9,954
25	4	65%	0	1	$ 400	$ 22,950	$ 3,443	$ 22,950	$ 10,875
26	5	65%	0	1	$ 400	$ 22,950	$ 3,443	$ 22,950	$ 9,062
27	6	65%	0	1	$ 400	$ 22,950	$ 3,443	$ 22,950	$ 7,552
28	7	65%	0	1	$ 400	$ 22,950	$ 3,443	$ 22,950	$ 6,293
29	8	65%	0	1	$ 400	$ 22,950	$ 3,443	$ 22,950	$ 5,244
30	9	65%	0	1	$ 400	$ 22,950	$ 3,443	$ 22,950	$ 4,370
31	10	65%	0	1	$ 400	$ 22,950	$ 3,443	$ 22,950	$ 3,642

FIGURE 7.17 Model in LifetimeValueModel.xls for computing customer lifetime values for two different customer segments.

Cells C9:C18 and C22:C31 are Crystal Ball yes-no assumptions that take the value 1 if the customer quits buying from Buford during the year and 0 otherwise. We assume that Buford receives the revenues and pays the retention costs during the year that a customer quits, but the customer never returns after quitting in any year. For each yes-no assumption, the probability of quitting is the complement of the retention rate in the same row of column B in the spreadsheet. Cells D10:D18 and D23:D31 use Excel =IF formulas to model the fact that once a customer quits, he does not return in a later year. The actual margins in cells H9:H18 and H22:H31 are gross profit margins earned from the customer if he is retained that year. These are normally distributed random variables with means and standard deviations given in columns F and G.

The values in cells I9:I18 and I22:I31 are the profits (Actual Margin minus Retention Cost) for each year, discounted to reflect the time value of money. Cells A4

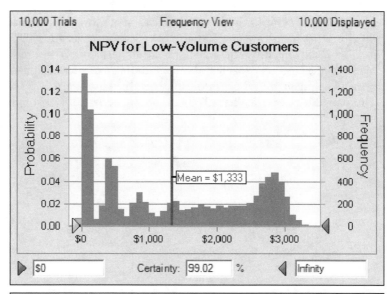

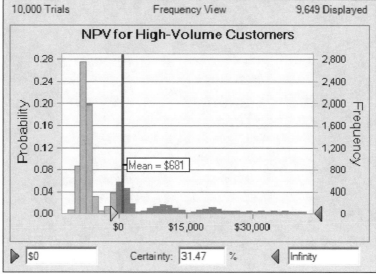

FIGURE 7.18 Forecast charts for CLVs of two customer segments in LifetimeValueModel.xls.

and **A5** use Excel's =SUMPRODUCT formula to compute the NPV of each customer segment, which are defined as Crystal Ball forecasts.

Results

Figure 7.18 shows the results from 10,000 simulation trials. The low-volume customer segment is more profitable on average than the high-volume segment, and the distribution of NPV for high-volume customers shows that a significant proportion (nearly 70 percent) are unprofitable, that is, have negative NPV. This difference in CLV is explained by the higher retention costs and lower retention rates of the high-volume customer segment. Some authors advocate a management approach to proactively identify and abandon unprofitable customers. See Blattberg, Getz, and Thomas (2001) or Haenlein, Kaplan, and Schoder (2006) for more details about this approach.

CHAPTER 8

Modeling Financial Statements

P erhaps the most widely used financial models are the pro forma income statement and balance sheet. Most companies use deterministic versions of these models for planning, and they are a natural place to start when constructing a Crystal Ball model. Especially when decision makers are first exposed to risk analysis with Crystal Ball, it is best to make your stochastic models resemble as much as possible the deterministic models to which decision makers in your company are already accustomed.

In this chapter, we start with deterministic pro forma statements from Chapter 6 of Sengupta (2004), which is an excellent source for more information on constructing deterministic financial models in Excel. In this chapter, we will focus on using Crystal Ball with an existing deterministic model, just as you might do on the job. We walk through use of the basic tools to get you started. As you gain experience, you will be tempted to make your models far more complex than those presented here. However, do not add complexity just for its own sake. It is far better to start with a simple model, and add complexity only if necessary to help make a sound decision.

DETERMINISTIC MODEL

Figure 8.1 shows the historical income statement for 1999–2002 for the Vitex Corporation example from Chapter 6 of Sengupta (2004). Figure 8.2 shows the balance sheets for 1999–2002 for the Vitex Corporation. Our job is to project these measures forward using historical data and input from management about the future uncertainty.

We begin thinking about the uncertain future by looking to the past. While it is always true that there are no guarantees the future will resemble the past, historical data are often the best information you will have available. Furthermore, if you do have available to you a better source of information about what portends for your company's fortunes, then you can easily incorporate it in a Crystal Ball model using the methodology described here.

Figure 8.3 shows the common size statements for 1999–2002 for the Vitex Corporation from Sengupta (2004). These are created by dividing each year's

	A	B	C	D	E
1	**Sengupta.xls**				
2					
3	Historical Income Statements and Balance Sheets for Vitex Corp.				
4					
5	**Income Statement ($ Million)**				
6			Year Ending Dec. 31,		
7		1999	2000	2001	2002
8	Sales	$1,234.9	$1,251.7	$1,300.4	$1,334.4
9	Cost of Sales	$679.1	$659.0	$681.3	$667.0
10	Gross Operating Income	$555.8	$592.7	$619.1	$667.4
11					
12	Selling, Gen. & Admn. Expenses	$339.7	$348.6	$351.2	$373.3
13	Depreciation	$47.5	$52.0	$55.9	$75.2
14	Other net (Income)/Expenses	($11.8)	($7.6)	($7.0)	($8.2)
15	EBIT	$180.4	$199.7	$219.0	$227.1
16					
17	Interest (Income)	($1.3)	($1.4)	($1.7)	($2.0)
18	Interest Expense	$16.2	$15.1	$20.5	$23.7
19	Pre-Tax Income	$165.5	$186.0	$200.2	$205.4
20					
21	Income Taxes	$56.8	$64.2	$67.5	$72.6
22	**Net Income**	**$108.7**	**$121.8**	**$132.7**	**$132.8**

FIGURE 8.1   Historical income statement in Sengupta.xls.

income statement line items by the corresponding year's sales so that each line item in the common size statement is expressed as a percentage of sales. By looking at the variability of common size line items over the years, we gain an idea of how much variability to expect in each line item. Then we can quantify the impact of each item on the bottom line.

TORNADO CHART AND SENSITIVITY ANALYSIS

Figure 8.4 shows a Crystal Ball model for 2002–2006 for the Vitex Corporation income statement from Sengupta (2004), which we use to create a tornado and sensitivity chart. Cell J6 models the average changes in sales across years as a uniform(1%,10%) Crystal Ball assumption based on information provided by management on the possible variation they see for sales. Cells J7, J10, and J12 are uniform(48%,52%), uniform(27%,30%), and uniform(−1%,0%) assumptions, respectively. These parameters were selected based on the common size statements, and were defined to facilitate use of the tornado chart and sensitivity chart to see which variables had the greatest impact on the forecast, EBIT in 2006.

Figure 8.5 shows a tornado chart for the Crystal Ball model for 2002–2006 for the Vitex Corporation income statement from Sengupta (2004). This shows that the sales forecasting factor had the largest impact, then cost of sales, followed by sales, general and administrative (SG&A) expenses.

	A	B	C	D	E
27	**Balance Sheet ($ Million)**				
28	**Assets**				
29	Cash and Marketable Securities	$25.6	$23.0	$32.1	$28.4
30	Accounts Receivable	$99.4	$102.9	$107.3	$120.1
31	Inventories	$109.6	$108.0	$114.9	$116.8
32	Other Current Assets	$96.7	$91.4	$103.7	$97.5
33	Total Current Assets	$331.3	$325.3	$358.0	$362.8
34					
35	Property, Plant and Equipment, Gross	$680.9	$734.3	$820.8	$913.1
36	Accumulated Depreciation	$244.8	$296.8	$352.7	$427.9
37	Property, Plant and Equipment, Net	$436.1	$437.5	$468.1	$485.2
38					
39	Other Non-Current Assets	$203.2	$205.1	$407.0	$456.3
40	Total Non-Current Assets	$639.3	$642.6	$875.1	$941.5
41					
42	**Total Assets**	$970.6	$967.9	$1,233.1	$1,304.3
43					
44	**Liabilities and Shareholders' Equity**				
45	Accounts Payable	$82.8	$77.1	$71.8	$80.5
46	Short-Term Debt	$39.1	$29.7	$79.8	$110.3
47	Other Current Liabilities	$152.0	$123.8	$172.1	$111.3
48	Total Current Liabilities	$273.9	$230.6	$323.7	$302.1
49					
50	Long-Term Debt	$163.5	$145.0	$201.8	$218.1
51	Deferred Income Taxes	$22.3	$19.6	$15.0	$12.7
52	Other Non-Current Liabilities	$100.6	$80.1	$115.0	$94.5
53	Total Liabilities	$560.3	$475.3	$655.5	$627.4
54					
55	Paid-In Capital	$46.9	$46.1	$38.2	$44.8
56	Retained Earnings	$363.4	$446.5	$539.4	$632.1
57	Total Shareholders' Equity	$410.3	$492.6	$577.6	$676.9
58					
59	**Total Liabilities and Equity**	$970.6	$967.9	$1,233.1	$1,304.3

FIGURE 8.2 Balance sheet in Sengupta.xls.

	A	G	H	I	J	K	L	M
1	Historical IS and BS for Vitex Corp.							
2								
3	**Income Statement ($Million)**	**Common Size Statements**						
4		Year Ending Dec. 31,						
5		1999	2000	2001	2002	Average	Min	Max
6	Sales	100.0%	100.0%	100.0%	100.0%	100.0%	100.0%	100.0%
7	Cost of Sales	55.0%	52.6%	52.4%	50.0%	52.5%	50.0%	55.0%
8	Gross Operating Income	45.0%	47.4%	47.6%	50.0%	47.5%	45.0%	50.0%
9								
10	Selling, General & Admn. Expenses	27.5%	27.9%	27.0%	28.0%	27.6%	27.0%	28.0%
11	Depreciation	3.8%	4.2%	4.3%	5.6%	4.5%	3.8%	5.6%
12	Other Net (Income)/Expenses	-1.0%	-0.6%	-0.5%	-0.6%	-0.7%	-1.0%	-0.5%
13	EBIT	14.6%	16.0%	16.8%	17.0%	16.1%	14.6%	17.0%
14								
15	Interest (Income)	-0.1%	-0.1%	-0.1%	-0.1%	-0.1%	-0.1%	-0.1%
16	Interest Expense	1.3%	1.2%	1.6%	1.8%	1.5%	1.2%	1.8%
17	Pre-Tax Income	13.4%	14.9%	15.4%	15.4%	14.8%	13.4%	15.4%
18								
19	Income Taxes	4.6%	5.1%	5.2%	5.4%	5.1%	4.6%	5.4%
20	**Net Income**	8.8%	9.7%	10.2%	10.0%	9.7%	8.8%	10.2%

FIGURE 8.3 Common-size statements in Sengupta.xls.

	A	E	F	G	H	I	J
1	**Income Statement and Balance Sheet for Vitex Corp.**						
2							
3	**Income Statement ($ Million)**						
4				Forecast Period			Forecasting
5		2002	2003	2004	2005	2006	Factor
6	Sales	$1,334.4	$1,401.1	$1,471.2	$1,544.7	$1,622.0	5.0%
7	Cost of Sales	$667.0	$700.6	$735.6	$772.4	$811.0	50.0%
8	Gross Operating Income	$667.4	$700.6	$735.6	$772.4	$811.0	
9							
10	Selling, General & Admn. Expenses	$373.3	$406.3	$426.6	$448.0	$470.4	29.0%
11	Depreciation	$75.2	$78.9	$85.2	$92.0	$99.4	8.0%
12	Other Net (Income)/Expenses	($8.2)	($9.8)	($10.3)	($10.8)	($11.4)	-0.7%
13	EBIT	$227.1	$225.2	$234.0	$243.2	$252.6	
14							
15	Interest (Income)	($2.0)	($1.7)	($1.8)	($1.9)	($2.0)	6.0%
16	Interest Expense	$23.7	$20.1	$19.4	$20.3	$21.3	7.0%
17	Pre-Tax Income	$205.4	$206.8	$216.4	$224.7	$233.3	9.0%
18							
19	Income Taxes	$72.6	$72.4	$75.7	$78.7	$81.6	35.0%
20	**Net Income**	**$132.8**	**$134.4**	**$140.7**	**$146.1**	**$151.6**	
21							10%
22	Dividends	$40.1	$43.1	$46.0	$49.3	$53.1	40.0%
23	Addition to Retained Earnings	$92.7	$91.3	$94.7	$96.8	$98.6	

FIGURE 8.4 Crystal Ball model for income statement in Sengupta2.xls. Cells J6, J7, J10, and J12 are Crystal Ball assumptions, and I3 is a forecast.

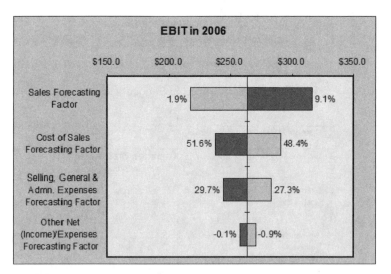

FIGURE 8.5 Tornado chart for Crystal Ball model in Sengupta2.xls. The values of the Crystal Ball assumptions were varied from the 1st percentile to the 99th percentile in five equally spaced steps.

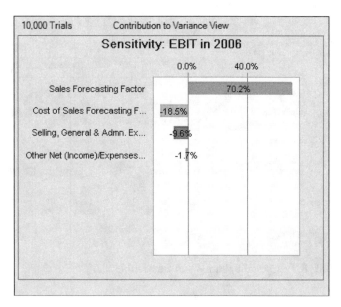

FIGURE 8.6 Sensitivity analysis chart for Crystal Ball model in Sengupta2.xls.

CRYSTAL BALL SENSITIVITY CHART

Figure 8.6 shows a sensitivity chart for the Crystal Ball model for 2002–2006 for the Vitex Corporation income statement from Sengupta (2004). This chart shows results similar to those obtained from the tornado chart, but indicates an even larger impact from the sales forecasting factor. See Chapter 2 for an explanation of the differences between these two types of charts.

Figure 8.7 shows a Crystal Ball model for 2002–2006 for the Vitex Corporation income statement from Sengupta (2004). Note that this models the annual changes in sales and cost of sales as a percentage year-by-year as Crystal Ball assumptions. In Chapter 11, we look closer at modeling financial time series with this sort of multiplicative random walk model, and introduce more models for simulating financial time series.

Figure 8.8 shows a forecast chart for the Crystal Ball model for 2002–2006 for the Vitex Corporation income statement from Sengupta (2004). A 95 percent certainty interval for earnings before interest and taxes (EBIT) in 2006 is from $201.5 to $309.2.

CONCLUSION

In modeling financial statements, our intent is to project financial measures into the future to help make informed decisions about the activities that result in these

	A	B	C	D	E	F	G	H	I	J
1	**Sengupta3.xls**									
2	Income Statement and Balance Sheet for Vitex Corp.									
3	Income Statement ($ Million)									
4			Historical period				Forecast Period			Forecasting
5		1999	2000	2001	2002	2003	2004	2005	2006	Factor
6	Sales	$1,234.9	$1,251.7	$1,300.4	$1,334.4	$1,401.1	$1,471.2	$1,544.7	$1,622.0	
7	Sales Percentage Increase					5%	5%	5%	5%	
8	Cost of Sales	$679.1	$659.0	$681.3	$667.0	$700.6	$735.6	$772.4	$811.0	
9	Cost of Sales as Percent					50%	50%	50%	50%	
10	Gross Operating Income	$555.8	$592.7	$619.1	$667.4	$700.6	$735.6	$772.4	$811.0	
11										
12	Selling, General & Admn. Expenses	$339.7	$348.6	$351.2	$373.3	$406.3	$426.6	$448.0	$470.4	29.0%
13	Depreciation	$47.5	$52.0	$55.9	$75.2	$78.9	$85.2	$92.0	$99.4	8.0%
14	Other Net (Income)/Expenses	($11.8)	($7.6)	($7.0)	($8.2)	($9.8)	($10.3)	($10.8)	($11.4)	-0.7%
15	EBIT	$180.4	$199.7	$219.0	$227.1	$225.2	$234.0	$243.2	$252.6	
16										
17	Interest (Income)	($1.3)	($1.4)	($1.7)	($2.0)	($1.7)	($1.8)	($1.9)	($2.0)	6.0%
18	Interest Expense	$16.2	$15.1	$20.5	$23.7	$20.1	$19.4	$20.3	$21.3	7.0%
19	Pre-Tax Income	$165.5	$186.0	$200.2	$205.4	$206.8	$216.4	$224.7	$233.3	9.0%
20										
21	Income Taxes	$56.8	$64.2	$67.5	$72.6	$72.4	$75.7	$78.7	$81.6	35.0%
22	**Net Income**	**$108.7**	**$121.8**	**$132.7**	**$132.8**	**$134.4**	**$140.7**	**$146.1**	**$151.6**	

FIGURE 8.7   Crystal Ball model in Sengupta3.xls.

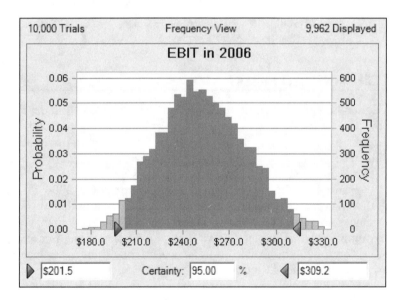

FIGURE 8.8   Forecast chart for Crystal Ball model in Sengupta3.xls.

measures. Deterministic versions of pro forma statements have long been used for answering "what-if" questions about the bottom-line impact of managerial decisions, and a Crystal Ball model can be viewed as a type of more-sophisticated what-if analysis from which decision makers can gain more insight than from a deterministic model.

The procedure for modeling financial statements is to identify the key inputs, as we did with the tornado chart, which varied many inputs one at a time to see the impact on the key output, EBIT in 2006. Any output may be specified depending on the decision maker's interest. Because we used sales-driven forecasting, it is no surprise that we found sales growth to be the most important driver of 2006 EBIT. This emphasizes the need to come up with a good model for defining sales assumptions.

We started with common-size statements to see which percentages are stable over time and which are variable. We usually base our projections on historical data where they are available, but can incorporate other educated guesses too, if they are encapsulated in probability distributions that are used to define Crystal Ball assumptions. When historical data are available, a popular technique is to obtain subjective estimates from subject matter experts for the parameters of Uniform or Triangular assumptions.

The procedure for modeling financial statements is to identify the key inputs, as we did with the Tornado Chart, then observe key outputs like EBIT in 2006. Any output may be specified depending on the decision maker's interest. Because we used sales-driven forecasting, it is no surprise that we found sales growth to be the most important driver of 2006 EBIT. This emphasizes the need to come up with a good model for defining sales assumptions.

CHAPTER 9

Portfolio Models

Crystal Ball is very useful for investigating different allocations of investment funds to a set of risky assets. This chapter demonstrates the use of Crystal Ball and OptQuest for determining the optimal allocation of funds in an investment portfolio based on the decision maker's risk tolerance. We use Crystal Ball and OptQuest to find an optimal allocation for a situation where we know the true optimal allocation, and one where we do not.

SINGLE-PERIOD CRYSTAL BALL MODEL

In this example, we consider investing in the five asset classes listed in Table 9.1. Figure 9.1 shows a segment of the single-period Crystal Ball model in **Portfolio.xls**. Cells **B12:E88** contain annual rates of return in percent on four asset classes. These rates of return were calculated from the indices contained in the **Indices** worksheet of **Portfolio.xls**. The indices were constructed from data collected from various sources for use only in the examples presented in this book. For more specific data on asset returns available to investors during the period 1926–2002 (and more), see the Center for Research in Security Prices (**www.crsp.com**), Ibbotson Associates (2006), or Bodie, Kane and Marcus (2008).

   Overview.   Assume that you have four asset classes from which to choose for an investment portfolio. These classes are listed in Table 9.1 along

TABLE 9.1 Means and standard deviations for annual total returns, $1 + r_i$, during the period 1926–2002 for four asset classes.

Asset Class	Name	Mean Return	Std. Dev.
Large-Company Stocks	LCS	1.1212	0.2052
Small-Company Stocks	SCS	1.1734	0.3607
Corporate Bonds	CB	1.0595	0.0794
U.S. Government Bonds	USGB	1.0559	0.0699

	A	B	C	D	E	F
1	**Portfolio.xls**					
2						
3	Initial Investment					
4	$ 10,000					
5		Large Company Stocks	Small Company Stocks	Corporate Bonds	U.S. Government Bonds	Portfolio Value
6		LCS	SCS	CB	USGB	
7	Return	1.1212	1.1734	1.0595	1.0559	
8	Allocation	27%	11%	0%	62%	$ 10,864.64
9						
10		Historical Returns				
11	Year	LCS	SCS	CB	USGB	
12	1926	11.91	-4.32	5.96	6.04	
13	1927	36.74	27.16	7.78	5.60	
88	2002	-22.10	-17.43	16.56	13.35	
89						
90	Mean	12.12	17.34	5.95	5.59	
91	Std. Dev	20.52	36.07	7.94	6.99	

FIGURE 9.1 Spreadsheet segment from model to simulate a portfolio.

TABLE 9.2 Pearson correlation matrix for annual total returns during the period 1926–2002 for four asset classes.

	LCS	SCS	CB	USGB
LCS	1			
SCS	0.787	1		
CB	0.174	0.035	1	
USGB	0.104	−0.032	0.948	1

with their historical mean total returns, and standard deviations. The Pearson correlations for the five asset classes are in Table 9.2. The data from which these parameters were estimated are in Cells **B12:E88** of the **Stochastic Model** tab of **Portfolio.xls**.

To keep things simple we will assume that you have $10,000 to invest (Cell **A4**) and wish to find the optimal percentage of your $10,000 to invest in each of the asset classes (**B8:E8**). We ignore the effects of inflation for now.

Forecast. The forecast for this example is portfolio value in cell **F8**, the value of the portfolio in Year 1.

Stochastic assumptions. The assumptions are defined in cells **N13:Q13** by using Batch Fit to find the distributions and Spearman correlations.

TABLE 9.3 Spearman correlation matrix for annual total returns during the period 1926–2002 for four asset classes.

	LCS	SCS	CB	USGB
LCS	1			
SCS	0.811	1		
CB	0.124	0.047	1	
USGB	0.013	-0.045	0.936	1

The assumptions are referenced in cells **B7:E7**. Batch Fit was limited to considering only normal or lognormal distributions for the historical returns. The normal distributions used for LCS and SCS were truncated at zero to reflect the limited liability of investing in equities. Batch Fit found that lognormal distributions fit better to CB, and USGB. Lognormal distributions are bounded by zero from below by definition, so needed no truncation. The Spearman correlation matrix computed by Batch Fit is shown in Table 9.3.

Decision variables. Each decision variable in cells **B8:E8** represents the percent of the initial investment allocated to the corresponding asset class. Each decision variable is defined with a lower bound of 0 percent, an upper bound of 100 percent, and a step size of 1.0 percent. By assuming a lower bound of 0 percent we are precluding the possibility of selling short any of the asset classes. The upper bound of 100 percent precludes borrowing to buy on margin or selling short. The step size of 1 percent is specified to make the optimization converge on a solution more quickly than with a smaller step size.

Summary. The results shown here were found when using OptQuest to maximize the mean of the total return forecast in cell **F8**, with the additional requirement that the standard deviation of total return be no more than $1,000. The optimal allocations are (27 percent, 11 percent, 0 percent, 62 percent) for (LCS, SCS, CB, USGB) as shown in cells **B8:E8** in Figure 9.1. For these allocations, the mean portfolio value is $10,865 with a standard deviation of $998.87. By running OptQuest for longer than the 60 minutes used to obtain these results, one may be able to improve on the results slightly.

SINGLE-PERIOD ANALYTICAL SOLUTION

The worksheet Analytical Solution in Portfolio.xls shows the the optimal allocation to each asset class based on using Solver in Excel to maximize the mean return subject to the standard deviation of the portfolio remaining less than or equal to 10 percent. The optimal allocation is (.22, .13, .00, .65) for (LCS, SCS, CB, USGB). This is the solution to the following mathematical programming problem:

$$\max_{\alpha_1,\alpha_2,\alpha_3,\alpha_4} E(P) = \sum_{i=1}^{4} \alpha_i E(1+r_i)$$

subject to

$$\sum_{i=1}^{4} \alpha_i = 1$$

$$\sqrt{\alpha^T S \alpha} = \sigma(P) \leq 10\%$$

$$0 \leq r_i \leq 1 \text{ for all } i,$$

where $E(P)$ is the expected return on the portfolio, $\sigma(P)$ is the standard deviation of the portfolio return, α_i is the portfolio weight allocated to asset $i = 1, 2, 3, 4$ for the ordering of assets (LCS, SCS, CB, USGB) as shown in cells J18:J21, and r_i is the mean rate of return for asset i. The 4×4 matrix S is the covariance matrix shown in cells H4:K7. For the optimal allocation, the expected return is 8.6 percent with a standard deviation of 10 percent.

It is not surprising, but is reassuring that this allocation agrees with the OptQuest allocation. For this simple problem, we can be certain that the deterministic solution gives us the optimal allocation for the given values of the means, standard deviations, and correlations. Because OptQuest is a heuristic technique subject to sampling variation, there is no guarantee that it will find the globally optimal solution. However, the fact that the OptQuest solution is so close to the known deterministic solution in this simple case encourages us to believe that OptQuest will also find solutions that are very close to the global optimum in problems that are too complicated for deterministic solutions to be used.

MULTIPERIOD CRYSTAL BALL MODEL

For investment advisors, a major consideration in planning for a client in retirement is the determination of an appropriate asset allocation that will enable the client to withdraw funds necessary to maintain his or her desired standard of living. If a client withdraws too much or if investment returns fall below expectations, there is a danger of either running out of funds or reducing the desired standard of living. In the model presented in this section we assume that the client is a woman. As women have slightly longer life expectancies than men, our results are conservative when applied to the retirement portfolio planning problem for a man of the same age.

The sustainable retirement withdrawal is the amount a client can withdraw periodically from her retirement funds for a selected planning horizon. This amount cannot be determined with complete certainty because of the stochastic nature of investment returns. In practice, the sustainable retirement withdrawal is determined by limiting the probability of running out of funds to some specified level, such as

5 percent. The sustainable retirement withdrawal amount is typically expressed as a percentage of the initial value of the assets in the retirement portfolio, but is actually the inflation-adjusted monetary amount that the client will use each year for living expenses.

Suppose that at the end of 2002, a 60 year-old woman has $1 million in a tax-deferred retirement account, and that she would like to withdraw $40,000 per year in 2002 dollars. Assume that she has a life expectancy of 30 years, and that the inflation rate will be 3.12 percent. Her withdrawal in each year is $40,000 adjusted by the inflation rate. That is, her withdrawal at the end of 2003 will be $41,248, at the end of 2004 will be $42,535, and so on.

In this scenario, her retirement withdrawal, or "spending rate" is specified at 4 percent based on the initial balance of her total retirement funds. Her retirement portfolio planning problem is to allocate her initial $1 million to the asset classes available to her for investment, while maximizing her spending rate without running out of funds before she dies. An optimal choice of spending rate and allocations can be defined as one that limits to 5 percent the chance that she spends all of her accumulated wealth at the end of a deterministic, 30-year planning horizon. As a secondary issue, she may also be concerned with the value of her estate that is bequeathed to her heirs when she dies.

For this model, the data in **Portfolio.xls** were used to parameterize the Crystal Ball model by using Crystal Ball's Batch Fit tool. Table 9.1 shows the means and standard deviations of the annual returns (in percent) during the period 1926–2002 for four asset classes: large-company stocks (LCS), small-company stocks (SCS), corporate bonds (CB), and U.S. government bonds (USGB). Table 9.3 shows the Spearman correlation matrix for these four asset classes during the same period. The annual rate of inflation during 1926–2002 averaged 3.12 percent.

The model in **SustainableRetirementWithdrawals.xls** generates stochastic returns in cells **I11:L71** for the assets LCS, SCS, CB, and USGB in years 2003–2063. The four returns in each row are correlated with each other, but each row is statistically independent of the other rows. The Spearman correlations, in cells **G78:J81**, were computed by the Batch Fit tool. Crystal Ball's Correlation Matrix tool was used to create the upper triangular matrix in cells **K78:N81**, which references the Spearman correlations. These are the values used by Crystal Ball during the simulation trials.

The portfolio weights of the asset classes in cells **I8:L8** are defined as decision variables in the range [0, 1] (i.e., no short sales nor margin purchases are allowed) in steps of 1 percent. At the end of each simulated year, a constant real amount (in 2002 dollars) is withdrawn for living expenses. The withdrawal amount is defined as both a decision variable and a forecast variable in Crystal Ball. The portfolio is assumed to be composed entirely of tax-deferred dollars and the effects of taxes on the amounts withdrawn are not considered.

We consider two different planning horizons: (1) a deterministic 30-year horizon, and (2) a stochastic horizon equal to the remaining lifetime of the woman

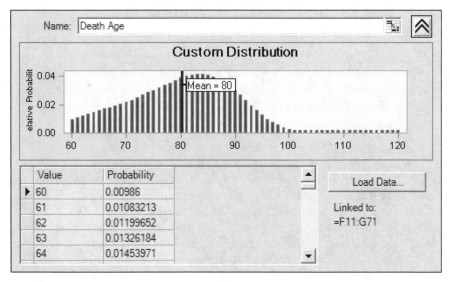

FIGURE 9.2 Custom distribution representing the death age of a 60-year-old female as given by the 2001 CSO mortality table.

characterized by the 2001 Commisioner's Standard Ordinary (CSO) mortality table. The distribution of the death age of a 60 year-old woman is shown in Figure 9.2.

In OptQuest, the percentage allocation to each asset class and the withdrawal rate are specified as decision variables. The percentage allocations are bounded by 0 and 100 and are constrained to sum to 100 percent. An indicator variable is defined as a Crystal Ball forecast for the event that wealth at the end of each planning horizon is positive. The withdrawal rate forecast variable in cell **H4** is specified as the objective to be maximized with an additional requirement that the mean of the positive-wealth indicator variable have a lower bound of 0.9540. To account for sampling error in the estimates used by OptQuest in its optimization algorithm, this lower bound exceeds 0.9500 by approximately two standard errors of the mean of the positive-wealth indicator variable resulting from 4,000 trials. Table 9.4 shows the allocations obtained for two different planning horizons:

1. A deterministic horizon of 30 years.
2. A stochastic horizon equal to the woman's remaining lifetime.

From a final run of 10,000 trials of the Crystal Ball model for the deterministic, 30-year horizon, the estimated median value of the woman's wealth is $3.79 million, with a 95.30 percent probability of being solvent (wealth greater than zero) at the end of 30 years. Figure 9.3 shows the distribution of wealth at the end of 30 years. For the stochastic, remaining lifetime horizon, the estimated median value of her

TABLE 9.4 Optimal asset allocations and sustainable
withdrawal rates for two planning horizons.

Horizon	LCS	SCS	CB	USGB	Spend
30-year	.25	.12	0	.63	4.08%
Rem. life	.23	.13	0	.64	4.53%

estate is $1.78 million, with a 95.25 percent probability of leaving to her heirs an estate greater than zero. Figure 9.4 shows the distribution of her estate.

Her spending rate is 4.08 percent with a fixed 30-year horizon, and 4.53 percent with a stochastic horizon. With an initial investment of $1 million, the difference between the spending rates amounts to an additional $4,500 in 2002 dollars to spend each year. This differential stems primarily from the fact that the retiree has a high likelihood of dying before she reaches age 90. For the assumptions stated above, our analysis quantifies the risk of dying broke if one chooses to withdraw more to live better during retirement.

From comparison of the results in Table 9.4 and Figures 9.3 and 9.4, it is evident that very large stock allocations are not necessary for sustainability of withdrawals. In fact, allocation of a majority of the portfolio to equities will increase the likelihood of depleting the retiree's funds during her lifetime. For both planning horizons, the split between debt and equity in the retirement portfolio is roughly 60–40.

FIGURE 9.3 Distribution of wealth after 30 years with asset allocations listed in Table 9.4 for the 30-year planning horizon.

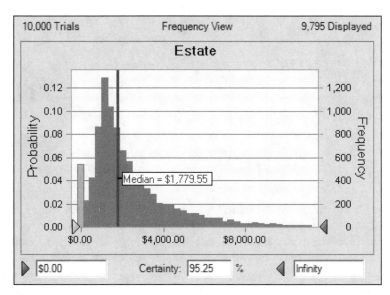

FIGURE 9.4 Distribution of the retiree's estate with asset allocations and withdrawal rate listed in Table 9.3 for the remaining-lifetime planning horizon.

This example is intended only to demonstrate the use of Crystal Ball and Opt-Quest for financial planning. A more thorough analysis would include analyses of other potential investments, such as real estate or international equities, and more specific and recent data on the components of the asset classes used in this chapter. However, the analysis presented here does serve to inform individuals who are facing retirement about the tradeoffs involved in the retirement portfolio planning problem, and gives financial planners an idea of how to use Crystal Ball and OptQuest to demonstrate to their clients the risks involved in retirement planning.

CHAPTER 10

Value at Risk

Many times one wants to know for planning purposes what is the "worst that can happen." In many situations, the worst that can happen is to lose one's entire investment; however, this usually has an extremely low probability of occurrence. The concept of Value at Risk (VaR) was devised to obtain a risk measure that associates a severe loss with a probability level of reasonable interest to the decision maker, such as 1 percent or 5 percent. See Jorion (2001) for more about VaR. In this chapter, we see how to use Crystal Ball to find VaR and a related measure, Conditional VaR (CVaR).

VAR

In practice, we can think of a potential loss L as the worst that can happen if the probability of losing L or more during a selected time period is a specified amount such as 5 percent. In that case, L is called the "5 percent Value at Risk (VaR)." More precisely, let R denote the total return (in dollars) on an investment, I, and let c denote the α percentile of the distribution of R. Then the α percent VaR is defined as $L = I - c$.

Figure 10.1 shows a segment of the one-year Crystal Ball model in PortfolioVaR. xls, which is adapted from the file Portfolio.xls described in Chapter 9. The potential loss from investing in the portfolio, $I - R$, is measured directly in cell B11 with the Excel formula =A4-A11, which is simply the difference between the initial investment and the final value of the portfolio. A copy of the forecast window for this quantity is shown at the bottom of the spreadsheet segment in Figure 10.1. Because the certainty is 95 percent that portfolio loss is between −Infinity and $792.47, we say that the 5 percent VaR for one year is $792.47. Note that when we find the α percent VaR from the loss $(I - R)$ distribution, we use the $(1 - \alpha)$ percentile in the upper tail rather than the α percentile, c, in the lower tail of the distribution of R.

VaR is used by regulators to compute capital requirements for financial institutions, and by managers as an input to risk-management decisions. VaR can also be used by managers to assess the quality of their models. For example, if a model provides that there is a 5 percent chance that a bank's trading operations will lose $1 million over a 1-day horizon, then on average the trading operation should lose

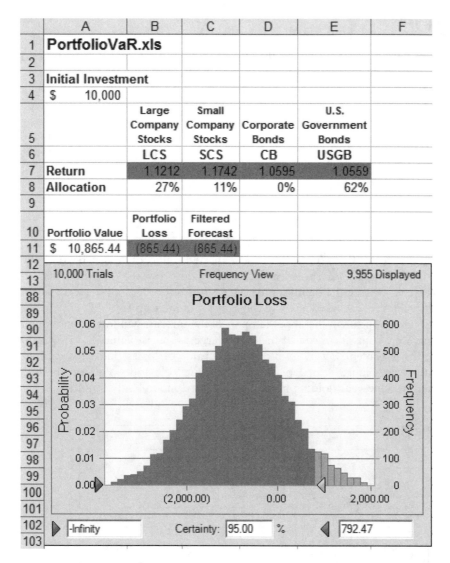

FIGURE 10.1 Spreadsheet segment from model to illustrate the concept of Value at Risk (VaR).

$1 million or more on 5 percent of the days in a randomly selected period. If there are many more losses, it implies that the model assigns too little risk to the situation. If there are many fewer losses, it implies that the model assigns too much risk. In this sense, VaR can therefore be used to check the validity of a model.

Some regulators have adopted VaR as part of their risk management guidelines, but critics of this measure have pointed out some of its shortcomings, which are discussed in the next section.

SHORTCOMINGS OF VAR

VaR provides no information about the extent of losses that might occur beyond the threshold level. In that sense it is very optimistic because it gives a lower bound on potential loss at the α percent level. Further, it is not always subadditive, which means that the VaR of the combination of two or more investments can exceed the sum of the individual VaR for each investment. This is contrary to the basic principle of diversification, which holds that risk will *decrease* when more assets are held, not increase. This failure to reward diversification is perceived as the greatest shortcoming of VaR. An alternate risk measure, Conditional Value at Risk (CVaR), overcomes these shortcomings.

CVAR

Conditional Value at Risk (CVaR) is the expected value of losses beyond the threshold level. Figure 10.2 shows a forecast window for the portfolio loss in PortfolioVaR.xls. During the definition of cell **C11** as a forecast, a filter was set on the forecast values to exclude values in the range −Infinity up to $792.47. That is why "500 Trials" appears in the upper left part of the forecast window, even though 10,000 trials were run. The mean of these 500 largest forecast values is $1,192.56. In general, the α percent CVaR is the expected value of losses that exceed the α percent VaR level. Figure 10.3 depicts the 5 percent VaR and CVaR on the loss distribution for a one-year holding period for the portfolio in PortfolioVaR.xls.

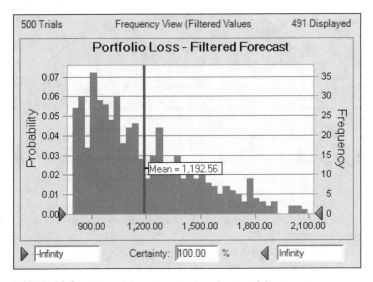

FIGURE 10.2 Filtered forecast window for Portfolio Loss in Figure 10.1.

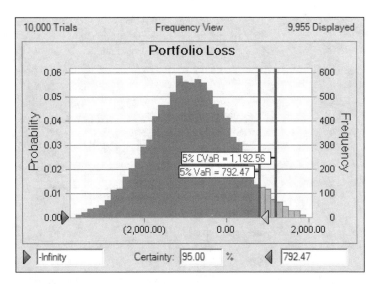

FIGURE 10.3 Forecast window for Portfolio Loss in Figure 10.1 showing the 5 percent VaR over one year of $1,967 and the corresponding CVaR of $2,794.

Investments with high CVaR will necessarily have high VaR as well. CVaR, which is also called *Conditional Tail Expectation, Expected Tail Loss, Mean Excess Loss, Mean Shortfall,* or *Tail VaR,* is considered to be a more "coherent" measure of risk than VaR. Artzner, Delbaen, Eber, and Heath (1999) describe subadditivity and other coherent measures of risk in detail. Uryasev (2000) and Hardy (2006) are good references on the basics of CVaR.

CVaR.xls

The file **CVaR.xls**, a segment of which is shown in Figure 10.4, contains a simulation model of a three-asset portfolio. Assets 1, 2, and 3 have mean returns of 10 percent, 12 percent, and 13 percent, respectively, with variance-covariance matrix

$$\begin{bmatrix} 0.10 & 0.04 & 0.03 \\ 0.04 & 0.20 & -0.04 \\ 0.03 & -0.04 & 0.30 \end{bmatrix}.$$

The variance-covariance matrix is contained in cells **B9:D11**, and the corresponding Pearson correlation matrix is computed in cells **B14:D16**. As correlation matrices are symmetric, it appears as a lower triangular matrix. The variance-covariance matrix is used in an Excel array formula in this example (cell **C32**), so the entire symmetric matrix is in the file.

The Crystal Ball model simulates returns from a portfolio with weights 0.30, 0.25, and 0.45, invested in Assets 1, 2, and 3, respectively. Asset rates of return are

	A	B	C	D	E
1	**CVaR.xls**	Mean	Portfolio		
2		Returns	weights		
3	Asset1	10%	0.30		
4	Asset2	12%	0.25		
5	Asset3	13%	0.45		
6	Initial investment	$ 100.00			
7	VaR level desired	1%			
8	**Var-Cov Matrix**	**Asset1**	**Asset2**	**Asset3**	
9	**Asset1**	0.10	0.04	0.03	
10	**Asset2**	0.04	0.20	-0.04	
11	**Asset3**	0.03	-0.04	0.30	
12					
13	**Correlation matrix**	**Asset1**	**Asset2**	**Asset3**	
14	**Asset1**	1			
15	**Asset2**	0.283	1		
16	**Asset3**	0.173	-0.163	1	
17					
18	**Crystal Ball Model**	**Asset1**	**Asset2**	**Asset3**	**Total**
19	Mean rate of return	10%	12%	13%	
20	St. dev. rate of return	32%	45%	55%	
21	Rate of return	0%	0%	0%	
22	Weight	0.3	0.25	0.45	
23	Investment	$ 30.00	$ 25.00	$45.00	$ 100.00
24	Value	$ 30.00	$ 25.00	$45.00	$ 100.00
25	1.00% quantile	$ 10.98	$ 4.03	$ 4.20	$ 49.05
26	VaR at 1.00% level	$ 19.02	$ 20.97	$40.80	$ 50.95
27	Conditional mean	$ 8.14	$ 2.28	$ 2.24	$ 43.25
28	1.00% CVaR	$ 21.86	$ 22.72	$42.76	$ 56.75

FIGURE 10.4   Crystal Ball model to find VaR and CVaR.

normally distributed, but truncated at -100 percent. The model has four forecast cells: Asset1 Value, Asset2 Value, Asset3 Value, Total Value. To reproduce the results tabulated below, run 10,000 Trials with LHS and Seed = 813.

To get the 1 percent VaR and CVaR values from Crystal Ball, first find the 1st percentile of each forecast using using the command

$$=CB.GetForePercentFN(Range, Percent)$$

as shown in cells B25:E25. Then use

$$Preferences \rightarrow Forecast \dots \rightarrow Filter Tab$$

to set a filter on the forecast values to include values in the range $-$Infinity to the 1st percentile (entered as a number) of each forecast. The means of the filtered values are used to compute the $\alpha = 1$ percent CVaR for each asset and the portfolio as shown in Table 10.1. Again, CVaR is preferred by some analysts because it is subadditive, which means that the CVaR of the portfolio is always less than or equal to the sum

TABLE 10.1 VaR and CVaR for three assets and portfolio modeled in CVaR.xls.

	1st Percentile	Investment	VaR	CVaR
Asset1 Value	$ 10.98	$ 30.00	$ 19.02	$ 21.86
Asset2 Value	$ 4.03	$ 25.00	$ 20.97	$ 22.72
Asset3 Value	$ 4.20	$ 45.00	$ 40.80	$ 42.76
Portfolio Value	$ 49.05	$ 100.00	$ 50.95	$ 56.75

of the individual CVaRs of the portfolio components. VaR is not always subadditive (although it is so in this example), which means that the risk of a portfolio can be larger than the sum of the stand-alone risks of its components when measured by VaR. The CVaR is also less sensitive to changes in the defining percentile α than is VaR.

CVaRSubadditivity.xls

The model in Figure 10.5 is a Crystal Ball simulation of an analytical result presented by Tasche (2002). The model simulates investments in each of two independent

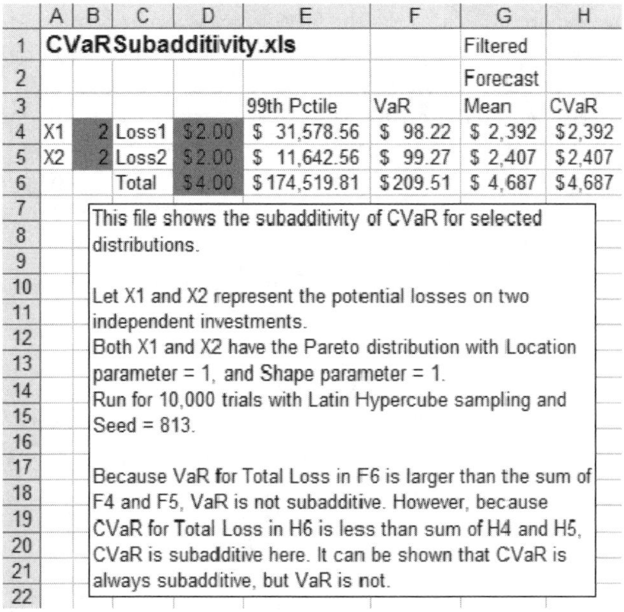

FIGURE 10.5 Crystal Ball model to demonstrate subadditivity of CVaR in a situation for which VaR is not subadditive.

TABLE 10.2 VaR and CVaR for independent investments modeled in CVaRSubadditivity.xls.

	1% VaR	1% CVaR
Total Loss	$ 209.51	$ 4,687
Loss1	$ 98.22	$ 2,392
Loss2	$ 99.27	$ 2,407

opportunities with potential losses X_1 and X_2. Both X_1 and X_2 loss distributions have Pareto distributions with **Location Parameter** = 1 and **Shape Parameter** = 1. Cell **D4** is a Crystal Ball forecast representing the loss on the first opportunity, **Loss1** = X_1. Cell **D5** is a Crystal Ball forecast representing the loss on the second opportunity, **Loss2** = X_2. Cell **D6** is a Crystal Ball forecast representing the total loss, **Loss1** + **Loss2**. The VaR and CVaR of the Loss1, Loss2, and Total Loss are shown in Table 10.2. The table shows that CVaR is subadditive because the CVaR for Total Loss, $4687 is less than the sum of the CVaRs for Loss1 and Loss2, $4799 = $2392 + $2407. However, VaR is not subadditive because the VaR for the Total Loss, $209.51, is greater than the sum of the VaRs for Loss1 and Loss2, $197.49 = $98.22 + $99.27.

In other words, the 1 percent VaR for the portfolio is greater than the sum of the 1 percent VaRs of the investments considered individually. The principle of diversification holds that risk is lower when two or more assets are combined into a portfolio. As VaR indicates in this example that the risk of holding the portfolio is greater than the sum of the risks of holding each portfolio component individually, VaR is not a satisfactory measure of risk in this example. However, CVaR indicates correctly that the risk of holding the portfolio is lower than the sum of the component risks, and so it *is* a satisfactory measure of risk from this point of view.

CHAPTER 11

Simulating Financial Time Series

I n financial modeling, we encounter two main types of time-series data:

1. Observations that appear to be independent and identically distributed (IID).
2. Observations that do not appear to be IID because they follow a trend or some other pattern over time.

Financial theory provides a compelling argument—the *efficient markets hypothesis*—that returns on investments must be independent over time because no one has access to information not already available to someone else. If returns are independent, however, prices will be dependent over time and we will require a way to model that dependence. This chapter presents some models that can be used for projecting future returns, asset prices, and other financial times series in simulation models for risk analysis.

WHITE NOISE

A *white noise process* is defined to be one that generates data appearing to be IID. It takes its name from the fact that no specific frequency or pattern dominates in a spectral analysis of the observations, similar to white light, or the noise of static emitted from an AM radio that is not tuned in to a station.

The model for a white noise process is

$$W_t = \mu + \epsilon_t, \tag{11.1}$$

where μ is a constant, and ϵ_t is a sequence of uncorrelated random variables identically distributed with mean zero and finite variance for $t = 1, \ldots, T$. The probability distribution of ϵ_t is not necessarily normal, but if it is the process is said to be *Gaussian white noise* named after the eighteenth-century mathematician, Carl F. Gauss, who studied the properties of the normal distribution.

For example, we can simulate observations from a Gaussian white noise process with Crystal Ball by placing several uncorrelated Normal(0,10) assumptions in a column, adding a constant, say $\mu = 200$, and plotting the results as was done in the file RandomWalk.xls. Figure 11.1 shows the model. In cells **B6:B35** are Crystal Ball

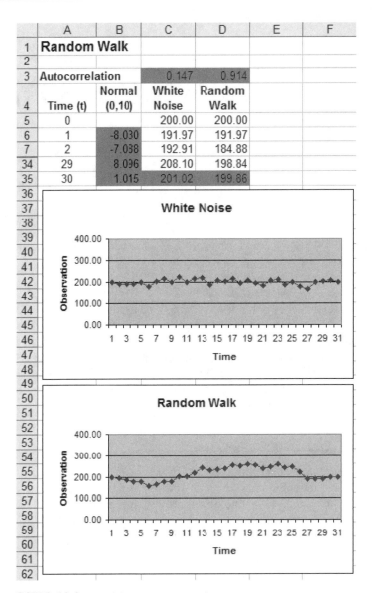

FIGURE 11.1 Model to compare a white noise process to a random walk. Note that rows 8 through 33 are hidden.

normal(0,10) assumptions that we denote as ϵ_t for $t = 1, \ldots, 30$. A Gaussian white noise process was generated in cells C6:C35 using Expression 11.1, and a time series plot of one realization of the process appears in the center of Figure 11.1. Notice how the independence of the observations in the white noise process is manifested in the choppiness of its plot. For the white noise process, no matter where each observation falls, the next observation is equally likely to be above or below the mean of 200. This characteristic causes the choppy look.

RANDOM WALK

One form of a non-IID process is the additive random walk process defined by

$$Y_t = Y_{t-1} + \epsilon_t \tag{11.2}$$

for $t = 1, \ldots, T$. For example, in RandomWalk.xls, we set $T = 30$ and $Y_0 = 200$, then generated observations from the process in Expression 11.2 in cells D6:D35, using the values in B6:B35 for ϵ_t, $t = 1, \ldots, 30$.

A time series plot of one realization of the random walk process appears in the lower time series plot in Figure 11.1. Notice how the random walk process exhibits a meandering pattern. The first few points are below the mean, then once the plot goes above the mean, it tends to stay above for a while, then heads down and goes below the mean again before eventually heading back up. Even though the changes in the level of the random walk are independent, the levels themselves are dependent over time. This dependence causes more variability in the levels of the random walk process than is evident in the levels of the white noise process.

The aggregate effect of the dependence of the levels of the random walk compared to the white noise process can be seen in Figures 11.2 and 11.3. Because the observations in the white noise process are IID, the forecast chart in Figure 11.2 has a mean of $\mu = 200$ and standard deviation of $\sigma = 10$, as do all of the observations

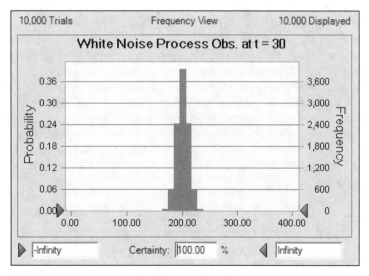

FIGURE 11.2 Forecast chart for the observation at time $t = 30$ for the random process.

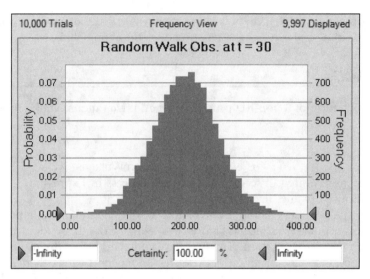

FIGURE 11.3   Forecast chart for the observation at time $t = 30$ for
the random walk.

W_t in the white noise process for $t \geq 1$. The mean of the additive random walk
process is also 200 for every observation, but the standard deviation grows larger
every time period because we are adding on another random change. It can be
shown that each value Y_t of the random walk process has a mean of $\mu = 200$ and
a standard deviation of $\sigma \sqrt{t}$. In Figure 11.3 you can see that the standard deviation
($10\sqrt{30} = 54.77$) is much greater than the standard deviation (10) of the forecast
in Figure 11.2. The scales of the horizontal axes of these two plots were specified
to be equal so that the difference in variability between the white noise process and
random walk was apparent. However, the scales of the vertical axes in Figures 11.2
and 11.3 are different. Figure 11.4 is another illustration of the differences in these
forecasts with an overlay chart for cells **C35** and **D35**.

For a dynamic illustration of the difference between white noise and a random
walk, see the file **RandomWalk.xls**. In **Run Preferences**, set **Run Mode** to **Demo**
and watch the time series plots to see the difference in behavior when the simulation
is running. The white noise process will bounce almost entirely within the 3σ bounds
of 170 to 230 at every point in time, while the random walk will exhibit increasing
variability as t gets larger.

AUTOCORRELATION

Chapter 4 showed how to calculate both Pearson and Spearman correlations between
two variables with Excel. When checking for independence of a series of values over
time, we calculate the *autocorrelation*, which is the correlation coefficient of the
values in the series that are separated by a specific length of time. In this context,

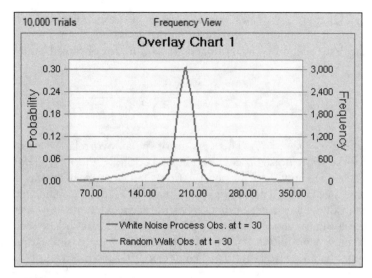

FIGURE 11.4 Overlay chart to compare the time $t = 30$ observations from a white noise process and a random walk.

the prefix *auto*–means *same*, so the autocorrelation is the correlation of the values in a time series with other values within the same series. Sometimes authors refer to autocorrelation by the term *serial correlation* to emphasize the correlation within a time series.

While the correlation coefficients for values separated by two or more time periods are also of interest in time series analysis, for our purposes it is sufficient to think only about *first-order autocorrelation*, which is the correlation between values in a time series that are separated by one unit of time. Thus, first-order autocorrelation is also called *Lag-1 autocorrelation*. Unless specified otherwise, the term *autocorrelation* in this chapter is meant to refer to first-order autocorrelation. It is usually true with financial time series that if the first-order autocorrelation is near zero, then the rest of the autocorrelation coefficients will also be near zero. However, for time series that exhibit seasonality, higher-order autocorrelation could be significant while lag-1 autocorrelation is low.

To calculate the first-order autocorrelation coefficient for the white noise process values in cells C5:C35, we entered into cell C3 the Excel formula =CORREL(C5:C34, C6:C35). As shown in Chapter 4, this calculates the Pearson correlation for the two arrays C5:C34 and C6:C35. Likewise, cell D3 holds the Excel formula =CORREL(D5:D34,D6:D35) to find the first-order autocorrelation coefficient for the random walk time series in cells D6:D35. Note that there are other methods to calculate the autocorrelation coefficient having more appeal to purists, but Excel does not yet include these other methods in its arsenal of statistical functions. For more discussion of this point and other methods for calculating autocorrelation coefficients, see pages 330–340 of Priestley (1981), or section 2.2 of Tsay (2002).

Of course, with more work, you can always use Excel to calculate the autocorrelation coefficient by one of the other methods. For example, another way to calculate the first-order autocorrelation coefficient, $\hat{\rho}_1$, for observed values y_t, $t = 1, 2, \ldots, T$ is

$$\hat{\rho}_1 = \frac{\sum_{t=2}^{T}(y_t - \bar{y})(y_{t-1} - \bar{y})}{\sum_{t=1}^{T}(y_t - \bar{y})^2},$$

where $\bar{y} = \sum_{t=1}^{T} y_t/T$. This version of the autocorrelation was calculated in cell **Q6** for the white noise process in cells **C6 : C35** of RandomWalk.xls.

To see how these autocorrelation coefficients vary during simulation trials, they have been defined as Crystal Ball forecasts. Figure 11.5 shows the forecast chart for cell **C3**, the autocorrelation coefficient for the white noise process values. By the way these values were generated, we know that they are independent over time, so their true autocorrelation is zero. However, in any given simulation trial the calculated (sample) autocorrelation coefficient can differ from zero simply because of sampling error. It can be shown that the sampling error for the first-order autocorrelation coefficient calculated for an IID time series of length T has a standard deviation of approximately $1/\sqrt{T}$, so we would expect the standard deviation of the 10,000 values plotted in Figure 11.5 to be $1/\sqrt{30} = 0.183$ and roughly 95 percent of the values to fall within the two standard error interval $(-0.366, 0.366)$. Figure 11.5 shows that 95.86 percent of the observations actually fell within that interval during the 10,000 simulation trials, which agrees with what we expect. Furthermore, the

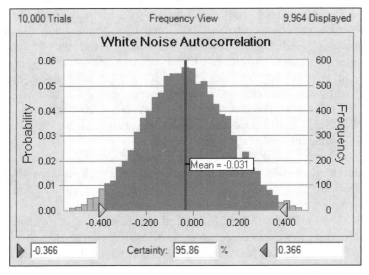

FIGURE 11.5 Forecast chart for the autocorrelation coefficient for the random process.

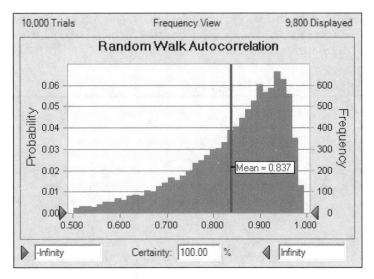

FIGURE 11.6 Forecast chart for the first-order autocorrelation coefficient for the random walk process.

sample standard deviation of the distribution in Figure 11.5 is 0.178, which is also close to its expected value of 0.183.

Figure 11.6 shows the autocorrelation for cell **D3**, the autocorrelation coefficient for the random walk time series. All values of the random walk autocorrelation coefficient were significantly larger than zero, which is what we expect because the levels of the random walk process are not independent over time.

To check for a white noise process in practice, you can use the following test statistic. First, calculate the first-order autocorrelation coefficient, $\hat{\rho}_1$, from the T time-series observations. Then find $Z = \hat{\rho}_1 \sqrt{T}$. If the absolute value of Z is greater than two ($|Z| > 2$), conclude that the observations do not come from a white noise process. If you reach this conclusion, then you must decide how best to model the time series if you want to use Crystal Ball to generate potential future values of the time series. The rest of this chapter describes some models for you to consider. There are many models that might be applied, but we show a few of the more popular models for generating future values of financial times series with Crystal Ball.

Selected models for simulating financial time series are popular because of some "stylized facts" recognized by finance practitioners, and listed in McNeil, Frey, and Embrechts (2005). For series of daily returns, exchange rates, and commodity prices:

- Return series are not IID although they show little serial correlation.
- Conditional expected returns are close to zero.
- Volatility appears to vary over time.
- Return series are leptokurtic or heavy-tailed.
- Extreme returns appear in clusters.

Varying volatility and clustered, leptokurtic returns can be modeled with some type of mixture model. The remainder of this chapter describes some models that can be incorporated in risk analysis spreadsheet models.

ADDITIVE RANDOM WALK WITH DRIFT

The model for an additive random walk with drift is

$$Y_t = \mu + Y_{t-1} + \epsilon_t \tag{11.3}$$

for $t = 1, \ldots, T$, where μ is the mean change per time period and ϵ_t is an IID sequence of random variables that is not necessarily normally distributed.

By subtracting Y_{t-1} from both sides of Expression 11.3, we get

$$Y_t - Y_{t-1} = \mu + \epsilon_t,$$

which means that changes in the levels of a random walk with drift process follow a white noise process.

Generating Values from a Scalar Random Walk with Drift Process

To simulate potential future values of a time series that you think follows an additive random walk with drift process, take the first differences of the time series and fit a Crystal Ball assumption to them. This is illustrated in Figure 11.7.

The values of the time series Y_t for $t = 1, 2, \ldots, 20$ in cells **B4:B23** of RandomWalkWithDrift.xls are quarterly sales of an industrial product. The first differences are found by entering =B5-B4 in Cell **C5** and copying this formula down through cell **C23**. The autocorrelation coefficient of the first differences is calculated in cell **D4** as 0.184, which is smaller than the two-standard-error value of 0.447 calculated in cell **D7**. This, combined with the apparent statistical stationarity we see in the time series plot of the differences in Figure 11.7 lets us conclude that the differences can be modeled with Crystal Ball as though they are IID.

To generate potential future values of the sales time series, we used Crystal Ball's distribution-fitting procedure to fit a **Triangular(-69.54,17.99,100.93)** distribution to the values in cells **C5:C23** and used that distribution to specify Crystal Ball assumptions in cells **C25:C29**. The values in **B25:B29** are calculated using Expression 11.3. Cell **B25** has the formula =B23+C25. Cell **B26** has the formula =B25+C26, and this was copied and pasted to cells **B27** and **B28**.

You can forecast as many steps ahead as desired using the random walk model, but realize that in doing so you are assuming implicitly that the distribution generating the differences remains stationary over the future period for which you generate values. The adequacy of this assumption depends on the context. It may well be adequate for a few steps ahead, but the variance of the random walk model increases linearly with time, so for prolonged use of the model you will want to update the model by fitting distributions to the new data value changes as you observe them.

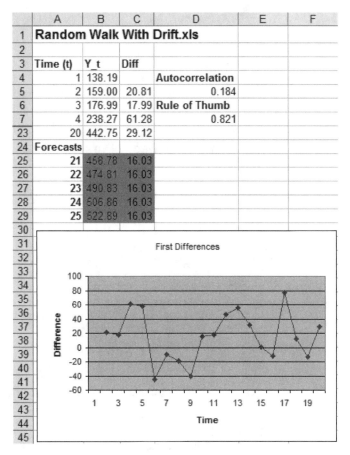

FIGURE 11.7 Crystal Ball model on the "Scalar Random Walk" worksheet of RandomWalkWithDrift.xls for forecasting a time series with a random walk with drift process. Cells C25:C29 are Crystal Ball assumptions, and B25:B29 are Crystal Ball forecasts. Note that rows 8 through 22 are hidden.

Forecasting with Vector Random Walk Model

You can also use the random walk model to simulate observations from time series that have both autocorrelation and correlation between series. This is illustrated in Figure 11.8 for the sales of three industrial products labeled X, Y, and Z in columns B, C, and D. The procedure for forecasting more than one (that is, a vector) time series is similar to forecasting a single (scalar) time series. However, with a vector random walk model, we take into account the correlation between changes in time series at the same time period as well as using the random walk model to induce autocorrelation among the levels of the time series.

	A	B	C	D	E	F	G
1	**Correlated Random Walk Model**						
2							
3	Time	X	Y	Z			
4	1	138.2	159.2	135.1	Diff.X	Diff.Y	Diff.Z
5	2	158.4	189.2	152.6	20.3	30.0	17.5
6	3	182.8	161.5	113.6	24.3	-27.6	-39.0
7	4	233.3	193.2	96.1	50.6	31.7	-17.5
8	5	259.9	215.7	98.8	26.6	22.5	2.7
9	6	254.7	176.7	70.6	-5.2	-39.0	-28.2
10	7	261.3	182.9	75.3	6.6	6.2	4.7
11	8	240.9	155.2	75.2	-20.4	-27.7	-0.1
12	9	294.1	171.8	42.1	53.2	16.6	-33.1
13	10	279.0	178.9	65.8	-15.1	7.1	23.7
14	11	298.7	176.1	88.0	19.7	-2.8	22.2
15	12	323.9	158.1	57.8	25.2	-18.0	-30.2
16	13	357.2	214.3	80.1	33.3	56.2	22.2
17	14	387.6	235.6	73.7	30.4	21.2	-6.4
18	15	419.1	232.3	32.7	31.5	-3.3	-40.9
28	25	442.7	333.5	205.7	-14.4	-13.0	-14.2
29	26	481.6	340.7	208.6	38.9	7.3	2.9
30	27	520.5	348.0	211.6	38.9	7.3	2.9
31	28	559.4	355.2	214.5	38.9	7.3	2.9
32	29	598.3	362.5	217.4	38.9	7.3	2.9
33	30	637.2	369.8	220.4	38.9	7.3	2.9
34							
35				Autocorrelation	0.036	0.028	-0.083
36				Rule of Thumb	0.178	0.138	-0.414

FIGURE 11.8 Crystal Ball model on the "Vector Random Walk" worksheet of RandomWalkWithDrift.xls for forecasting a vector time series with a random walk with drift process. Cells E29:G33 are Crystal Ball assumptions, and B29:D33 are Crystal Ball forecasts. Note that rows 19 through 27 are hidden.

In cells E5:G28 of Figure 11.8, we found the first differences of the X, Y, and Z time series in cells B4:B28. The autocorrelations in cells E35:G35 indicate that the differences follow a random process. Using Crystal Ball's Batch Fit feature, we modeled the changes in X, Y, and Z as Normal distributions with parameters that you will find in the file. Figure 11.9 shows the correlation matrix for the changes in cells M11:O13.

Again, you can forecast as many steps ahead as desired using the vector random walk model, but realize that you are assuming implicitly that the random processes generating the differences remain stationary in regard to their distributions and their cross correlations.

	L	M	N	O
4	Data Series:	Diff.X	Diff.Y	Diff.Z
5	Anderson-Darling:	0.293	0.202	0.191
6	Distribution:	0.00	0.00	0.00
7	Best fit:	Min Extreme	Beta	Beta
8				
9				
10	Correlations	Diff.X	Diff.Y	Diff.Z
11	Diff.X	1.000	0.465	-0.564
12	Diff.Y	0.465	1.000	0.223
13	Diff.Z	-0.564	0.223	1.000

FIGURE 11.9 Information generated by Crystal Ball's Batch Fit tool on the first differences of the X, Y, and Z times series in file RandomWalkWithDrift.xls.

MULTIPLICATIVE RANDOM WALK MODEL

If the time series of returns on a financial asset are IID, then we can use a multiplicative model to generate potential future prices of the asset. This is illustrated in Figure 11.10, which has data obtained from finance.yahoo.com. Cells B8:B170 hold the monthly adjusted closing prices of the exchange traded fund (ETF) based on the Standard & Poor's 500 Composite Stock Price Index with sticker symbol SPY. Denote these prices as S_t for $t = 1, \ldots, 163$. Note that the historical prices are listed in reverse chronological order, with S_{163} in cell B8, down to S_1 in cell B170. In cells C8:C169, we have calculated the gross returns $R_t = S_t/S_{t-1}$ for $t = 2, \ldots, 163$.

The multiplicative model used here to generate potential future prices is

$$S_{t+1} = S_t \times R_{t+1}, \tag{11.4}$$

for $t = 164, \ldots, 168$. These prices are calculated chronologically in cells G9:G13. The gross returns $R_{164}, \ldots, R_{168}$ are calculated as Crystal Ball assumptions in cells F9:F13. Each assumption is a lognormal distribution with mean 1.0088 and standard deviation 0.0409, as determined by Crystal Ball's distribution-fitting feature. The lognormal distribution was chosen because of its adequate fit to the data and its appealing property that it is bounded below by zero. This bound represents well the limited liability of owning shares of SPY, from which an owner cannot lose more than the total amount invested. The parameters of the fitted distribution tell us that on average during the period February 1, 1993, through August 1, 2006, the ETF had a monthly rate of return of 0.88 percent with a monthly standard deviation of 4.09 percent. These monthly figures annualize to a mean rate of return of $12 \times 0.88 = 10.56$ percent with a standard deviation of $\sqrt{12} \times 4.09 = 14.17$ percent.

Cell G13 is defined as a Crystal Ball forecast, and its chart is shown in Figure 11.11. Using our methodology, a 95 percent certainty interval for the price

	A	B	C	D	E	F	G
1	SPY.xls						
2							
3			SPY				
4		Autocorr	-0.025				
5		Abs(Z)	0.324				
6							
7	Date	SPY Adj. Close*	SPY Gross Return		Date	SPY Gross Return	SPY Adj. Close*
8	1-Aug-06	127.22	0.9952		1-Aug-06		127.22
9	3-Jul-06	127.84	1.0044		1-Sep-06	1.0000	127.22
10	1-Jun-06	127.28	1.0026		2-Oct-06	1.0000	127.22
11	1-May-06	126.95	0.9699		1-Nov-06	1.0000	127.22
12	3-Apr-06	130.89	1.0126		1-Dec-06	1.0000	127.22
13	1-Mar-06	129.26	1.0165		2-Jan-07	1.0000	127.22
14	1-Feb-06	127.16	1.0057				
169	1-Mar-93	36.23	1.0252				
170	1-Feb-93	35.34					

FIGURE 11.10 Crystal Ball model for forecasting with a multiplicative model the January 2, 2007, adjusted closing value of SPY. Note that rows 15 through 168 are hidden.

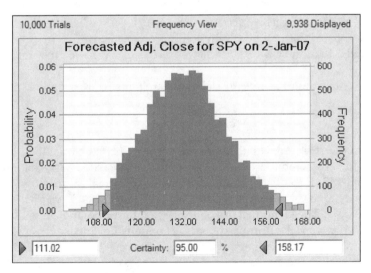

FIGURE 11.11 Crystal Ball forecast for the 2-Jan-07 adjusted closing value of SPY, based on the file SPY.xls. The actual closing value of SPY on 3-Jan-07 was 141.37. Note that the new York Stock Exchange was closed on 2-Jan-07 in observance of a national day of mourning for the death of former U. S. president Gerald R. Ford.

is from \$111.02 to \$158.17. Because we used the lognormal distribution for gross returns, it is possible to have come up with this forecast analytically. However, we saw in Chapter 9 how the multiplicative model is used along with annual withdrawals to come up with a retirement planning model for which a forecast cannot easily be obtained analytically. Ibbotson Associates (2006) describes wealth forecasting with Monte Carlo simulation and provides historical data from which to estimate the necessary parameters.

The multiplicative model can also be used with assets whose returns are correlated within the same time period, but are serially uncorrelated. Figure 11.12 is a model for three ETFs based on data for the period November 1, 2002, through August 1, 2006, obtained from finance.yahoo.com. The adjusted closing price data are in cells B8:D53 (not shown in Figure 11.12), and were used to calculate gross returns in cells E8:G52. From these gross returns the lognormal distributions with means, standard deviations, and correlations indicated in cells I15:L22 were fit using Crystal Ball's Batch Fit tool. Again, see Chapter 9 for an example of how the multiplicative model was used for retirement planning.

	I	J	K	L	M	N	O
6	**ETFs.xls**						
7	Date	SPY Gross Return	ADRA Gross Return	ADRU Gross Return	SPY Adj. Close*	ADRA Adj. Close*	ADRU Adj. Close*
8	1-Aug-06				127.22	28.92	26.53
9	1-Sep-06	1.0000	1.0000	1.0000	127.22	28.92	26.53
10	2-Oct-06	1.0000	1.0000	1.0000	127.22	28.92	26.53
11	1-Nov-06	1.0000	1.0000	1.0000	127.22	28.92	26.53
12	1-Dec-06	1.0000	1.0000	1.0000	127.22	28.92	26.53
13	2-Jan-07	1.0000	1.0000	1.0000	127.22	28.92	26.53
14							
15	Parameters	SPY	ADRA	ADRU			
16	Mean	1.0086	1.0146	1.015			
17	Std. Dev	0.0269	0.0450	0.0459			
18							
19	Correlations	SPY Gross Return	ADRA Gross Return	ADRU Gross Return			
20	SPY Gross Return	1.00	0.63	0.63			
21	ADRA Gross Return	0.63	1.00	0.59			
22	ADRU Gross Return	0.63	0.59	1.00			

FIGURE 11.12 Crystal Ball model for forecasting with a multiplicative model the January 2, 2007, adjusted closing values of SPY, ADRA, and ADRU. The Crystal Ball assumptions in cells J9:L13 have means and standard deviations shown in cells I15:L17, and cross correlations shown in cells I19:L22. Cells M13:O13 are Crystal Ball forecasts.

GEOMETRIC BROWNIAN MOTION MODEL

A special type of multiplicative random walk process is the *geometric Brownian motion* (GBM) process, which is used widely for simulating stock prices. It is also called *exponentiated Brownian motion*, and indeed to simulate GBM processes we generate values from a Brownian motion process and then exponentiate them. Brownian motion takes its name from botanist Robert Brown, who observed in 1827 that pollen particles floating in water under a microscope exhibited a "jittery" motion even though they were inanimate. Work by Albert Einstein and others in the early 1900s associated the normal distribution with the jittery movements observed by Brown.

In his 1900 doctoral thesis, Louis Bachelier described the movement of stock prices with what we now call Brownian motion in order to find the value of options. In the 1950s, economist Paul Samuelson rediscovered Bachelier's thesis and went on to popularize the use of GBM as a model of stock prices and other financial assets. See Wilmott (2000) for a good, not-too-technical explanation of how GBM can be developed from tossing coins.

Whereas it is possible for Brownian motion to take on negative values, GBM is always positive because exponentiation always results in positive values. This is a desirable feature because the limited liability of stock ownership implies that prices cannot be negative. Also, it turns out that for GBM it is the percentage changes that are IID rather than the absolute changes as in the additive random walk. This implies that the stochastic percentage return is independent of the stock's price level for GBM. This is an appealing feature. If an investor desires a 10 percent return on her investment, then with all else equal she will not care whether the 10 percent is earned from holding 3,000 shares of General Electric purchased for $30 per share or one share of Berkshire Hathaway Inc. purchased for $90,000.

The non-negativity of the prices it generates, the independence of the percentage changes, and the relative simplicity and good empirical fit all account for the popularity of GBM for simulating stock prices. To learn more about the derivation of GBM, see Duffie (1996). To read more about its development and use in finance, see Rubinstein (2006).

Generating Stock Prices with GBM

To simulate stock prices using the GBM model, we generate independent replications of the stock price at time $t + \delta$, from the formula

$$S_{t+\delta} = S_t e^{(\mu - \sigma^2/2)\delta + \sigma\sqrt{\delta}Z}, \tag{11.5}$$

where S_t is the stock price at time t, μ is the rate of return parameter stated on an annual basis, σ is the volatility parameter stated on an annual basis, δ is the time step (in years), and Z is a standard normal random variate. The parameter σ is also known simply as the *volatility* of the stock price, and is an important quantity in

	A	B	C	D	E	F	G
1	**SPYwithGBM.xls**						
2							
3			SPY				
4		**Autocorr**	-0.025				
5		**Abs(Z)**	0.324				
6							
7	Date	SPY Adj. Close*	SPY Gross Return	Log Return		Monthly	
8	1-Aug-06	127.22	0.9952	-0.005		**Mean**	0.007907
9	3-Jul-06	127.84	1.0044	0.0044		**Std Dev**	0.040524
10	1-Jun-06	127.28	1.0026	0.0026			
11	1-May-06	126.95	0.9699	-0.031		**Annualized**	
12	3-Apr-06	130.89	1.0126	0.0125		**Mean**	0.134294
13	1-Mar-06	129.26	1.0165	0.0164		**Std Dev**	0.140379
14	1-Feb-06	127.16	1.0057	0.0057			
169	1-Mar-93	36.23	1.0252	0.0249			
170	1-Feb-93	35.34					
171							
172	Date	N(0,1)	SPY Adj. Close*				
173	1-Aug-06		127.22				
174	1-Sep-06	0.0000	128.55				
175	2-Oct-06	0.0000	129.89				
176	1-Nov-06	0.0000	131.24				
177	1-Dec-06	0.0000	132.61				
178	2-Jan-07	0.0000	133.99	< Result of five one-month steps			
179			133.99	< Result of one five-month step			

FIGURE 11.13 Crystal Ball model for forecasting SPY prices with GBM.

modeling financial time series. Some authors refer to μ simply as the rate of return, but its interpretation takes some care as explained below.

Because $\ln(S_{t+\delta})$ is normally distributed, stock prices generated with GBM follow a lognormal distribution. Figure 11.13 shows a model used to generate SPY prices with GBM having $\mu = 9.49$ percent and $\sigma = 14.04$ percent in cells **G12** and **G13**, respectively. A forecast chart for the price of SPY on 2-JAN-07, is shown in Figure 11.14. We arrived at this price by generating prices in five steps of one month ($\delta = 1/12$), but could have obtained similar results with just one step of five months ($\delta = 5/12$) in Expression 11.5. The next section explains how the values of the parameters μ and σ were selected.

Estimating GBM Parameters

Given a time series of stock prices, $S_0, S_1, S_2, \ldots, S_n$ observed at equally spaced time periods with interval δ (stated in years), we can estimate the values of μ and σ as

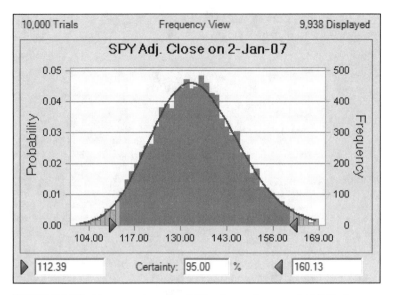

FIGURE 11.14 Forecast chart for SPY price on January 2, 2007. A lognormal density function is superimposed on the histogram.

	A	B	C	D	E	F	G
1	**Correlated GBM**						
2							
3	Time	Market	Stock	Market Epsilon	Stock Epsilon	Parameters	
4	1/1/2000	100.00	100.00	0.0000	0.0000	Mkt_Mu	8%
5	1/3/2000	100.03	100.03	0.0000	0.0000	Mkt_Sigma	12%
6	1/4/2000	100.06	100.06	0.0000	0.0000	Stock_Mu	10%
7	1/5/2000	100.09	100.08	0.0000	0.0000	Stock_Sigma	25%
8	1/6/2000	100.12	100.11	0.0000	0.0000	Correlation	0.96
9	1/7/2000	100.15	100.14	0.0000	0.0000	Beta	2
10	1/10/2000	100.17	100.17	0.0000	0.0000		
102	5/17/2000	102.89	102.73	0.0000	0.0000		
103	5/18/2000	102.92	102.76	0.0000	0.0000		

FIGURE 11.15 Correlated GBM. Cells D4:E103 are assumptions. Cells B103 and C103 are forecasts.

was done in SPYwithGBM.xls. Define R_i as the gross return per period and r_i as the continuously compounded rate of return per period on the stock. To estimate μ and σ, first find

$$R_i = S_i/S_{i-1} \quad \text{and} \quad r_i = \ln(R_i) \text{ for } i = 1, 2, \ldots, n.$$

Using the standard formulas for sample mean and standard deviation, compute

$$\bar{r} = \frac{1}{n}\sum_{i=1}^{n} r_i \quad \text{and} \quad s_r = \sqrt{\frac{1}{n-1}\sum_{i=1}^{n}(r_i - \bar{r})}.$$

Then the GBM parameters are estimated as

$$\hat{\mu} = \frac{\bar{r}}{\delta} + \frac{s_r^2}{2\delta} \quad \text{and} \quad \hat{\sigma} = \frac{s_r}{\sqrt{\delta}}$$

Note the difference between the GBM rate of return parameter μ and the expected annual return on the stock. Suppose that stock price S_T is generated by a GBM process with parameters μ and σ, starting at price S_t, where $T > t$ and both are stated in years. Then S_T is lognormally distributed with mean and variance

$$E(S_T) = S_t e^{\mu(T-t)}$$

$$Var(S_T) = S_t^2 e^{2\mu(T-t)}(e^{\sigma^2(T-t)} - 1)$$

For the SPY example, the expected mean and variance are 132.35 and 144.42, respectively. The sample mean and variance of the forecast in cell **C178** are 134.54 and 149.49, respectively. Furthermore, let r be the continuously compounded rate of return stated on an annual basis from time t to T, that is, $S_T = S_t e^{r(T-t)}$. Then r is normally distributed with mean and variance

$$E(r) = \mu - \frac{\sigma^2}{2}$$

$$Var(r) = \frac{\sigma^2}{(T-t)}$$

This is verified by the simulation results in SPYwithGBM.xls.

There are other methods for estimating volatility that use more information, such as the daily high and low prices as well as the closing prices. See Wilmott (2000) and the references therein for more information.

Generating Correlated Stock Prices

Figure 11.15 shows part of a Crystal Ball model for generating correlated geometric Brownian motion in CorrelatedGBM.xls. This model lets you specify parameters for means, standard deviations, and correlation for a market return and a stock. It also calculates sample statistics for means, standard deviations, and correlation for a market return and a stock, as well as showing time-series plots of stock and market prices and a scatterplot of returns.

MEAN-REVERTING MODEL

The mean-reverting model is used for modelling commodity prices, foreign exchange rates, interest rates and other financial time series. Unlike the random walk with drift model, which increases (or decreases) on average over time, the mean-reverting model has the characteristic that its level tends to fluctuate around the mean value, μ. One type of mean-reverting model is the autoregressive model, which takes advantage of the autocorrelation in a time series to predict future values from past values of the series.

AR(1) Process

An autoregressive (AR) model of order 1, known as an AR(1) model, is

$$Y_t = \phi_0 + \phi_1 Y_{t-1} + a_t, \tag{11.6}$$

where a_t is a white noise series with mean zero and variance σ_a^2. Expression 11.6 is in the same form as a simple regression model, so we can use Excel's Data Analysis tool to find estimates of the parameters, ϕ_0, ϕ_1, and σ_a^2, then use these estimates to simulate future values of the time series.

For example, the model in Figure 11.16 shows the market yield on 10-year U.S. Treasury bonds for 2005. In order to use Excel's regression capabilities, the data in cells B4:B252 were copied and pasted to cells C5:C253. The values in column C are then called the Lag1 values simply because for each value of the series in rows 5 through 253 of column B, the previous value of the series is in the same row of column C.

To estimate the parameters of the AR(1) model, mouse to Tools > Data Analysis ... > Regression in Excel and you will get the dialog window shown in Figure 11.17. By specifying B5:B253 as the Y Range and C5:C253 as the X Range, and checking the box next to Residuals, we generated a New Worksheet Ply named "AR(1)" containing the output shown in Figures 11.18 and 11.19.

To simulate future values of the time series, we use the model

$$Y_t = 0.132 + 0.969Y_{t-1} + e_t,$$

where e_t is Normal with mean zero and standard deviation 0.045. The values 0.132, 0.969, and 0.045 are taken from cells B17, B18, and B7, respectively in Figure 11.18. To check whether the residuals appear to be white noise, their autocorrelation is found in cell D25 to be 0.011, which gives a rule of thumb value of 0.181 (much less than 2 in absolute value) in cell E25. Furthermore, using Crystal Ball's Distribution Fitting feature, we found that a normal(0,0.045) distribution fit the residuals well.

For the AR(1) model specified in Expression 11.6, the mean is $\mu = \phi_0/(1 - \phi_1)$. Therefore, the mean to which our simulated data will revert is estimated as

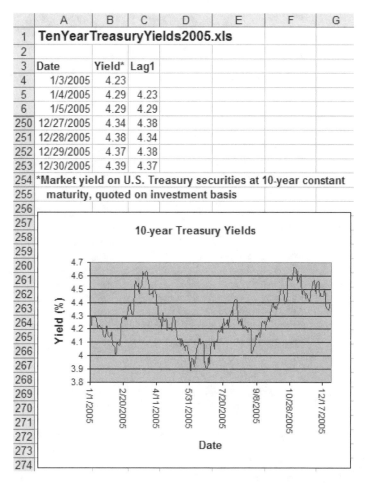

FIGURE 11.16 Market yield on 10-year U.S. Treasury bonds for 2005 obtained from www.federalreserve.gov/datadownload/ and their lag-1 values. Note that rows 7 through 249 are hidden.

$0.132/(1 - 0.969) = 4.31$. Although we can use this model to simulate future values for an indefinite period, it may be best to reestimate the model parameters as new data become available.

AR(p) Process

In the previous example, because the residuals in Figure 11.19 appeared to come from a white noise process, we concluded that an AR(1) process was suitable for simulating future values. In this section, we consider what to do when the residuals from an AR(1) model do not appear to be from a white noise process.

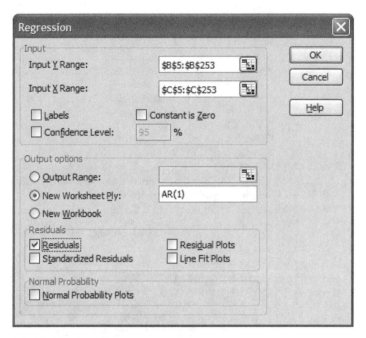

FIGURE 11.17 Excel regression fitting an AR(1) model to the data
dialog window used in Figure 11.16.

	A	B	C	D	E	F
1	SUMMARY OUTPUT					
2						
3	*Regression Statistics*					
4	Multiple R	0.969				
5	R Square	0.939				
6	Adjusted R Square	0.939				
7	Standard Error	0.045				
8	Observations	249				
9						
10	ANOVA					
11		*df*	*SS*	*MS*	*F*	*Significance F*
12	Regression	1	7.821	7.821	3805.037	0.000
13	Residual	247	0.508	0.002		
14	Total	248	8.329			
15						
16		*Coefficients*	*Standard Error*	*t Stat*	*P-value*	
17	Intercept	0.132	0.067	1.952	0.052	
18	X Variable 1	0.969	0.016	61.685	0.000	

FIGURE 11.18 Excel regression output from fitting an AR(1) model to the data
in Figure 11.16.

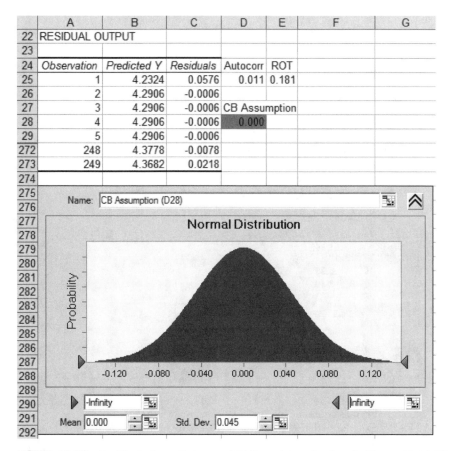

FIGURE 11.19 Residuals from fitting an AR(1) model to the data in Figure 11.16. Note that rows 30 through 271 are hidden.

Mean-reverting processes can be simulated as AR(p) processes, where the order p is identified from the data. The model for an AR(p) process is

$$Y_t = \phi_0 + \phi_1 Y_{t-1} + \ldots + \phi_p Y_{t-p} + a_t,$$

where a_t is a white noise series with mean zero and variance σ_a^2 as in the specification of an AR(1) model. Observations from an AR(p) model will revert to the mean level,

$$\mu = \phi_0/(1 - \phi_1 - \ldots - \phi_p).$$

One strategy for using an AR(p) model is to find the smallest order p such that the residuals from the AR(p) autoregression have no statistically significant first-order autocorrelation. This assumes that if the first-order autocorrelation is

	A	B	C	D	E	F	G
1	Title:	1-Year Treasury Constant Maturity Rate					
2	Series ID:	GS1					
3	Source:	Board of Governors of the Federal Reserve System					
4	Release:	H.15 Selected Interest Rates					
5	Seasonal Adjustment:	Not Applicable					
6	Frequency:	Monthly					
7	Units:	Percent					
8	Date Range:	1990-01-01 to 2005-01-01					
9	Last Updated:	2006-07-05 11:12 AM CT					
10	Notes: Averages of business days. For further information regarding treasury						
11	constant maturity data, please refer to						
12	http://www.federalreserve.gov/releases/h15/current/h15.pdf and						
13	http://www.treas.gov/offices/domestic-finance/debt-management/interest-rate/index.html						
14							
15	DATE	VALUE	LAG1	LAG2	LAG3		
16	1990-01-01	7.92					
17	1990-02-01	8.11	7.92				
18	1990-03-01	8.35	8.11	7.92			
19	1990-04-01	8.40	8.35	8.11	7.92		
20	1990-05-01	8.32	8.40	8.35	8.11		
207	2005-12-01	4.35	4.33	4.18	3.85		
208	2006-01-01	4.35				0	
209	2006-02-01	4.34				0	
210	2006-03-01	4.33				0	
211	2006-04-01	4.31				0	
212	2006-05-01	4.29				0	
213	2006-06-01	4.28				0	
214							

FIGURE 11.20 Data and lagged values contained on the "Data" worksheet of the file OneYearTreasuryYieldsData.xls. Note that rows 21 through 206 are hidden.

zero, then higher orders will be zero also. While not always a good assumption, this method is useful for generating potential future values from many time series used in financial models. For information about performing more thorough time series analyses of financial time series for inferential purposes, see Tsay (2002).

An example of identifying and using an AR(p) model is shown in the file OneYearTreasuryYields.xls for 1-Year Treasury Constant Maturity Rate data shown in cells **B16:B207** of the "Data" worksheet in the Excel file shown in Figure 11.20. The LAG1, LAG2, and LAG3 values were placed in Columns B, C, and D, respectively, on the "Data" worksheet. Worksheets "AR(1)", "AR(2)", and "AR(3)" show the output from fitting AR models of order 1, 2, and 3 to the time series values. Based on this output, we would select an AR(2) model for simulating potential future values. Figure 11.21 shows some of the output on the "AR(2)" worksheet.

We reach this conclusion because the residuals from the AR(1) model have autocorrelation of 0.462, which is large enough by our rule of thumb (because

	A	B	C	D	E	F	G
1	SUMMARY OUTPUT						
2							
3	*Regression Statistics*						
4	Multiple R	0.994					
5	R Square	0.987					
6	Adjusted R Square	0.987					
7	Standard Error	**0.200**					
8	Observations	189					
9							
10	ANOVA						
11		*df*	*SS*	*MS*	*F*	*Significance F*	
12	Regression	2	582.289	291.144	7250.435	0.000	
13	Residual	186	7.469	0.040			
14	Total	188	589.758				
15							
16		*Coefficients*	*Standard Error*	*t Stat*	*P-value*	*Lower 95%*	*Upper 95%*
17	Intercept	**0.075**	0.039	1.908	0.058	-0.003	0.152
18	X Variable 1	**1.442**	0.064	22.391	0.000	1.315	1.569
19	X Variable 2	**-0.461**	0.064	-7.241	0.000	-0.587	-0.336
20							
21	RESIDUAL OUTPUT		**Autocorrelation**	**ROT**			
22			**0.004**	0.053			
23	*Observation*	*Predicted Y*	*Residuals*				
24	1	8.373	0.027				
25	2	8.335	-0.015				
212	189	4.390	-0.040				

FIGURE 11.21 Worksheet "AR(2)" of the file OneYearTreasuryYieldsData.xls.

6.35 > 2) to conclude that they are not uncorrelated. However, the residuals from the AR(2) model have autocorrelation of 0.004 (see cell **C22** in Figure 11.21), which is small enough by the rule of thumb value (0.053 in cell **D22**) to conclude that they come from a white noise process. We reach the same conclusion by noting that the estimate of ϕ_3 in the AR(3) model, 0.010, is not statistically different from zero because its **P-value** in the Excel output is 0.891, which is much greater than the usual comparison value of 0.05.

In cells **B208:B213** of the "Data" worksheet, we see how to use the mean-reverting AR(2) model to simulate data for the first six months of 2006 with the equation

$$Y_t = 0.075 + 1.442 Y_{t-1} - 0.461 Y_{t-2} + e_t$$

where e_t is Normal with mean zero and standard deviation 0.200.

This chapter covered some of the basic models used in financial modeling and risk analysis. For more advanced models used for specialized purposes, see Tsay (2002), Fan and Yao (2003), or McNeil, Frey, and Embrechts (2005).

CHAPTER 12

Financial Options

A financial *option* is a security that grants its owner the right, but not the obligation, to trade another financial security at specified times in the future for an agreed amount. The financial security that can be traded in the future is called the underlying asset, or simply the *underlying*. An option is an example of a *derivative* security, so named because its value is derived from that of the underlying. The problem of placing a value on an option is made difficult by the asymmetric payoff that arises from the option owner's right to trade the underlying in the future if doing so is favorable, but to avoid trading when doing so is unfavorable.

Options allow for hedging against one-sided risk. However, a prerequisite for efficient management of risk is that these derivative securities are priced correctly when they are traded. Nobel laureates Fischer Black, Robert Merton, and Myron Scholes developed in the early 1970s a method to price specific types of options exactly, but their method does not produce exact prices for all types of options. In practice, Monte Carlo simulation is often used to price derivative securities. This chapter shows how to use Crystal Ball for option pricing.

The optionality leads to a nonlinear payoff that is convolved with the lognormally distributed stock price to result in a probability distribution for option value that is difficult for many analysts to visualize without Crystal Ball. The payoff diagrams familiar to options traders give the range and level of option value as a function of stock price but don't offer insights into the probabilities associated with payoffs. However, Crystal Ball forecasts do this readily. The next section provides brief background material on financial options. For more information, consult the books by Hull (1997), McDonald (2006), or Wilmott (1998, 2000).

TYPES OF OPTIONS

Denote the price of the underlying asset by S_t, for $0 \leq t \leq T$, where T is the expiration date of the option. The agreed amount for which the underlying is traded when the option expires is called the *strike price*, which is denoted by K. There are many different types of options. Some basic types are listed below.

Call. A call option gives its owner the right to *purchase* the underlying for the strike price on the expiration date. The payoff for a call option with strike price K when it is exercised on date T is max $(S_T - K, 0)$.

Put. A put option gives its owner the right to *sell* the underlying for the strike price on the expiration date. The payoff for a put option with strike price K when it is exercised on date T is max $(K - S_T, 0)$.

European. A European option allows the owner to exercise it *only at the termination date*, T. Thus, the owner cannot influence the future cash flows from a European option with any decision made after purchase.

American. An American option allows the owner to exercise *at any time on or before the termination date*, T. Thus, the owner of an American call (or put) option can influence the future cash flows with a decision made after purchase by exercising the option when the price of the underlying is high (or low) enough to compel the owner to do so.

Exotic. The payoffs for exotic options depend on more than just the price of the underlying at exercise. Some examples of exotics are: Asian options, which pay the difference between the strike and the average price of the underlying over a specified period; up-and-in barrier options, which pay the difference between the strike and spot prices at exercise only if the price of the underlying has exceeded some prespecified barrier level; and down-and-out barrier options, which pay the difference between the strike and spot prices at exercise only if the price of the underlying has not gone below some prespecified barrier level.

New types of options appear frequently. Because they are designed to cover individual circumstances, analytic methods to price new derivative securities are not always available when the securities are developed. However, it is possible to obtain good estimates of the value of most any type of option using Crystal Ball and the concept of risk-neutral pricing.

RISK-NEUTRAL PRICING AND THE BLACK-SCHOLES MODEL

Arbitrage is the purchase of securities on one market for immediate resale on another in order to profit from a price discrepancy. Because the sale of the security in the higher-price market finances the purchase of the security in the lower-price market, an arbitrage opportunity requires no investment capital. An arbitrage opportunity is said to exist when a combination of trades is available that requires no investment capital, cannot lose money, and has a positive probability of making money for the arbitrageur.

In an efficient market, arbitrage opportunities cannot last for long. As arbitrageurs buy securities in the market with the lower price, the forces of supply and demand cause the price to rise in that market. Similarly, when the arbitrageurs sell the securities in the market with the higher price, the forces of supply and demand cause the price to fall in that market. The combination of the profit motive and nearly instantaneous trading ensures that prices in the two markets will converge quickly if arbitrage opportunities exist.

Using the assumption of no arbitrage, financial economists have shown that the price of a derivative security can be found as the expected value of its discounted payouts when the expected value is taken with respect to a transformation of the original probability measure called the *equivalent martingale* measure or the *risk-neutral* measure. See Duffie (1996), Hull (1997), McDonald (2006), or Wilmott (1998, 2000) for more about risk-neutral pricing.

The price of a fairly valued European put option is the expected present value of the payoff $E\left[e^{-rT}\max(K - S_T, 0)\right]$, where the expectation is taken under the risk-neutral measure. To compute this expectation, Black and Scholes (1973) modeled the stochastic process generating the price of a non-dividend-paying stock as geometric Brownian motion (GBM).

The Black-Scholes price for a European call option on a non-dividend-paying stock trading at time t is

$$C_t(S_t, T - t) = S_t N(d_1) - Ke^{-r(T-t)}N(d_2), \tag{12.1}$$

where

$$d_1 = \frac{\log(S_t/K) + \left(r + \frac{1}{2}\sigma^2\right)(T - t)}{\sigma\sqrt{T - t}}, \tag{12.2}$$

$$d_2 = \frac{\log(S/K) + \left(r - \frac{1}{2}\sigma^2\right)(T - t)}{\sigma\sqrt{T - t}} = d_1 - \sigma\sqrt{T - t}, \tag{12.3}$$

$N(d_i)$ is the cumulative distribution value for a standard normal random variable with value d_i, K is the strike price, r is the risk-free rate of interest, and T is the time of expiration.

The Black-Scholes solution for a European put option on a non-dividend-paying stock trading at time t is:

$$P_t(S_t, T - t) = -S_t N(-d_1) + Ke^{-r(T-t)}N(-d_2), \tag{12.4}$$

where d_1 and d_2 are given by expressions (12.2) and (12.3) above.

Note that the variables appearing in the Black-Scholes equations are the current stock price, S_t; stock price volatility, σ; strike price, K; time of expiration, T; and the risk-free rate of interest, r; all of which are independent of individual risk preferences. This allows for the assumption that all investors are risk neutral, which leads to the Black-Scholes solutions above. However, these solutions are valid in all worlds, not just those where investors are risk neutral.

Option Pricing with Crystal Ball

In the Black-Scholes worldview, a fair value for an option is the present value of the option payoff at expiration under a risk-neutral random walk for the underlying asset prices. Therefore, the general approach to using simulation to find the price of the option is straightforward:

1. Using the risk-free measure, simulate sample paths of the underlying state variables (e.g., underlying asset prices and interest rates) over the relevant time horizon.
2. Evaluate the discounted cash flows of a security on each sample path, as determined by the structure of the security in question.
3. Average the discounted cash flows over sample paths.

In effect, this method computes an estimate of a multidimensional integral that yields the expected value of the discounted payouts over the space of sample paths. The increase in complexity of derivative securities has led to a need to evaluate high-dimensional integrals. Monte Carlo simulation is attractive relative to other numerical techniques because it is flexible, easy to implement and modify, and the error convergence rate is independent of the dimension of the problem.

To simulate stock prices using the assumptions behind the Black-Scholes model, generate independent replications of the stock price at time $t + \delta$ from the formula

$$S_{t+\delta}^{(i)} = S_t \exp\left((r - \sigma^2/2)\delta + \sigma \sqrt{\delta} Z^{(i)} \right), \tag{12.5}$$

for $i = 1, \ldots, n$, where S_t is the stock price at time t, r is the riskless interest rate, σ is the stock's volatility, and $Z^{(i)}$ is a standard normal random variate.

The Excel files EuroCall.xls in Figure 12.1 and EuroPut.xls in Figure 12.2 contain simulation models for pricing European Call and Put options on a stock with current price S_0 =$100 and annual volatility $\sigma = 40\%$. The options have strike price K =$100, and six months until expiration, in a world with risk-free rate $r = 5\%$. Of course, these are securities for which the Black-Scholes formulas (12.1) and (12.4) provide an exact answer, so there is no need to use simulation to price them. However, European options serve to help us see how well the Monte Carlo pricing approach works—since we know the exact solution, it becomes possible to check the accuracy of our simulation results against the exact solution provided by Black-Scholes. In the Excel file EuroCall.xls, the European call price estimated by simulation with 100,000 iterations is $12.33 (with standard error 0.06), while the Black-Scholes price is $12.39. In EuroPut.xls, the European put price estimated by simulation with 100,000 iterations is $9.92 (0.04), while the Black-Scholes price is also $9.92.

The increased availability of powerful computers and easy-to-use software has enhanced the appeal of simulation to price derivatives. The main drawback of Monte Carlo simulation is that a large number of replications may be required to obtain precise results. Fortunately, computer speeds have increased greatly in the last

	A	B	C	D	E
1	EuroCall.xls				
2					
3	Inputs			Black-Scholes Solution	
4	S_0	$ 100.00		d_1	0.2298
5	K	$ 100.00		d_2	-0.0530
6	Sigma	40%		N(d_1)	0.5909
7	T	0.5		N(d_2)	0.4789
8	R_f	5%		C(S,T)	$ 12.39
9	Z	0.0000			
10					
11	S_T	$ 98.51			
12	Payoff	$ -			
13	Present value of call	$ -		Mean PV	$ 12.39

FIGURE 12.1 Spreadsheet segment from model to simulate a European call option.

	A	B	C	D	E
1	EuroPut.xls				
2					
3	Inputs			Black-Scholes Solution	
4	S_0	$ 100.00		d_1	0.2298
5	K	$ 100.00		d_2	-0.0530
6	Sigma	40%		N(-d_1)	0.4091
7	T	0.5		N(-d_2)	0.5211
8	R_f	5%		P(S,T)	$ 9.92
9	Z	0.0000			
10					
11	End price (S_T)	$ 98.51			
12	Payoff	$ 1.49			
13	Present value of put	$ 1.45		Mean PV	$ 9.92

FIGURE 12.2 Spreadsheet segment from model to simulate a European put option.

30 years and software algorithms such as Crystal Ball's Extreme Speed feature have become more efficient. Furthermore, variance reduction techniques can be applied to sharpen the inferences and reduce the number of replications required. Variance reduction techniques are covered in Appendix C.

PORTFOLIO INSURANCE

In this section, we use Crystal Ball to simulate the combination of holding a put option with the underlying asset. This limits the upside potential, but protects against potential losses and so is a form of portfolio insurance. We will see how this strategy lowers the risk and expected value from the levels obtained when holding

	A	B	C	D	E
1	**VFH.xls**				
2					
3	Drift	11.50%			
4	Vol	11.75%			
5	Date	Adj. Close*	Return	Put Option	
6	21-Aug-06	59.33	-0.29%	Purchased	8/21/2006
7	18-Aug-06	59.5	0.08%	Price	1.95
8	17-Aug-06	59.45	0.32%	Expires	3/16/2007
9	16-Aug-06	59.26	0.51%	Strike	58.00
10	15-Aug-06	58.96	1.62%	Stock	
11	14-Aug-06	58.01	0.14%	Purchased	8/21/2006
12	11-Aug-06	57.93	-0.46%	Price	59.33
13	10-Aug-06	58.2	0.60%	Holding Period	0.57
14	9-Aug-06	57.85	-1.08%	Z	0.00
15	8-Aug-06	58.48	-0.87%		
16	7-Aug-06	58.99	-0.41%	Stock Price on Expiration Date	
17	4-Aug-06	59.23	0.37%	$	68.68
18	3-Aug-06	59.01	0.56%	Put Value on Expiration Date	
19	2-Aug-06	58.68	0.12%	$	-
20	1-Aug-06	58.61	-0.26%	Return on Stock Alone	
21	31-Jul-06	58.76	-0.41%	15.76%	
22	28-Jul-06	59	1.76%	Return on Stock and Put	
23	27-Jul-06	57.97	-0.52%	12.08%	
24	26-Jul-06	58.27	0.00%		
649	2-Feb-04	47.67	0.44%		
650	30-Jan-04	47.46			

FIGURE 12.3 Spreadsheet segment from model in VFH.xls to simulate the return on holding a stock and a put option.

the underlying asset by itself. Although this strategy lowers risk for any selected underlying asset, it might induce a money manager to purchase a riskier underlying with a higher expected return if it can be protected with a put.

Figure 12.3 shows a spreadsheet segment from the model in file **VFH.xls** used for estimating the return on a portfolio composed on August 21, 2006, of one share of the exchange-traded fund (ETF) tracking stock VFH and a put option on VFH that expires on March 16, 2007. The holding period is calculated as 0.57 years in cell **E13**. VFH tracks the performance of the Morgan Stanley (MSCI) U.S. Investable Market Financials benchmark index. This index consists of stocks of large, medium-size, and small U.S. companies within the financial sector, which is composed of companies involved in activities such as banking, mortgage finance, consumer finance, specialized finance, investment banking and brokerage, asset management and custody, corporate lending, insurance, financial investment, and real estate. The drift and volatility parameters were estimated as 11.50 percent and 11.75 percent, respectively, from the monthly closing prices of VFH for the previous 31 months. Cell **D21** has the rate of return earned if the stock alone was held from

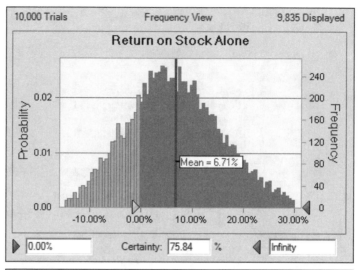

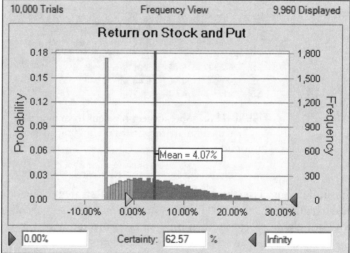

FIGURE 12.4   Forecast charts from model in VFH.xls to simulate the return on holding a stock and a put option.

August 21 through March 16, and cell **D23** has the rate of return earned on the portfolio of the stock and the put option held during the same period.

Figure 12.4 shows the forecast charts for cells **D21** and **D23**, specified to have the same scale on the horizontal axes. Note how the option to sell VFH for the exercise price, if its price falls below that, limits the downside value of the portfolio but not the upside. However, this protection comes at the cost of the price of the option, so the mean percentage return on the portfolio of 4.07 percent is lower than that on holding the stock alone, which is 6.71 percent. This is similar to buying insurance coverage to protect against a loss, so the strategy of purchasing a put along with stock is a form of portfolio insurance.

AMERICAN OPTION PRICING

Whereas a European option grants its holder the right, but not the obligation, to buy or sell shares of a common stock for the exercise price, K, at expiration time T, an *American* option grants its holder the right, but not the obligation, to buy or sell shares of a common stock for the exercise price, K, *at or before* expiration time T. The Black-Scholes expressions (12.1) and (12.4) are for European options and thus yield approximations for the values of American call and put options. In practice, numerical techniques are used to obtain closer approximations of options that can be exercised at or before expiration time T.

The fair value of an American put option is the discounted expected value of its future cash flows. The cash flows arise because the put can be exercised at the next instant, dt, or the following instant, $2dt$, if not previously exercised, ... , *ad infinitum*. In practice, American options are approximated by securities that can be exercised at only a finite number of opportunities, k, before expiration at time T. These types of financial instrument are called *Bermudan options*. By choosing k large enough, the computed value of a Bermudan option will be practically equal to the value of an American option.

Geske and Johnson (1984) develop a numerical approximation for the value of an American option based on extrapolating values for Bermudan options having small numbers (1, 2, and 3) of exercise opportunities. Their results are exact in the limit as the number of exercise opportunities goes to infinity. Broadie and Glasserman (1997) used simulation to price American options by generating two estimators, one biased high and one biased low, both asymptotically unbiased and converging to the true price. Avramidis and Hyden (1999) discuss ways to improve the Broadie and Glasserman estimates. Longstaff and Schwartz (1998) provide an alternate method for pricing American options.

The early exercise feature of American options makes their valuation more difficult because the optimal exercise policy must be estimated as part of the valuation. This *free–boundary* aspect of the pricing problem led some authors to conclude that Monte Carlo simulation is not suitable for valuing American options (for example, Hull 1997). However, we'll see next how to use Crystal Ball and OptQuest for this purpose.

The file **BermuPut.xls** contains an example of valuing an Bermudan put option with initial stock price $S_0 = 40$, risk-free rate $r = 0.0488$, time to expiration $T = 0.5833$ (seven months), volatility $\sigma = 0.4$, strike price $K = 45$, and six early-exercise opportunities at Months 1 through 6. From Geske and Johnson (1984), the true value of this option is $7.39.

The spreadsheet in Figure 12.5 illustrates a method to price this option using Crystal Ball and OptQuest. This method uses OptQuest's tabu search to identify an

	A	B	C	D	E	F	G	H
1	**BermuPut.xls**							
2								
3	Inputs							
4	S_0	$40.00						
5	K	$45.00						
6	Sigma	40%						
7	T	0.5833						
8	R_f	4.88%						
9								
10	Month	Time	Z	S	Bound	Sell	Sold	PV(Payoff)
11	0	0		$40.00				
12	1	0.08	0.00	$39.90	$30.05	0	0	$ 5.08
13	2	0.17	0.00	$39.79	$30.10	0	0	$ 5.17
14	3	0.25	0.00	$39.69	$30.36	0	0	$ 5.25
15	4	0.33	0.00	$39.59	$34.53	0	0	$ 5.33
16	5	0.42	0.00	$39.48	$35.88	0	0	$ 5.41
17	6	0.50	0.00	$39.38	$36.85	0	0	$ 5.48
18	7	0.58	0.00	$39.28	$45.00	1	1	$ 5.56
19								
20	Value at Time 0							
21	$5.56							

FIGURE 12.5 Spreadsheet segment from model to simulate a Bermudan put option.

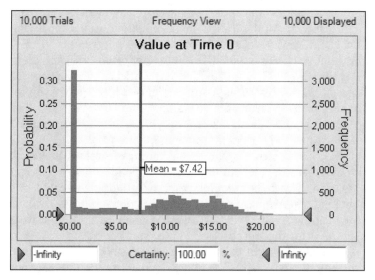

FIGURE 12.6 Forecast from model to simulate a Bermudan put option. The values of the decision variables in cells E12:E17 were selected by OptQuest.

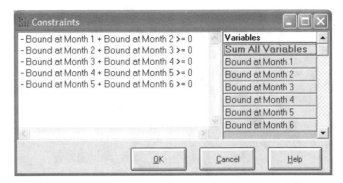

FIGURE 12.7   Constraints from model to simulate a Bermudan put option.

optimal policy, then a final set of iterations to estimate the value of the option under the identified policy. The estimated price for the option described above is shown in Figure 12.6 as $7.42. The standard error of this estimate is $0.06.

Figure 12.7 shows the only constraints on the decision variables. Because the longer the time left until expiration, the greater the chance of the stock price falling below the exercise price, so the early-exercise boundary value should also be less than the value at a later time. These constraints are imposed in Figure 12.7 by requiring the bound at month t to be greater than or equal to the bound in the previous month, $t - 1$, for $t = 2, 3, 4, 5, 6$.

EXOTIC OPTION PRICING

Exotic options are financial instruments having more complicated payoff structures than "plain vanilla" puts and calls. As the term *exotic* is used to describe options in the sense of *unusual*, there is not a well-accepted categorization of exotic options. What are exotic options to one trader may be traded on a daily basis by another, and therefore not unusual. For our purposes, we use the term to apply to any option other than the European or American puts and calls we have described thus far.

There are far too many exotic options to list here, but the next three subsections show how to model some options that are representative of those you might encounter.

Digital options

Digital options pay either a prespecified amount of an asset, or nothing at all. For example, a European cash-or-nothing digital (also called a binary) call option pays $1 if and only if the price of the underlying exceeds the strike price on the exercise date. That is, the payoff is

$$\$1 \text{ if } S_T > K,$$
$$0 \text{ otherwise.}$$

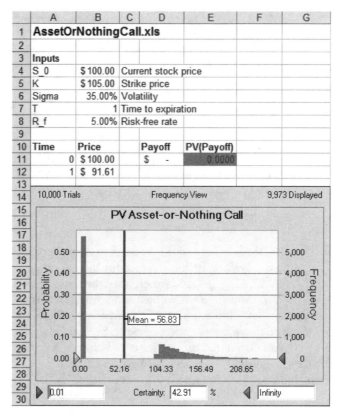

FIGURE 12.8　Spreadsheet segment from model in AssetOrNothingCall.xls to simulate the return on an asset-or-nothing call option.

A European asset-or-nothing digital call option pays one share of the underlying asset if and only if the price of the underlying exceeds the strike price on the exercise date. That is, the payoff is

$$S_T \ \text{if} \ S_T > K,$$
$$0 \ \text{otherwise.}$$

Figure 12.8 shows a model to value an asset-or-nothing call option with strike price $105 expiring in one year. It can also be used to model a cash-or-nothing option having payoff $1 by inserting into cell **D11** the formula =IF(B12>K,1,0).

Barrier Options

On September 28, 1998, the *New York Times* reported that Sprint chairman William T. Esrey stood to earn call options having a strike price of $47.94 for one

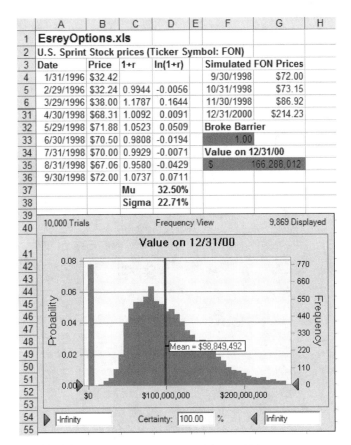

FIGURE 12.9 Spreadsheet segment from model in EsreyOptions.xls to simulate the return on an up-and-in barrier call option.

million shares of Sprint stock if the stock price reached a barrier price of $95.875 sometime in the future. On September 30, 1998, Sprint's stock price closed at $72.00. The file EsreyOptions.xls in Figure 12.9 contains a model to estimate the value of Mr. Esrey's up-and-in barrier call options on December 31, 2000, based on the historical drift and volatility of Sprint stock estimated from monthly closing prices during the period January 31, 1996, through September 30, 1998, which was a period of very dynamic growth in the telecommunications industry.

Asian Options

Figure 12.10 shows a model used to determine the price of an Asian average-price call option for a stock with $S_0 = \$40$, $K = \$40$, $\sigma = 30\%$, $r = 8\%$, and $T = 0.25$.

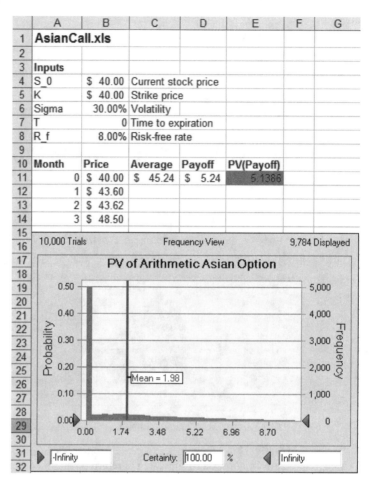

FIGURE 12.10 Spreadsheet segment from model in AsianCall.xls to simulate the return on an average-price call option.

The value of $1.98 (with a standard error of $0.03) is consistent with McDonald (2006), who gets a price of $2.03 ($0.03).

Denote the price of the stock at time t as S_t. Then for this option, which pays off on the arithmetic average of the monthly prices, the option price is found by simulating the stock prices S_1, S_2, and S_3, then taking the mean over all iterations of the quantity

$$e^{-rT}\mathrm{E}\left(\max\left[(S_1 + S_2 + S_3)/3 - K, 0\right]\right).$$

Analytic solutions exist for pricing Asian options that pay off on the geometric average (see McDonald 2006). To price this as a geometric Asian option with Crystal

Ball, simulate stock prices S_1, S_2, and S_3, then take the mean over all iterations of the quantity

$$e^{-rT}E\left(\max\left[\sqrt[3]{S_1 S_2 S_3)} - K, 0\right]\right).$$

BULL SPREAD

Options traders often hold more than one option on the same stock. This is called an option strategy. Figure 12.11 shows a model for a bull-spread strategy in which a trader buys a call with strike price $K = \$130$ and writes a call with strike price $K = \$140$. Both calls expire on December 15, 2006.

Figure 12.11 shows a mean return of -5.96 percent on the bull spread if the assumed μ and σ parameters of the stock are 5 percent and 11 percent, respectively.

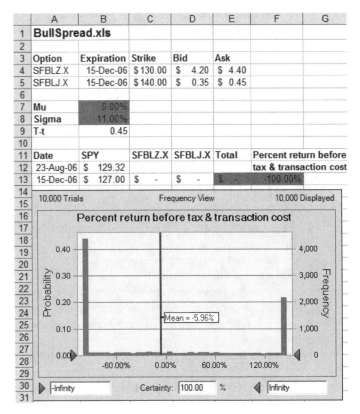

FIGURE 12.11 Spreadsheet segment from model in BullSpread.xls to simulate the return on a bull spread.

	A	B	C	D	E	F	G	H
	Trend Chart	Mu (0.00%)	Mu (2.00%)	Mu (4.00%)	Mu (6.00%)	Mu (8.00%)	Mu (10.00%)	
	Overlay Chart							
1	Forecast Charts							
2	Sigma (6.00%)	-58%	-44%	-29%	-11%	7%	27%	1
3	Sigma (8.00%)	-45%	-33%	-20%	-6%	9%	25%	2
4	Sigma (10.00%)	-35%	-25%	-14%	-2%	10%	23%	3
5	Sigma (12.00%)	-28%	-19%	-9%	1%	11%	22%	4
6	Sigma (14.00%)	-23%	-15%	-6%	2%	11%	21%	5
7	Sigma (16.00%)	-19%	-12%	-4%	4%	12%	20%	6
8	Sigma (18.00%)	-16%	-9%	-3%	5%	12%	19%	7
9	Sigma (20.00%)	-14%	-8%	-1%	5%	11%	18%	8
10	Sigma (22.00%)	-12%	-6%	0%	5%	11%	17%	9
11	Sigma (24.00%)	-10%	-5%	0%	6%	11%	16%	10
12	Sigma (26.00%)	-9%	-4%	1%	6%	11%	16%	11
13		1	2	3	4	5	6	

FIGURE 12.12 Decision table from model in BullSpread.xls to simulate the return on a bull spread for several values of μ and σ.

Because different traders have different expectations for μ and σ, Figure 12.12 shows estimates of the bull-spread strategy's mean return as a function of different levels of μ and σ. In general, the mean return increases as a function of both parameters.

PRINCIPAL-PROTECTED INSTRUMENT

While not strictly an option, the analysis of principal-protected instruments (PPIs) is included here to demonstrate how to model another derivative security recently introduced in the marketplace.

PPIs are sold to risk-averse investors who wish to contractually guarantee that they will not lose any of their initial investment, but also wish to participate to some extent in upward movements of the price of a financial investment. They are hybrid securities that combine a fixed income instrument with a series of derivative components. PPIs have been engineered for assets such as equities, currencies, interest rates or commodities.

Figure 12.13 shows a model for valuing a PPI with the following characteristics: For every quarter of its five-year life, the PPI quarterly return tracks the quarterly return on the underlying asset XYZ. However, if the quarterly rate of return on XYZ exceeds 15 percent for any quarter, the PPI return for that quarter is capped at 15%. At the end of five years, the PPI will deliver a final amount determined by the 20 quarterly returns specified in the contract.

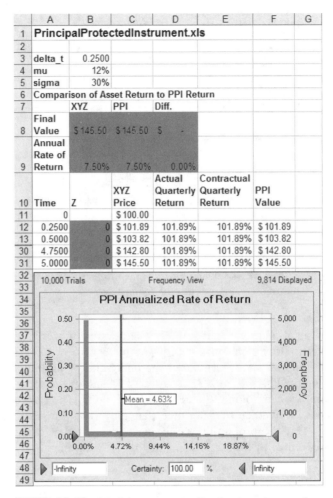

FIGURE 12.13 Model to compute distribution of rates of return on a principal-protected instrument.

Denote the initial investment as I, the final value of XYZ as F_{xyz}, the final value of PPI as F_{ppi}, and the quarterly rate of return on XYZ stock as R_i for $i = 1, 2, \ldots, 20$. The final value of XYZ is

$$F_{xyz} = I \prod_{i=1}^{20} (1 + R_i),$$

while the final value of PPI is

$$F_{ppi} = \max \left[I \prod_{i=1}^{20} \min(1 + R_i, 1.15), I \right].$$

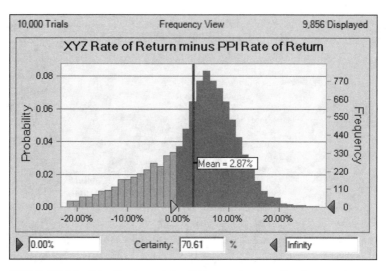

FIGURE 12.14 Distribution of the difference in annualized rates of return on a PPI and the underlying asset.

The simulation model in Figure 12.13 generates quarterly values for asset XYZ using geometric Brownian motion with parameters $\mu = 12$ percent and $\sigma = 30$ percent. The "Report" worksheet shows the final values and annualized rates of return on holding the PPI and on XYZ. Figure 12.14 shows the difference in annualized rates of return when holding the PPI and XYZ alone. The risk-averse investor pays 2.87 percent on average to guarantee that the principal is not lost. Figure 12.14 also shows that the probability is about 70 percent that the investor would realize a greater return by holding XYZ alone than by holding the PPI.

CHAPTER 13

Real Options

This chapter describes a recent topic in finance called real options analysis (ROA) and shows how Crystal Ball and OptQuest can help you determine the value of real options. As we have seen, a financial option is the right, but not the obligation, to buy (or sell) an asset at some point within a predetermined period of time for a predetermined price. ROA is used as an alternate methodology for evaluating capital investment decisions involving a high degree of managerial flexibility, such as research and development projects or new product decisions. Unlike the simple net present value (NPV) method used in traditional finance theory, ROA treats an investment opportunity as either a single option or a compound option (a sequence of options). The traditional NPV method does not value managerial flexibility correctly when it relies on the false assumption that the investment is either irreversible or that it cannot be delayed.

In this chapter, we will see the similarity between financial and real options, then discuss applications of ROA and some analytical methods that have been used with real options. The real option valuation (ROV) tool described in the final sections combines the use of Crystal Ball and OptQuest to determine the value of opportunities that contain real options.

FINANCIAL OPTIONS AND REAL OPTIONS

With a *financial option* the initial investment in an option contract buys the potential opportunity to enjoy positive cash flow when future spot price changes of the underlying financial asset favor doing so, but does not carry the obligation to realize negative cash flow if unfavorable conditions prevail. For example, the holder of a call option is not obligated to purchase the underlying at the strike price if its spot price is below the strike price on the expiration date, and the holder of a put option is not obligated to sell the underlying at the strike price if the spot price is above the strike price on the expiration date. This flexibility to limit one's losses adds value to a financial option contract when there is uncertainty about the future spot price of the underlying.

Contrast the flexibility of an option contract to a *futures contract*, which specifies a price and a future date for a transaction that both parties are obligated to complete.

For example, if you are to be paid a fixed amount of Indian rupees (INR) one year from now, but you want to lock in the amount of American dollars (USD) you will gain at that time, you can enter into a futures contract (at some cost to you) that specifies an exchange rate for the amount of USD to receive in exchange for INR one year from now. Once you are locked into the exchange rate, you are shielded from fluctuations in the USD/INR spot exchange rate. If the spot exchange rate is lower next year than the rate you locked in, you will end up with more USD than you would otherwise receive at the spot exchange rate, but if the spot exchange rate is higher next year, you will end up with fewer USD than you would otherwise. With a futures contract, you bear the risk of losing more than just the cost of the contract if the USD/INR exchange rate rises—you also lose the opportunity to benefit from the higher exchange rate.

With a rupee *put option* contract, you can simply choose not to complete the transaction if the spot exchange rate exceeds the strike price. You will lose the cost of entering into the option contract, but you will benefit from selling your INR at the higher spot exchange rate. With all else equal, an option contract is worth more than a futures contract because an option contract offers more flexibility than a futures contract. Chapter 12 describes how to use Crystal Ball to determine option values. For more information about options and futures contracts, see McDonald (2006) or Wilmott (2000).

With a *real option*—an option on a real asset—the initial investment related to the asset buys the potential opportunity to continue, expand, or abandon the use of the asset when it is favorable to do so, but does not carry the obligation to realize some losses when unfavorable conditions prevail. Because efforts such as testing potential oil-drilling sites can be viewed as learning options, financial models similar to those used for determining financial option values can be used to determine the value of the real options embedded in the opportunity to test for oil at a particular site.

To learn more about the theory underlying real options, see the texts by Dixit and Pindyck (1994), or Trigeorgis (1996), which summarize much of the early work done in applying financial options valuation methodology to real options problems. The next section describes how real options have been applied in various contexts.

APPLICATIONS OF ROA

For a good, nontechnical introduction to real options analysis, see Copeland and Keenan (1998a, 1998b), who categorize real options into the three broad categories described below.

1. **Investment/growth options.** These include (1) *scale-up* options, where early entrants can scale up later through sequential investments as their market grows; (2) *switch-up* options, where speedy commitments to the first generation of a product or technology give managers a preferential position to switch to the next generation of the product or technology; and (3) *scope-up* options, where

investments in proprietary assets in one industry enables managers to enter another industry with a competitive cost advantage.

For example, a venture capitalist (VC) who invests in stages uses ROA of the growth option to value a start-up company. By structuring the contract properly, the VC retains exclusive rights to a portion of the profits from the start-up venture. However, if the VC decides later not to invest further, any loss is limited to the amount already invested. The VC is not obligated to pay the start-up's debts if the venture fails.

2. **Deferral/learning options.** Also called *study/start* options, these are opportunities to delay investment until more information or skill is acquired. For example, an oil company uses ROA to evaluate exploration investment strategies, in which drilling sites undergo various types of testing before the decision whether or not to drill is made. A pharmaceutical firm uses ROA to evaluate drug development projects, in which investments are made in several phases of experimentation with the drug compound before seeking regulatory approval and going to market.

3. **Disinvestment/shrinkage options.** These include (1) *scale-down* options, where new information that changes the expected payoffs can cause managers to shrink or shut down a project before completion; (2) *switch-down* options, where managers have the ability to switch to more cost-effective and flexible assets as new information is obtained; and (3) *scope-down* options, where the scope of operations is decreased or even ceased when managers see no further potential in a business opportunity.

   For example, a manufacturing firm uses ROA to evaluate three types of power generators that use (1) natural gas, (2) fuel oil, or (3) both for fuel. The higher cost of a dual-fuel generator may be offset by future savings obtained when the cost per energy unit of natural gas is lower than fuel oil, or vice versa. ROA can determine a value for the flexibility to use the cheaper fuel when the dual-fuel generator is installed.

Myers (1984) is often credited with being the first to publish in the academic literature the notion that Black and Scholes (1973) results could be applied to strategic issues concerning real assets rather than just financial assets. In the practitioner literature, Kester (1984) suggested that the discounted cash flow valuation methods in use at that time ignored the value of important flexibilities inherent in many investment projects and that methods of valuing this flexibility were needed. ROA is most effective when competing projects have similar values obtained with the simple NPV method.

One difficulty in applying ROA is that real asset investments are usually affected by more than one source of uncertainty, whereas all of the uncertainty driving financial options is characterized by the volatility in spot prices of the underlying financial asset. As we saw in Chapter 12, the historical volatility of a financial asset is readily obtained from publicly available market prices. Options with values driven by multiple sources of uncertainty are called *rainbow options*. Combinations of rainbow and learning options often exist in practice.

Thinking about investment projects in option terms encourages managers to decompose an investment into its component options and risks, which can lead to valuable insights about sources of uncertainty and how uncertainty will resolve over time (Brabazon 1999). Options thinking also encourages managers to consider how to enhance the value of their investments by building in more flexibility where possible. Bowman and Moskowitz (2001) suggest that ROA is useful because it challenges the type of investment proposals that are submitted and encourages managers to think proactively and creatively.

ROA has the potential to allow companies to examine programs of capital expenditures as multi-year investments, rather than as individual projects (Copeland 2001). Such programs of investments are strategic and highly dependent on market outcomes, which is just the decision climate under which Miller and Park (2002) find ROA to be most useful. However, ROA and NPV are complementary techniques, with NPV being suitable for basic replacement decisions.

Early work on real options valuation suggests that if the analogous real options parameters can be estimated, any method used to value financial options can potentially be used to value real options. Often though, many of the assumptions must be relaxed to make the connection. Amram and Kulatilaka (1999), Copeland and Antikarov (2001), and Mun (2002) provide guidelines for analyzing real options with financial-option pricing techniques. The remainder of this section describes two early techniques for ROA: the Black-Scholes method, and lattice methods.

Black-Scholes Method

The Black-Scholes method relies on the assumption that project values follow a geometric Brownian motion (GBM) stochastic process. While useful in the abstract, GBM is difficult to use in practical real options problems involving many sources of uncertainty and interrelated decisions. In order to use this method, one must somehow encapsulate the random effects of all the important real-world complications into one summary measure—the volatility parameter of the GBM process. Relatively few managers have the background or inclination to estimate the values of the volatility parameters that are necessary for using Black-Scholes formulas to value complicated real options in industry. However, the Black-Scholes model is useful for gaining insights into real options valuation and how projects can be managed to increase their real option value.

Lattice Methods

Lattice methods also rely on the assumption that project values follow a GBM stochastic process. While the equations used in lattice methods are perhaps easier to grasp than those underlying Black-Scholes, lattice methods are simply a way to approximate a GBM process and thus suffer from the same limitations as

Black-Scholes—namely, that so many important real-world complications must be encapsulated in the volatility parameter. Hence, many managers are uncomfortable with the estimation of the volatility parameters necessary to use lattice methods for ROA in industry. However, those trained in finance theory may well be comfortable using this technique. Mun (2002) has developed software for evaluating real options with lattice models that Decisioneering markets as the Real Options Analysis Toolkit.

BLACK-SCHOLES REAL OPTIONS INSIGHTS

The Black-Scholes model provides insights into the factors affecting the value of real options and how managers can manage their opportunities to increase this value. To see this, consider the Black-Scholes formula for a European call option on a stock that pays dividends at the continuous rate δ:

$$C(S, K, \sigma, T, \delta, r) = Se^{-\delta T}N(d_1) - Ke^{-rT}N(d_2), \qquad (13.1)$$

where

$$d_1 = \frac{\ln(S/K) + (r - \delta + \frac{1}{2}\sigma^2)T}{\sigma\sqrt{T}} \qquad (13.2)$$

$$d_2 = d_1 - \sigma\sqrt{T} \qquad (13.3)$$

and $N(x)$ is the cumulative normal distribution function, which is the probability that a number drawn randomly from the standard normal distribution (i.e., a normal distribution with mean 0 and variance 1) will be less than x.

The Black-Scholes formula for a European put option on a dividend-paying stock is

$$P(S, K, \sigma, T, \delta, r) = Ke^{-rT}N(-d_2) - Se^{-\delta T}N(-d_1), \qquad (13.4)$$

where $N(x)$ is the cumulative normal distribution function, and d_1 and d_2 are given by equations (13.2) and (13.3).

According to the Black-Scholes option-pricing models (13.1) and (13.4), options derive their value from six main factors. These factors are most easily expressed in terms of financial options, but the analogy to real options provides insights into the factors associated with strategic investment decisions. The factors are:

Stock price, S. The value of the underlying stock on which an option is purchased. This is the stock market's estimate of the present value of all future cash flows arising from ownership of the stock. Its analog in a real options analysis is the present value of cash flows expected from the investment opportunity under consideration. Some examples of the sources of uncertainty that affect the present value of cash flows from investment are: market demand for products and services, labor supply and cost, or materials supply and cost.

Exercise price, *K*.   The predetermined price at which the option can be exercised. Its real options analog is the present value of all the investment costs that are expected over the lifetime of the investment opportunity. The availability, timing, and price of real assets to be purchased all affect the uncertainty in this parameter.

Volatility, *σ*.   A measure of the unpredictability of stock price movements, usually expressed as the standard deviation of the growth rate of the value of future cash flows associated with the stock. Its real options analog is a measure of uncertainty of the cash flows associated with the investment opportunity. This uncertainty arises from volatility in market demand, labor supply and cost, and materials supply and cost. The correlations between these factors also affects the volatility parameter.

Time to expiration, *T*.   The period during which the option can be exercised. Its real options analog is the period during which the investment opportunity is available. This period depends on the product life cycle, the firm's competitive advantages, and the contractual arrangements made by the firm.

Dividends.   Sums paid regularly to stockholders at a constant continuous rate, *δ*. Dividends reduce a financial option payoff when the option is exercised after a dividend payout, which reduces the stock value. Their real options analogs are the expenses that drain away potential project value over the duration of the option. The cost of waiting could be high if competitors enter the market. Thus, the cost of waiting to invest might be reduced by locking-in key customers, or lobbying for regulatory constraints when possible to discourage competitors from exercising their options to enter the market.

Interest rate, *r*.   The yield on financial securities with the same maturity as the duration of the option. The risk-free rate of interest is used in the Black-Scholes model, but a different rate might be appropriate for an alternate option valuation method.

According to the Black-Scholes model, increases in stock price, volatility, time to expiration, and interest rates increase financial option values, while increases in exercise prices and dividends reduce financial option values. These qualitative relationships are generally true for real options as well. See Leslie and Michaels (1997), who describe how to apply options thinking to strategic situations by using the qualitative relationships as guidelines for managerial action.

However, real options have additional features that distinguish them from the type of financial options for which the Black-Scholes model was derived. The Black-Scholes model is an exact solution to a pricing problem that was simplified to make it solvable. The main simplification is called the European feature of the option, which means that the option is assumed to be exercisable at only a single time point in the future. Most financial and real options are said to have American features, which means that those options can be exercised at any point in time between their purchase and expiration. The valuation of American-style options is more difficult than the valuation of European options.

In practice, the difficulty introduced by the American exercise feature can be overcome partially by assuming a Bermudan feature, which means that an option can exercise at one of several discrete points between purchase and expiration (rather than continuously as with an American option). The Bermudan assumption is consistent with ROA if the decisions to make investments will be implemented only at discrete times (e.g., quarterly). The real options valuation (ROV) tool described in the next section uses Crystal Ball and OptQuest to value real options in a manner similar to the valuation of financial Bermudan options in Chapter 12. The ROV tool analyzes real-options investment opportunities by modeling cash flows occurring over a period of time, punctuated by key decisions to be made by management about whether to make additional investments, continue with no further investment, or abandon the investment opportunity.

ROV TOOL

The ROV tool is simply the use of Crystal Ball to add stochastic assumptions, decision variables, and forecasts to a deterministic spreadsheet, then finding the optimal values of the decision variables using OptQuest. Thus, describing how to use the ROV tool serves as a summary of financial modeling and risk analysis with Crystal Ball. See Charnes, et al. (2004) for a description of how the ROV tool was applied in the telecommunications industry.

The tool is used by following the eight steps in Figure 13.1, which diagrams the ROV modeling process. This process expands on the simulation modeling process detailed in Chapter 3. Each step is explained next.

ROV Modeling Process

Step 1: Identify Options   The first task in any ROV modeling effort is to identify the options in the problem in such a way that they can be modeled with decision variables in a spreadsheet. If this cannot be done, Crystal Ball cannot be used to help you make a decision. However, because of the versatility and flexibility of spreadsheets, many option problems can be modeled with Crystal Ball. Next, be sure you can quantify the uncertainty in the model's variables and any statistical relationships between them. Again, if this cannot be done, then building a spreadsheet ROV model is not possible. While these two tasks might seem obvious, making sure at the outset that a Crystal Ball model can be used to help solve the problem is critical to the success of any ROV project.

Step 2: Build or Revise Model   Be sure to design your model so that it will help solve the problem you've identified. Again, this sounds obvious, but some analysts get so

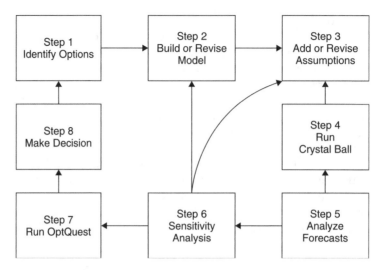

FIGURE 13.1   ROV modeling process diagram.

caught up in the details of modeling that they lose sight of the big picture. Do not let this happen to you.

Wherever possible, model the uncertain variables in the smallest component for which you have historical data collected. For example, suppose monthly sales revenue is a variable in your model. If you have data collected on both units sold and monthly sales revenue, in general it will be better to make units sold into a Crystal Ball assumption rather than monthly sales revenue. Revenue can be calculated in the spreadsheet as units sold times price, and by breaking revenue into its components, you have more flexibility by modeling the uncertainty in units sold rather than monthly sales revenue if you decide later to investigate a change in price, for example.

Another important point to keep in mind is to have each assumption included only once in your model, and have any calculations that depend on the assumption's value make reference to that cell. Novices sometimes put the same probability distribution in two or more cells in a model, thinking that as long as the same distribution—say a uniform(4000,6000), for example—is used in two places it will give the same value in both places during a simulation trial. However, including a distribution in two places means that Crystal Ball will generate independent values in each cell—for example, two different numbers drawn from the uniform(4000,6000) distribution—and the model will not represent the real-life situation the novice is trying to model.

You may also reach Step 2 in the process as the result of previous analyses. In particular, sensitivity analysis (Step 6) sometimes leads to changes in the model. This is both a natural and good thing to happen, because it usually means that the insights you have gained are helping you to improve the model you are building.

Some analysts build an initial model to work with for a while as a prototype, then throw it out and begin anew once they have a better understanding of the situation. Sometimes it is better to start over with a redesigned model than to continue working with an inefficient design that you can't bear to give up because you've been working on it for so long. An alternate approach advocated by some authors is to map out your spreadsheet on paper before you even open Excel. See Powell and Baker (2007) for their take on this approach.

Step 3: Add or Revise Assumptions   For novices, choosing a distribution and its parameter values is usually the hardest part of simulation modeling. However, choosing which variables to make into assumptions and which to leave as deterministic can also be a challenge. Choosing the assumption variables is a matter of using your best judgment, intuition, and any data that you have available to identify those you think are most important. After you have run the simulation you can use sensitivity analysis to measure the effect of each assumption on the forecast(s), and change your initial choices later in the modeling process when appropriate.

The Crystal Ball tornado chart is used to measure the effect of changes in any variable (including deterministic variables) on a selected forecast. If you are having a difficult time deciding which input variables should be probabilistic, and which should be deterministic, try using the tornado chart, which helps to identify the most important variables in terms of impact on the forecasts.

If you have no idea of which distribution family to select from the distribution gallery, consider using the triangular or uniform distributions. By default, the parameters of these distributions will be set so that the mean of your assumption is equal to the simple value in the cell when you click the Define Assumption icon. The minimum and maximum values will be set by default to 10 percent below the mean, and 10 percent above the mean, respectively. If no historical data are available, you can ask a subject matter expert (e.g., an engineer, cost analyst, or project manager) to help you choose the parameters of a triangular or uniform distribution. See the descriptions of these distributions in Appendix A for more information about setting the parameters.

If you are fortunate enough to have historical data available for a variable used in your model, you can have Crystal Ball analyze the historical data to suggest a distribution as described in Chapter 4. For some models, the nature of the process or underlying physics of the situation will suggest a distribution. See Appendix A for specific examples of when each distribution might be used.

Step 4: Run Crystal Ball   Click on Run > Single Step in the top menu of Crystal Ball to run just one iteration of the simulation. Look at the values of the assumptions and forecasts to make sure they are realistic for your model. If they are not realistic values (meaning that they represent a combination of values that could not occur in real life), then you have an error somewhere in your spreadsheet model.

Verify that your assumptions have the correct parameters, and that the Excel formulas are correct. Make any necessary changes, then use Single Step again to check your changes. Repeat this process until you are comfortable with the results you get on each step. Once you have verified that your model is correct, make sure Crystal Ball's sensitivity analysis feature is turned on (click on Run > Run Preferences, then click the Options button, put a check in the box next to Calculate Sensitivity, and click OK). Run the simulation for an initial number of trials. Try using 10,000 trials if you are using Extreme Speed (ES) mode. If you are unable to use ES mode because you have a large, complicated model, try using at least 2,000 trials in Normal Speed mode.

Step 5: Analyze Forecasts   Check the forecasts to see if they contain outcome values that could occur in real life. Because the combined effects of the probabilistic assumptions can be very large, don't be surprised if the range of outcomes is very wide. Click on Analyze > Extract Data... to extract the values generated by Crystal Ball for the assumptions and the corresponding forecast values. Investigating the extreme points in a forecast and the assumption values that led to them can yield useful insights.

Step 6: Sensitivity Analysis   Click on Run > Open Sensitivity Chart in the top menu to bring up the Sensitivity Chart. The model's assumptions are listed on this chart from top to bottom in descending order of the magnitude of their effects on the selected forecast. The magnitude of the effects is measured by the Spearman rank correlation statistic (see Chapter 4). Use the sensitivity analysis information to revise the assumptions (Step 3) or the model itself (Step 2). Begin with the top assumption listed on the chart, and work your way down. For each assumption, make sure you are satisfied that the distribution and its parameters represent the situation adequately. Draw upon subject matter experts for guidance.

Step 7: Run OptQuest   You might have to go through Steps 2–6 many times before you are satisfied with the model. However, this will help you understand the problem much better. Many analysts claim that at this point of the process they feel like they know enough about the problem to make a decision just because they have studied it so intensely to get this far. However, when you are comfortable with the results, and have obtained buy-in from the others involved in the decision-making process, you are ready to run OptQuest. Refer to Chapter 5 for the details of running OptQuest.

Step 8: Make Decision   If the model has helped to completely solve the problem you faced, congratulations! However, oftentimes the process of modeling leads to the identification of other problems to solve. If so, begin the process again to solve the new problem by returning to Step 1.

Value Added by Using ROV Tool

A major advantage of using Crystal Ball and OptQuest as the ROV tool is that it can be applied to a large number of existing spreadsheet models. These existing models serve as "calculation engines" that are used by Crystal Ball to transform the stochastic inputs into random outputs for specified values of the decision variables. An analyst comfortable with the ROV tool can use it with existing spreadsheet models without necessarily having to understand all of the minute details of the calculation engine. This makes the tool highly reusable, as it only requires the analyst to be able to link the top-level worksheet to the calculation engine in existing spreadsheets.

In Figure 13.2, the calculation engine is represented by the existing spreadsheets depicted on the right side. The calculations that go into the determination of NPV are usually very complex and can involve links to many of the worksheets composing the Excel model. Some high-level knowledge of the business case represented by the calculation engine is required to make the link to the top-level worksheet. However, the ROV tool can be used with spreadsheets built by others if you understand how the decision variables and stochastic assumptions are involved in the calculation of NPV. The function $g(d_1, d_2, \ldots, d_k; a_1, a_2, \ldots, a_n)$ in Figure 13.2 represents the result of all the calculations taking place in the business case that lead to a value of NPV for the decision variable values $d_1, d_2, \ldots, d_k$ and the assumption values $a_1, a_2, \ldots, a_n$. If you understand the calculation of the function $g(\cdot)$ well enough to know how $d_1, d_2, \ldots, d_k$ and $a_1, a_2, \ldots, a_n$ affect the calculation of NPV, then you can use the ROV tool independently of the analysis leading to the construction of the calculation engine. This feature allows the tool to be used with any existing or future financial worksheets.

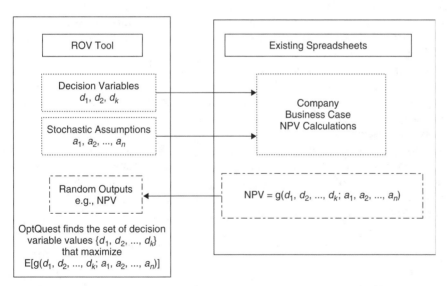

FIGURE 13.2 Depiction of links between the ROV tool and existing NPV calculations in your company's business cases. The function $g(d_1, d_2, \ldots, d_k; a_1, a_2, \ldots, a_n)$ represents the result of all the calculations taking place in the business case that lead to a value of NPV for the decision variable values $d_1, d_2, \ldots, d_k$ and the assumption values $a_1, a_2, \ldots, a_n$.

Because the ROV tool is independent of the calculation engine, it is scalable to virtually any size desired. The only limits on the size of the model are those imposed by Microsoft Excel. Crystal Ball and OptQuest can handle a number of decision variables that is unlimited for most practical purposes. Note that the current version (available in 2006) of Extreme Speed mode takes longer to initialize when the business case is composed of many spreadsheets. For some complicated models, this initialization can take so long that you may be better off running Crystal Ball in Normal Speed mode.

For long-term projects, a company comprising many divisions may find that sharing the ROV tool across divisions brings benefits in terms of better communication and understanding among division managers. In particular, the benefits of using the ROV tool to monitor progress in a cross-divisional project include:

- The spreadsheets become living documents that are updated continually to reflect current assumptions and the prevailing business environment. If many divisions understand and share the same model, discussions between divisions can be far more productive than they otherwise might be. By discussing the assumptions underlying a common model, disagreements can focus on specific assumptions in the model. This is more productive than discussions that occur sometimes in which the discussants argue about different underlying assumptions without realizing that they are doing so.
- The tool documents all assumptions to ensure consistency between decisions. As some projects take years to develop, changing conditions in the business climate can cause the company-wide assumptions about the conditions affecting future cash flow to change considerably over time. The ROV tool helps to document the changes in these assumptions so that everyone stays "on the same page."
- The modeling process itself leads to greater understanding. By decomposing the project into its components and the relationships between them, managers see the problem from many different aspects, which helps to gain understanding. Yet when the model is run in Steps 4 or 7 in Figure 13.2, the big picture will also be easily seen.
- The tool enables risk analysis of outcomes. As discussed in Chapter 7, by generating distributions of present value rather than a point estimate, managers gain a better idea of the riskiness of the projects they manage. Further, the distributions allow for calculation of VaR or CVaR, as described in Chapter 10, or other measures of risk as desired in specific situations.
- Crystal Ball enables sensitivity analysis of inputs. Sensitivity analysis can be accomplished in several ways, including the use of the sensitivity chart to see how each stochastic assumption affects the forecast(s), as well as an analysis of how the changes in the assumed parameters of the model will affect the results. This helps the managers to understand the problem better.
- The ROV tool finds optimal solutions for specified assumptions. As with any mathematical model, its usefulness must be judged in the context of its specific application. OptQuest may find the optimal solution(s) for the assumptions it is

fed, but there may well be non-quantifiable factors (political issues, for example) that also affect the decision. These non-quantifiable factors may cause the values of the decision variables chosen for implementation to be different from the values indicated by OptQuest, but by using it to compare expected NPV from both sets of decision variable values, the ROV tool will be able to provide an idea of the cost of the nonquantifiable factors.

Use of ROV Tool in New Product Development

As an example of how the ROV tool can be used at various phases throughout the product development process, consider the process depicted in Figure 13.3, which is intended to represent a generic new product development project. Assume that there are two competing technologies available initially that can be used in the product.

During Phase 1 the two technologies under consideration are evaluated along with two market segments and three sources of costs that have some uncertainty. The widths of the boxes representing the technologies and markets in the tornado graph at Phase 1 are wider than the boxes for costs because the uncertainty surrounding technology and markets is greater at this earliest phase. The ROV model helps to quantify the uncertainties and measure their impact on expected net present value. At Decision 1, decisions about which technologies to employ are made, and some of the uncertainty is resolved as decision makers learn more about the project in part through building and revising the ROV model.

During Phase 2, the reduced uncertainty regarding the technology is depicted by the "Tech" bars having smaller widths and thus moving down in the tornado graph. At this phase, most of the uncertainty is in regard to markets and operating costs. Decisions regarding the design of the product are made at Decision 2. Matching product design to market opportunity is critical at this stage.

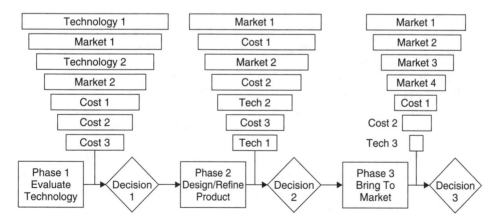

FIGURE 13.3 Managing risk and return throughout the product development process.

Because the technology has already been been chosen at Phase 3, the greatest uncertainties surround the markets for the product during this phase. Some uncertainty remains in regard to costs and a third competing technology that has emerged since Phase 1, but in this example, the ROV model is most useful for evaluating the options available for marketing the product. At Decision 3, the marketing decisions are made.

By linking the ROV model to stochastic demand, and taking into account the uncertainty surrounding technology and operating costs, the decision makers gain a better understanding of the impacts of these variables on their decisions. The ROV tool provides confidence bounds on its estimates, enables sensitivity analysis of its inputs, and leads to sound business decisions based upon expected net present value or other summary measures of interest to management.

The ROV tool is an extension of the business-case Excel models that are already in use at most companies. Thus it can be used with existing financial models for strategic planning, comparing products offered by different vendors, or estimating return on capital invested. Further, by adapting models to changing business conditions or decisions that have been made, the ROV tool helps to facilitate corporate memory and fosters consistency in decision making over time. With endorsement and commitment from top management, its use adds value to existing decision-making processes, encourages the establishment and monitoring of milestones for evaluating options resulting from managerial flexibility, and provides an ongoing framework within which learning from past successful and unsuccessful projects can be used to improve future decisions. Cooper, Edgett, and Kleinschmidt (2002) encourage managers to build in more effective go/kill decision points, and instill a regular management review process to make these decisions. The ROV tool is of great help in this process.

SUMMARY

This chapter has provided guidelines for developing business case models using the ROV tool. The tasks required include selecting inputs as stochastic assumptions, building and revising the model, adding and revising assumptions, and selecting and defining decision variables. Sensitivity analysis can be useful in identifying the assumptions that are most important for making a correct decision. The model building process is ongoing. Once a functional ROV model has been developed, additional information can be incorporated into the model as it becomes available. This helps to facilitate corporate memory, and fosters consistency in decision making over time.

The ROV tool approach to the valuation of managerial flexibility is itself highly flexible in its ability to support managerial decisions in a wide variety of situations involving real options. The greatest benefits from using the ROV tool will come to managers when the tool is adopted for making decisions on a company-wide basis. Using the structured approach of the ROV tool for decision making helps to ensure consistency in decision making and to facilitate corporate memory and learning.

The ROV tool can be used for strategic planning, comparing products offered by different vendors, or supplement the use of existing financial models for estimating return on invested capital. With endorsement and commitment from top management, its use adds tremendous value to existing decision-making processes and provide an ongoing framework that can be used to improve future decisions.

Crystal Ball's Probability Distributions

T his appendix lists a short description of each distribution in the Crystal Ball gallery along with its probability distribution function or probability density function (PDF), cumulative distribution function (CDF) where available, mean, standard deviation, and typical uses. For more information about these distributions, see Evans, Hastings, and Peacock (1993), Johnson, Kemp, and Kotz (2005), Johnson, Kotz, and Balakrishnan (1994), Law and Kelton (2000), or Pitman (1993).

All of Crystal Ball's distributions can be truncated on either or both ends to adapt to the circumstances of your model. Truncation is accomplished by entering the desired values in the truncation fields. For example, in Figure A.1, the normally distributed total return on a stock with nominal mean return 10 percent and nominal

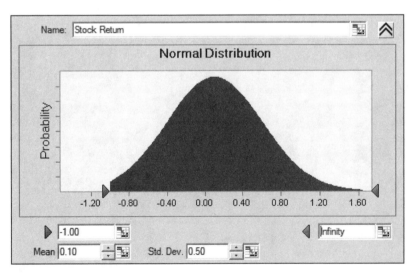

FIGURE A.1 Normal distribution of a stock return truncated at −100 percent to reflect the limited liability of stock ownership.

standard deviation 50 percent is truncated at −100 percent to reflect the limited liability of stock ownership.

When Crystal Ball truncates a distribution, the probability distribution is rescaled so that the total probability is 100% that a value will be generated within the range defined by the truncation points. For example, a random variable generated from the distribution shown in Figure A.1 has a 100 percent probability of falling between −100 percent and positive infinity. Therefore, truncation will affect the actual mean and standard deviation of a random variable. In general, it is not easy to determine the actual parameters of a truncated distribution analytically. However, you can obtain these values by selecting View → Statistics from the top menu in the assumption's dialog window. For example, even though the mean and standard deviation are specified in Figure A.1 to be 10 percent and 50 percent, the actual mean and standard deviation of the random values generated by this truncated distribution are 11.80 percent and 47.95 percent.

BERNOULLI

The Bernoulli distribution is the simplest discrete distribution. Among other uses, it represents the toss of a coin, if we define "1" to mean "heads" and "0" to mean "tails" (or vice versa). For a fair coin, the probability, p, of obtaining heads is 0.5 as depicted in Figure A.2. However, a Bernoulli trial can represent a biased (unfair) coin by specifying a different value for p. In financial modeling, it can be used to model the occurrence of a single event, such as the possible entry of a competitor into your market, for example.

The Bernoulli distribution is called the yes-no distribution in Crystal Ball. See the yes-no section of this appendix for more details. Bernoulli assumptions can be combined to generate values from other distributions. For example: the binomial distribution describes the number of successes in n Bernoulli trials; the geometric distribution describes the number of failures before the first success in a sequence of

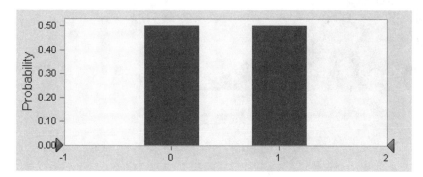

FIGURE A.2 Bernoulli distribution representing the number of heads obtained (0 or 1) with one flip of a fair coin.

Bernoulli trials; and the negative binomial describes the number of Bernoulli trials to get exactly β successes.

BETA

The standard beta distribution is defined for continuous values of x between 0 and 1, but Crystal Ball lets you select any minimum and maximum values, then it scales the distribution to fit on that range with a shape determined by the alpha and beta parameters you specify. The beta distribution can represent a random proportion or probability, the time to complete a task, or as a rough model when you have no historical data to use with Crystal Ball's distribution fitting routine. For much more information about the beta distribution, see Gupta and Nadarajah (2004).

> **Parameters:** Minimum, the minimum value, a; Maximum, the maximum value, b; Alpha, the first shape parameter, $\alpha > 0$; Beta, the second shape parameter, $\beta > 0$. See Figure A.3 for an example of the Beta PDF with $a = -10$, $b = 10$, $\alpha = 2$, and $\beta = 3$.
>
> **PDF:**

$$f(x) = \begin{cases} \dfrac{z^{\alpha-1}(1-z)^{\beta-1}}{B(\alpha,\beta)} & \text{if } 0 < x - a < b - a, \\ 0 & \text{otherwise} \end{cases}$$

where $z = \frac{x-a}{b-a}$, $B(\alpha, \beta)$ is the beta function, defined by $B(\alpha, \beta) = \int_0^1 t^{\alpha-1}(1-t)^{\beta-1} = \frac{\Gamma(\alpha)\Gamma(\beta)}{\Gamma(\alpha+\beta)}$ for any real numbers $\alpha > 0$, and $\beta > 0$, and $\Gamma(\cdot)$ is the

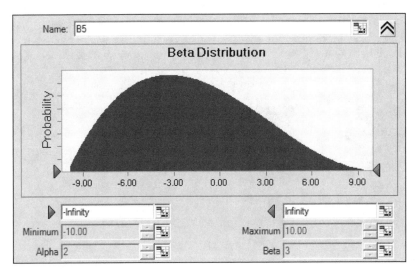

FIGURE A.3 Beta distribution with $a = -10$, $b = 10$, $\alpha = 2$, and $\beta = 3$.

Gamma function defined by $\Gamma(y) = \int_0^\infty t^{y-1}e^{-t}dt$ for any real number $y > 0$. Note that $\Gamma(k + 1) = k!$ for any nonnegative integer k, where $k! = k \cdot (k - 1) \cdots (2) \cdot (1)$ is read as "k-factorial."

CDF: No closed form.

Mean:

$$a + \frac{\alpha}{\alpha + \beta}(b - a)$$

Standard deviation:

$$(b - a)\sqrt{\frac{\alpha\beta}{(\alpha + \beta)^2(\alpha + \beta + 1)}}$$

Excel function: This distribution can be defined in two ways. Use

CB.Beta(Alpha,Beta,Scale,LowCutoff,HighCutoff,NameOf)

to define beta assumptions where $a = 0$, and $b = $ Scale. If the distribution has a minimum value not equal to zero, use

CB.Beta2(Min,Max,Alpha,Beta,HighCutoff,LowCutoff,NameOf).

where Min $= a$, Max $= b$, Alpha $= \alpha$, and Beta $= \beta$.

Notes: The beta distribution is U shaped if $\alpha > 1$ and $\beta > 1$, and is J shaped if $(\alpha - 1)(\beta - 1) < 0$. For all other permissible values of α and β it is unimodal.

BINOMIAL

The binomial distribution is a discrete distribution of the sum of n Bernoulli trials with constant probability of success, p, so it represents the number of successes in a specified number of attempts if the chance of success is the same for every attempt and the attempts are independent.

Parameters: Probability, the probability of success, p, such that $0 < p < 1$; Trials, the total number of trials, n, where n is an integer such that $1 \le n \le 1000$. See Figure A.4 for an example of the Binomial probability distribution function with $p = 0.5$, and $n = 50$.

PDF:

$$f(x) = \begin{cases} \dfrac{n!}{x!(n - x)!}p^x(1 - p)^{n-x} & \text{for } x = 0, 1, 2, \ldots, n \\ 0 & \text{otherwise} \end{cases}$$

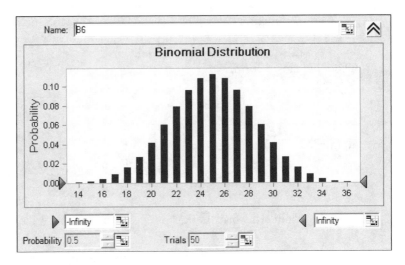

FIGURE A.4 Binomial(0.5,50) distribution.

CDF:

$$F(x) = \begin{cases} \sum_{y=0}^{x} \dfrac{n!}{y!(n-y)!} p^y (1-p)^{n-y} & \text{for } x = 0, 1, 2, \ldots, n \\ 0 & \text{otherwise} \end{cases}$$

Mean:

$$np$$

Standard deviation:

$$\sqrt{np(1-p)}$$

Excel function:

CB.Binomial(Prob,Trials,LowCutoff,HighCutoff,NameOf)

where **Prob** $= p$, and **Trials** $= n$.

Notes: The binomial distribution is equivalent to the distribution of a sum of Bernoulli random variables with the same probability of success, p. Thus, the sum of a binomial(p, n_1) variable and a binomial(p, n_2) variable has the binomial(p, $n_1 + n_2$) distribution. However, the sum of binomial distributions with different values of p does not follow a binomial distribution. The binomial distribution is symmetric when $p = 0.5$.

You cannot specify $n > 1000$ in Crystal Ball. To model such a situation, use as an approximation the Normal distribution with mean and standard deviation computed according to the expressions above, and truncated at 0 and $n + 0.99999$. Use Excel's =ROUNDOWN(number,num_digits) command to obtain a discrete value, if desired.

A beta binomial distribution can be simulated in Crystal Ball by defining the parameter p in a binomial distribution as a beta random variable. See file AppendixA.xls.

CUSTOM

The Custom distribution is defined by specifying a list of discrete values, continuous ranges of values, or discrete ranges of values, along with the associated probabilities. Once you choose the Custom from the Distribution Gallery, select **Parameters** from the top menu to specify the type of values you wish to use. You may enter the data values and probabilities directly in the dialog, or load them in from the worksheet by clicking the **Load Data...** button. You may also use the Excel function

$$CB.Custom(CellRange, NameOf)$$

where **CellRange** contains the data, and **NameOf** is the name of the assumption. See file AppendixA.xls for examples.

The custom distribution is very flexible, and is easily understood by inspection of the following examples:

■ See Figure A.5 for an example of the custom PDF with unweighted values. This is specified by a list of discrete values, each of which will occur with the same probability.

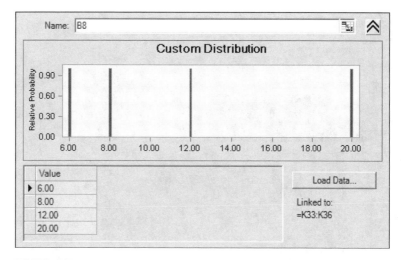

FIGURE A.5 Custom distribution specified with Unweighted Values parameters.

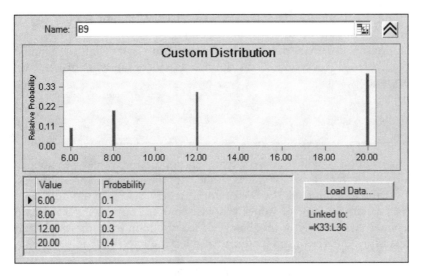

FIGURE A.6 Custom distribution specified with **Weighted Values** parameters.

- See Figure A.6 for an example of the custom PDF with weighted values. This is specified by a list of discrete values and their associated probabilities of occurrence.
- See Figure A.7 for an example of the custom PDF with continuous ranges. This is specified by ranges of values within which the continuous values have equal probability of occurrence by default.

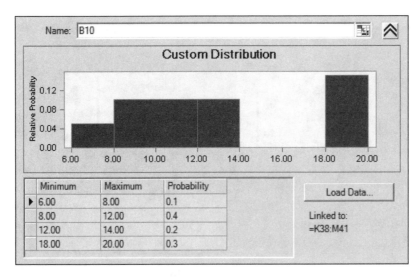

FIGURE A.7 Custom distribution specified with **Continuous Ranges** parameters.

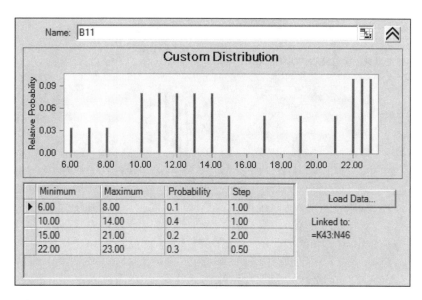

FIGURE A.8 Custom distribution specified with **Discrete Ranges** parameters.

- See Figure A.8 for an example of the custom PDF with discrete ranges values. This is specified by ranges of values within which the discrete values have equal probability of occurrence.
- See Figure A.9 for an example of the custom PDF with sloping ranges values. This is specified by ranges of discrete values within which the probabilities increase or decrease linearly.

Note that the vertical axes in Figures A.5 through A.9 are all labeled "Relative Probability." This means that the probabilities that you specify to define a custom distribution do not have to sum to 1.0; however, the specified probabilities are scaled by Crystal Ball such that the values used during the simulation do sum to 1.0.

DISCRETE UNIFORM

The discrete uniform distribution is used for modeling the random occurrence of one of several possible outcomes, each of which is equally likely. It may be used as a first model in the absence of data for modeling a quantity that varies among the integers $\{a, a + 1, a + 2, \ldots, b - 1, b\}$, but about which little else is known.

Parameters: Minimum, the minimum value, a, an integer where $-\infty < a < \infty$; and Maximum, the maximum value, b, and integer where $-\infty < b < \infty$, and $a < b$. See Figure A.10 for an example of this pdf.

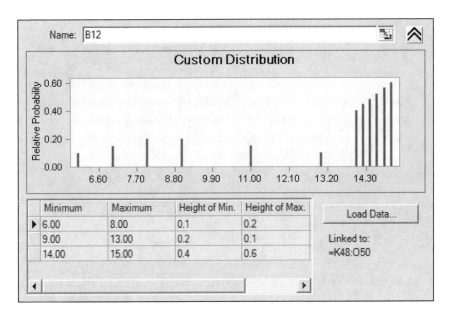

FIGURE A.9 Custom distribution specified with Sloping Ranges parameters.

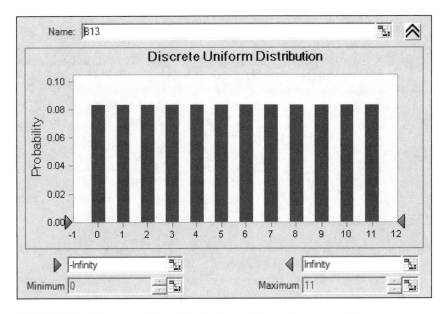

FIGURE A.10 Discrete uniform distribution with $a = 0$, and $b = 11$.

PDF:

$$f(x) = \begin{cases} \dfrac{1}{b-a+1} & \text{for } a < x < b, \\ 0 & \text{otherwise} \end{cases}$$

where x is an integer.

CDF:

$$F(x) = \begin{cases} 0 & \text{if } x < a, \\ \dfrac{\lfloor x \rfloor - a + 1}{b - a + 1} & \text{for } a < x < b, \\ 1 & \text{if } b < x \end{cases}$$

where $\lfloor x \rfloor$ denotes the greatest integer less than or equal to x.

Mean:

$$\frac{b-a}{2}$$

Standard deviation:

$$\sqrt{\frac{(b-a+1)^2 - 1}{12}}$$

Excel function:

CB.DiscreteUniform(Min,Max,LowCutoff,HighCutoff,

NameOf)

where Min $= a$, and Max $= b$.

Notes: The discrete uniform distribution for $a = 0$, and $b = 1$ is the same as the yes-no distribution with $p = 0.5$.

EXPONENTIAL

The exponential distribution is used to model continuous random variables that are nonnegative. It is used primarily to model the time between random events that occur at a constant average rate, such as the time between customer arrivals to service facilities.

Parameters: Rate, the constant average rate, $\lambda > 0$. See Figure A.11 for an example of the Exponential distribution with $\lambda = 10$.

PDF:

$$f(x) = \begin{cases} \lambda e^{-\lambda x} = & \text{for } x \geq 0 \\ 0 & \text{otherwise} \end{cases}$$

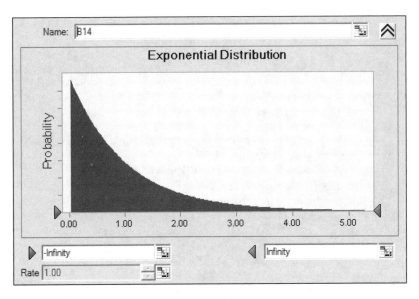

FIGURE A.11 Exponential distribution with $\lambda = 10$.

CDF:

$$F(x) = \begin{cases} 1 - e^{-\lambda x} & \text{for } x \geq 0 \\ 0 & \text{otherwise} \end{cases}$$

Mean:

$$1/\lambda$$

Standard deviation:

$$1/\lambda$$

Excel function:

CB.Exponential(Rate,LowCutoff,HighCutoff,NameOf)

where Rate $= \lambda$.

Notes: The exponential distribution with rate λ is a special case of the gamma distribution (with $L = 0$, $s = \lambda$, and $\beta = 1$), and the Weibull distribution (with $L = 0$, $s = \lambda$, and $\beta = 1$).

The exponential is the only continuous distribution with the *memoryless property*, which for the exponential random variable, X, is defined by

$$\Pr(X > s + t | X > s) = \Pr(X > t) \quad \text{for all } s, t > 0.$$

For customer arrivals occurring at a constant average rate λ, the memoryless property implies that no matter how long it has been since a customer has arrived, the time until the next arrival still follows the exponential distribution with rate λ.

Values from the Laplace, which is also known as the double exponential distribution, can be generated easily in Crystal Ball as follows. In one cell, define an assumption X as an exponential distribution with parameter λ, and in another cell define an assumption B as a yes-no distribution with $p = 0.5$. In a third cell, put in the formula $Y = (2B - 1)X$. Then Y follows the Laplace distribution with mean 0 and standard deviation $1/\sqrt{\lambda}$.

GAMMA

The gamma is a continuous distribution used often for modeling the time required to complete some task, such as repairing a machine or waiting on a customer in a service facility.

Parameters: Location, the location parameter, L; Scale, the scale parameter, $s > 0$; and Shape, the shape parameter, $\beta > 0$. See Figure A.12 for an example of the beta distribution with $L = 0$, $s = 1$, and $\beta = 2$.

PDF:

$$f(x) = \begin{cases} \dfrac{\left(\frac{x-L}{s}\right)^{\beta-1} e^{-\frac{x-L}{s}}}{\Gamma(\beta)s} & \text{for } x > L \\ 0 & \text{otherwise} \end{cases}$$

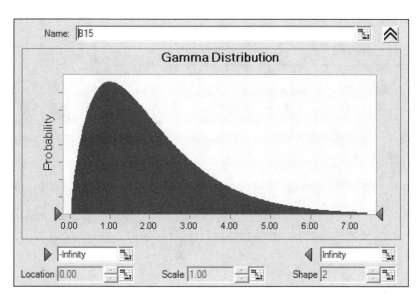

FIGURE A.12 Gamma distribution with $L = 0$, $s = 1$, and $\beta = 2$.

where $\Gamma(\cdot)$ is the gamma function defined in the beta distribution section of this appendix.

CDF: If β is not an integer, there is no closed form; for β an integer

$$F(x) = \begin{cases} 1 - e^{-\frac{x-L}{s}} \sum_{i=0}^{\beta-1} \frac{\left(\frac{x-L}{s}\right)^i}{i!} & \text{for } x > L \\ 0 & \text{otherwise} \end{cases}$$

Mean:

$$s\beta$$

Standard deviation:

$$s\sqrt{\beta}$$

Excel function:

CB.Gamma(Loc,Scale,Shape,LowCutoff,HighCutoff,NameOf)

Notes: The gamma distribution with $L = 0$, and $\beta = 1$ is the same as the Exponential distribution with rate s.

The gamma distribution with $L = 0$, and $\beta = k$, where k is a positive integer is called the k-Erlang distribution with rate s.

For a positive integer, k, the gamma distribution with $L = 0$, $\beta = k/2$, and $s = 2$ is the same as the chi-square distribution with k degrees of freedom.

GEOMETRIC

The geometric distribution is used to model the number of trials to get the first success in a sequence of IID Bernoulli trials with probability p of success on each trial. For example, it can be applied to model the number of calls a salesperson makes to obtain her first sale, the number of items in a batch of random size, or the number of items demanded by a customer.

Parameters: Probability, the probability of success, p. See Figure A.13 for an example of the geometric PDF with $p = 0.2$.

PDF:

$$f(x) = \begin{cases} p(1-p)^{x-1} & \text{for } x \in \{1, 2, 3, \ldots \\ 0 & \text{otherwise} \end{cases}$$

CDF:

$$F(x) = \begin{cases} 1 - (1-p)^{\lfloor x \rfloor} & \text{for } x \geq 1 \\ 0 & \text{otherwise} \end{cases}$$

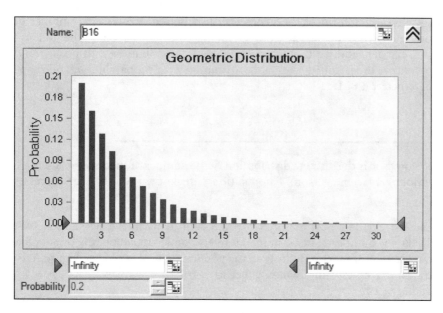

FIGURE A.13 Geometric distribution with $p = 0.2$.

Mean:

$$\frac{1}{p}$$

Standard deviation:

$$\frac{\sqrt{1-p}}{p}$$

Excel function:

CB.Geometric(Prob,LowCutoff,HighCutoff,NameOf)

where Prob $= p$.

Notes: The geometric distribution is a discrete analogue of the exponential distribution, and is the only discrete distribution with the *memoryless property*, which for the geometric random variable, Y, is defined by

$$\Pr(Y - k = m | Y \geq k) = \Pr(Y = m) \quad \text{for } k \geq 0 \text{ and } m = 0, 1, \ldots$$

For a gambler making the same bet on roulette that has probability p of winning, the memoryless property implies that no matter how many times the gambler has bet, the number of spins of the roulette wheel until the gambler wins still follows the geometric distribution.

An alternative form of the geometric distribution involves the number of Bernoulli trials up to, but not including, the first success. The random variable defined by a draw from a geometric distribution with probability, p, follows the negative binomial distribution with probability, p, and shape parameter, $\beta = 1$.

HYPERGEOMETRIC

The hypergeometric is the discrete distribution of the number of successes in a sample drawn without replacement from a population with known numbers of successes and failures.

Parameters: Success, the number of successful items in the population, N_x; Trials, the number of items in the sample, n; and Population, the population size, N. The number of failures in the population is $N - N_x$. See Figure A.14 for an example of the hypergeometric distribution with $N_x = 50$, $n = 50$, and $N = 100$.

PDF:

$$f(x) = \begin{cases} \dfrac{\binom{N_x}{x}\binom{N-N_x}{n-x}}{\binom{N}{n}} & \text{for } a \leq x \leq b \\[4mm] 0 & \text{otherwise} \end{cases}$$

where x is an integer, $a = \max[0, n - N + N_x]$, and $b = \min[N_x, n]$.

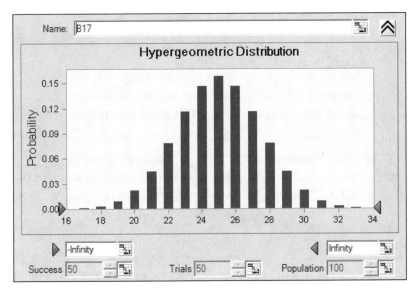

FIGURE A.14 Hypergeometric distribution with $N_x = 50$, $n = 50$, and $N = 100$.

CDF:

$$F(x) = \begin{cases} 0 & \text{for } a < x \\ \displaystyle\sum_{i=0}^{\lfloor x \rfloor} \frac{\binom{N_x}{i}\binom{N-N_x}{n-i}}{\binom{N}{n}} & \text{for } a \le x \le b \\ 1 & \text{for } b < x \end{cases}$$

Mean:

$$n\left(\frac{N_x}{N}\right)$$

Standard deviation:

$$\sqrt{n\left(\frac{N_x}{N}\right)\left(1 - \frac{N_x}{N}\right)\left(\frac{N-n}{N-1}\right)}$$

Excel function:

CB.Hypergeometric2(Success,Trials,Population,LowCutoff,HighCutoff,

NameOf)

where Success $= N_x$, Trials $= n$, and Population $= N$.

Notes: You cannot specify $N > 1000$ or $n > 1000$ for Crystal Ball's hypergeometric distribution. To model such a situation, use as an approximation the normal distribution with mean and standard deviation computed according to the expressions above, and truncated at 0 and $n + 0.99999$. Use Excel's =ROUNDDOWN(number,num_digits) command to obtain a discrete value.

LOGISTIC

The logistic is a continuous distribution that appears often near the top of the list of distributions Crystal Ball suggests when fitting distributions to stock returns and other financial data. It has fatter tails than the normal distribution. The excess kurtosis of the logistic distribution is 1.2. The logistic distribution has been applied to models in the areas of population growth, bioassay, medical diagnosis, and public health, among others. For much more about the logistic distribution, see Balakrishnan (1991).

Parameters: Mean, the mean of the distribution, μ; and Scale, the scale parameter, $s > 0$. See Figure A.15 for an example of the standard logistic distribution, which has $\mu = 0$ and $s = 1$.

PDF:

$$f(x) = \begin{cases} \dfrac{\operatorname{sech}^2\left[\dfrac{x-\mu}{2s}\right]}{4s} & \text{for } -\infty < x < \infty \end{cases}$$

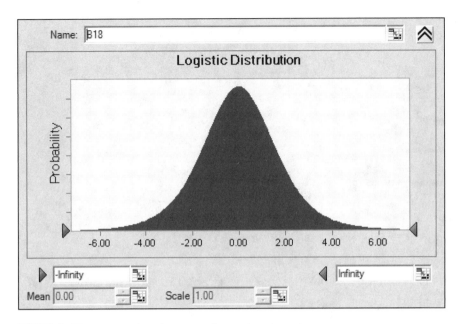

FIGURE A.15 Logistic distribution with $\mu = 0$ and $s = 1$.

or

$$f(x) = \left\{ \frac{z}{s(1+z)^2} \quad \text{for } -\infty < x < \infty \right.$$

where $z = e^{-(x-\mu)/s}$

CDF:

$$F(x) = \left\{ 1 - \frac{1}{1+z} \quad \text{for } -\infty < x < \infty \right.$$

Mean:

$$\mu$$

Standard deviation:

$$\frac{\pi s}{\sqrt{3}}$$

Excel function:

CB.Logistic(Mean,Scale,LowCutoff,HighCutoff,NameOf)

where **Mean** $= \mu$ and **Scale** $= s$.

Notes: Because the PDF of the logistic distribution can be expressed in terms of the square of the hyperbolic secant function, sech, it is sometimes called the sech-squared distribution.

LOGNORMAL

If $\ln(X)$, the natural logarithm of random variable X, follows a normal distribution, then X is said to follow the lognormal distribution. The lognormal distribution arises often in financial modeling and risk analysis because of the product version of the central limit effect (see section 4.1.7).

> **Parameters:** **Mean**, the mean, $\mu_L > 0$; and **Std. Dev.**, the standard deviation, $\sigma_L > 0$. See Figure A.16 for an example of the lognormal PDF with $\mu_L = 2.72$ and $\sigma_L = 1$.
>
> **PDF:**

$$f(x) = \begin{cases} \dfrac{1}{x\sqrt{2\pi\sigma^2}} e^{-(\ln x - \mu)^2/2\sigma^2} & \text{for } x > 0 \\ 0 & \text{otherwise} \end{cases}$$

where

$$\mu = \ln \mu_L - \frac{1}{2}\ln\left(1 + \frac{\sigma_L^2}{\mu_L^2}\right)$$

and

$$\sigma = \sqrt{\ln\left(1 + \frac{\sigma_L^2}{\mu_L^2}\right)}$$

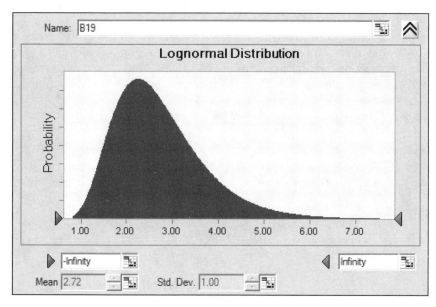

FIGURE A.16 Lognormal distribution with $\mu_L = 2.72$ and $\sigma_L = 1$.

CDF: No closed form.

Mean:

$$\mu_L = e^{\mu + \sigma^2/2}$$

Standard deviation:

$$\sigma_L = \sqrt{e^{2\mu + \sigma^2}\left(e^{\sigma^2} - 1\right)}$$

Excel function:

CB.Lognormal2(LogMean,LogStdDev,LowCutoff,HighCutoff,NameOf)

where LogMean $= \mu_L$, and LogStdDev $= \sigma_L$. You may also use

CB.Lognormal(Mean,StdDev,LowCutoff,HighCutoff,NameOf)

where Mean $= \mu$, and StdDev $= \sigma$.

Notes: Be sure to keep clear the difference between μ_L and σ_L, the mean and standard deviation of the lognormal random variable, X; and μ and σ, the mean and standard deviation of the normal distribution followed by $\ln(X)$, the natural logarithm of X.

MAXIMUM EXTREME

The maximum extreme distribution is the positively skewed form of the extreme value distribution. Crystal Ball's maximum extreme distribution is sometimes called the type 1 extreme value distribution. It has been applied to models in the areas of flood flows, radioactive emissions and human lifetimes, rupture of solids, earthquake magnitudes, estimation of insurance premiums, and stock market movements, among others. For more information, see de Haan and Ferreira (2006).

Parameters: Likeliest, the mode, m; and Scale, the scale parameter, $s > 0$. See Figure A.17 for an example of this PDF with $m = 0$ and $s = 1$, which is called the standard maximum extreme distribution, or the Gumbel distribution.

PDF:

$$f(x) = \begin{cases} \dfrac{z}{s}e^{-z} & \text{for } -\infty < x < \infty \\ 0 & \text{otherwise} \end{cases}$$

where $z = e^{-(x-m)/s}$.

CDF:

$$F(x) = \begin{cases} e^{-z} & \text{for } -\infty < x < \infty \\ 0 & \text{otherwise} \end{cases}$$

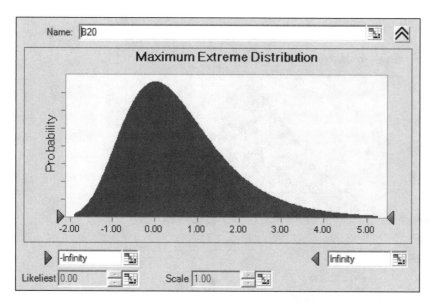

FIGURE A.17 Maximum extreme distribution with $m = 0$, and $s = 1$.

Mean:

$$m + 0.57722s$$

Standard deviation:

$$\frac{s\pi}{\sqrt{6}}$$

Excel function:

CB.MaxExtreme(Likeliest,Scale,LowCutoff,HighCutoff,NameOf)

where Likeliest $= m$, and Scale $= s$.

Notes: The maximum extreme distribution has skewness coefficient 1.139547, and excess kurtosis 2.4.

Because of the functional form of $f(x)$, the maximum extreme distribution is sometimes called the doubly exponential distribution. Do not confuse the doubly exponential distribution with the double exponential (aka Laplace) distribution.

MINIMUM EXTREME

Parameters: Likeliest, the mode, m; and Scale, the scale parameter, $s > 0$. See Figure A.18 for an example of this PDF with $m = 0$, and $s = 1$, which is called the standard minimum extreme distribution.

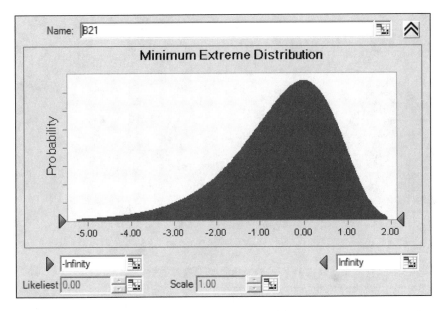

FIGURE A.18   Minimum extreme distribution with $m = 0$, and $s = 1$.

PDF:

$$f(x) = \begin{cases} \dfrac{z}{s}e^{-z} & \text{for } -\infty < x < \infty \\ 0 & \text{otherwise} \end{cases}$$

where $z = e^{\frac{(x-m)}{s}}$.

CDF:

$$F(x) = \begin{cases} e^{-z} & \text{for } x \geq 0 \\ 0 & \text{otherwise} \end{cases}$$

Mean:

$$m - 0.57722s$$

Standard deviation:

$$\frac{s\pi}{\sqrt{6}}$$

Excel function:

CB.MinExtreme(Likeliest,Scale,LowCutoff,HighCutoff,NameOf)

where Likeliest $= m$ and Scale $= s$.

Notes: The minimum extreme distribution has skewness coefficient -1.139547, and excess kurtosis 2.4.

NEGATIVE BINOMIAL

The negative binomial assumption in Crystal Ball is the discrete distribution of the total number of Bernoulli trials required to get exactly β successes where each Bernoulli trial has probability of success, p. Thus, the smallest value that a Crystal Ball negative binomial assumption can generate is β, and the largest potential number is infinitely large.

Parameters: Probability, the probability of success on each trial, p where $0 < p < 1$; and **Shape**, the number of successes, β, where $\beta > 0$ is an integer. See Figure A.19 for an example of the negative binomial PDF with $p = 0.2$, and $\beta = 10$.

PDF:

$$f(x) = \begin{cases} \binom{x-1}{\beta-1}p^{\beta}(1-p)^{x-\beta} & \text{for } x \geq \beta \\ 0 & \text{otherwise} \end{cases}$$

where x is an integer.

CDF:

$$F(x) = \begin{cases} \sum_{i=\beta}^{\lfloor x \rfloor} \binom{i-1}{\beta-1}p^{\beta}(1-p)^{i-\beta} & \text{for } x \geq \beta \\ 0 & \text{otherwise} \end{cases}$$

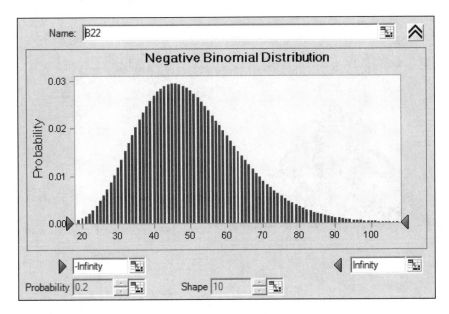

FIGURE A.19 Negative binomial distribution with $p = 0.2$, and $\beta = 10$.

Mean:

$$\beta/p$$

Standard Deviation:

$$\sqrt{\beta(1-p)}/p$$

Excel Function:

CB.NegBinomial(Prob,Shape,LowCutoff,HighCutoff,NameOf)

where **Prob** $= p$ and **Shape** $= \beta$.

Notes: The negative binomial distribution is also defined for noninteger β, but is not implemented in Crystal Ball for such values of β.

NORMAL

The normal is arguably the best known continuous distribution because of the Central Limit Theorem (see Chapter 4) and its application in many fields. The Normal is sometimes called the Gaussian distribution. For more information about the Normal distribution, see Patel and Read (1996).

Parameters: Mean, the location parameter, μ, where $-\infty < \mu < \infty$; and Std. Dev., the scale parameter, σ, where $\sigma > 0$. See Figure A.20 for an example of the standard normal distribution, which has parameters $\mu = 0$, and $\sigma = 1$.

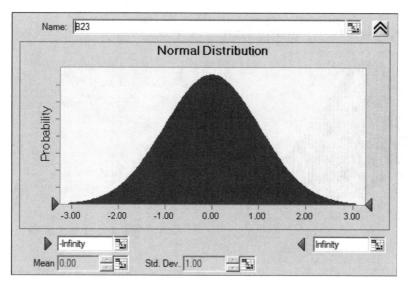

FIGURE A.20 Normal distribution with $\mu = 0$ and $\sigma = 1$.

PDF:

$$f(x) = \begin{cases} \dfrac{1}{\sqrt{2\pi}\sigma}e^{-(x-\mu)^2/2\sigma^2} & \text{for } -\infty < x < \infty \\ 0 & \text{otherwise} \end{cases}$$

CDF: No closed form.

Mean:

$$\mu$$

Standard deviation:

$$\sigma$$

Excel function:

CB.Normal(Mean,StdDev,LowCutoff,HighCutoff,NameOf)

where Mean $= \mu$ and StdDev $= \sigma$.

Notes: The normal distribution is symmetric, so has skewness coefficient 0. The kurtosis coefficient of any normal distribution is 3. Because the normal distribution is the standard to which the kurtosis coefficient of any other distribution is often compared, statisticians have defined the *excess kurtosis* coefficient to be equal to the kurtosis coefficient minus 3.

PARETO

The Pareto is a continuous distribution first used by economist Vilfredo Pareto in the late 1800s to describe the distribution of income over a population. For more information about the Pareto distribution, see Arnold (1983).

Parameters: Location, the location parameter, L, where $L > 0$; and Shape, the shape parameter, β, where $\beta > 0$. See Figure A.21 for an example of the Pareto distribution with $L = 1$, and $\beta = 2$.

PDF:

$$f(x) = \begin{cases} \beta L^\beta / x^{\beta+1} & \text{for } x \geq L \\ 0 & \text{otherwise} \end{cases}$$

CDF:

$$F(x) = \begin{cases} 1 - (L/x)^\beta & \text{for } x \geq L \\ 0 & \text{otherwise} \end{cases}$$

Mean:

$$\frac{\beta L}{\beta - 1} \quad \text{for } \beta > 1$$

Standard deviation:

$$\frac{\beta L^2}{(\beta - 1)^2(\beta - 2)} \quad \text{for } \beta > 2$$

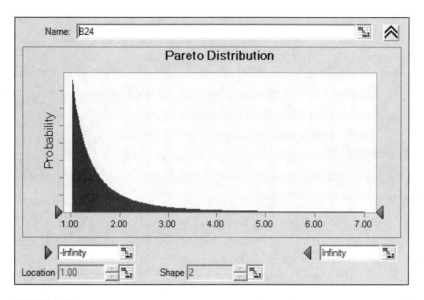

FIGURE A.21 Pareto distribution with $L = 1$ and $\beta = 2$.

Excel function:

CB.Pareto(Loc,Shape,LowCutoff,HighCutoff,NameOf)

where **Loc** $= L$, and **Shape** $= \beta$.

Notes: Pareto's work gave rise to the so-called 80–20 rule, whereby it is maintained that 80 percent of the wealth of a society is owned by 20 percent of the population. This rule has been expanded to other applications, and forms the basis of Pareto charts in Six Sigma quality management.

POISSON

The Poisson is the discrete distribution of the number of events that occur in a fixed area of opportunity when the events are occurring at a constant rate.

Parameters: **Rate,** the constant rate of occurrence, λ, where $\lambda > 0$. See Figure A.22 for an example of the Poisson distribution with $\lambda = 10$.

PDF:

$$f(x) = \begin{cases} \lambda^x e^{-\lambda}/x! & \text{for } x \geq 0 \\ 0 & \text{otherwise} \end{cases}$$

where x is an integer.

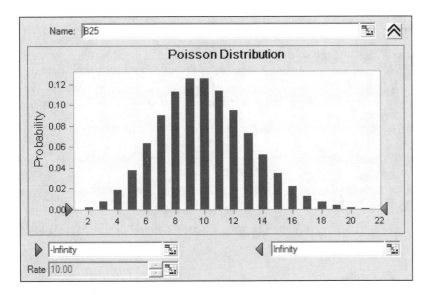

FIGURE A.22 Poisson distribution with $\lambda = 10$.

CDF:

$$F(x) = \begin{cases} \displaystyle\sum_{i=0}^{x} \lambda^i e^{-\lambda}/i! & \text{for } x \geq 0 \\ 0 & \text{otherwise} \end{cases}$$

Mean:

$$\lambda$$

Standard deviation:

$$\sqrt{\lambda}$$

Excel function:

CB.Poisson(Rate,LowCutoff,HighCutoff,NameOf)

where Rate $= \lambda$,

Notes: The Poisson distribution is usually applied to situations in which the number of potential opportunities for the outcomes to occur is large, but the probability of each occurrence is relatively small.

A notable application of the Poisson distribution was the number of deaths per year from kicks by horses in the Prussian Army Corps (Bortkiewicz 1898; see also Quine and Seneta 1987).

STUDENT'S T

Parameters: Midpoint, the midpoint of the distribution, m, where $-\infty < m < \infty$; Scale, the scale parameter, s, where $s > 0$; and Deg. Freedom, the number of degrees of freedom, d, an integer where $0 < d \leq 30$. See Figure A.23 for an example of the Student's t distribution with $m = 0$, $s = 1$, and $d = 5$.

PDF:

$$f(x) = \begin{cases} \dfrac{\Gamma\left(\dfrac{d+1}{2}\right)}{\sqrt{d\pi}\,\Gamma\left(\dfrac{d}{2}\right)\left(1 + \dfrac{z^2}{d}\right)^{\frac{d+1}{2}}} & \text{for } -\infty < x < \infty \\ \\ 0 & \text{otherwise} \end{cases}$$

where $z = \frac{x-m}{s}$, and $\Gamma(\cdot)$ is the Gamma function defined in the discussion of the beta distribution in this appendix.

CDF:

$$F(x) = \begin{cases} \dfrac{1}{2} + \tan^{-1}\left(\dfrac{z}{\sqrt{d}}\right) + \dfrac{z\sqrt{d}}{d+z^2} \times \displaystyle\sum_{j=0}^{(d-3)/2} \dfrac{a_j}{\left(1 + z^2/d\right)^j} \\ \qquad \text{for } d \text{ odd and } -\infty < x < \infty \\ \\ \dfrac{1}{2} + \dfrac{z}{2\sqrt{d+z^2}} \times \displaystyle\sum_{j=0}^{(d-2)/2} \dfrac{b_j}{\left(1 + z^2/d\right)^j} \\ \qquad \text{for } d \text{ even and } -\infty < x < \infty \\ \\ 0 \qquad\qquad\qquad\qquad\qquad\qquad\qquad \text{otherwise} \end{cases}$$

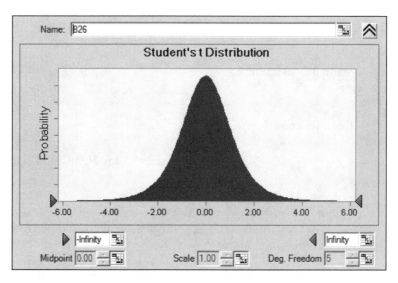

FIGURE A.23 Student's t distribution with $m = 0$, $s = 1$, and $d = 5$.

where $z = \dfrac{x - m}{s}$, $a_j = [2j/(2j + 1)]\,a_{j-1}$, $a_0 = 1$, $b_j = [(2j - 1)/2j]\,b_{j-1}$, and $b_0 = 1$.

Mean:

$$m, \text{ for } d > 1$$

Standard deviation:

$$\sqrt{sd/(d - 2)}, \text{ for } d > 2$$

Excel function:

CB.StudentT(Midpoint,Scale,Degrees,LowCutoff,HighCutoff,NameOf)

Notes: The Student's t distribution with $m = 0$ and $d = 1$ is called the standard Cauchy distribution, for which the mean and standard deviation do not exist (are infinite).

TRIANGULAR

The triangular distribution is used most often as a rough distribution in the absence of data. Its use as an approximation to the normal distribution is discussed in Bell (1962).

Parameters: Minimum, the minimum value, a, where $-\infty < a < \infty$; Likeliest, the mode, m, where $-\infty < a \le m < \infty$; and Maximum, the maximum value, b, where $-\infty < a \le m \le b < \infty$, but $a < b$. See Figure A.24 for an example of the Triangular distribution with $a = -10$, $m = 0$, and $b = 10$.

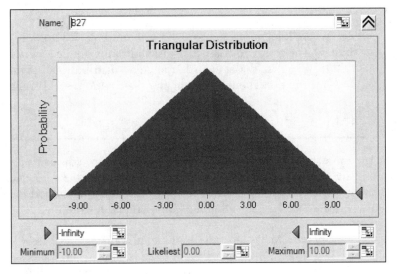

FIGURE A.24 Triangular distribution with $a = -10$, $m = 0$, and $b = 10$.

PDF:

$$f(x) = \begin{cases} \dfrac{2(x-a)}{(m-a)(b-a)} & \text{for } a \leq x \leq m \\ \dfrac{2(b-x)}{(b-m)(b-a)} & \text{for } m < x \leq b \\ 0 & \text{otherwise} \end{cases}$$

CDF:

$$F(x) = \begin{cases} 0 & \text{for } x < a \\ \dfrac{(x-a)^2}{(m-a)(b-a)} & \text{for } a \leq x \leq m \\ 1 - \dfrac{(b-x)^2}{(b-m)(b-a)} & \text{for } m < x \leq b \\ 1 & \text{for } b < x \end{cases}$$

Mean:

$$\frac{a+m+b}{3}$$

Standard deviation:

$$\sqrt{\frac{a^2 + m^2 + b^2 - am - ab - bm}{18}}$$

Excel function:

CB.Triangular(Minimum,Likeliest,Maximum,LowCutoff,HighCutoff,

NameOf)

where Minimum $= a$, Likeliest $= m$, and Maximum $= b$.

Notes: The standard triangular distribution is obtained when $a = 0$ and $b = 1$. If $m = 1/2$, the standard triangular distribution is symmetric. For more information about the triangular distribution, see Ayyangar (1941).

UNIFORM

The uniform distribution is used most often as a rough distribution in the absence of data. It applies to any continuous random variable for which the largest and smallest possible values can be specified, with equal likelihood for the occurrence of any value in between the minimum and maximum values.

Parameters: Minimum, the minimum value, a, where $-\infty < a < \infty$; and Maximum, the maximum value, b, where $-\infty < a < b < \infty$. See Figure A.25 for an example of the uniform distribution with $a = -10$ and $b = 10$.

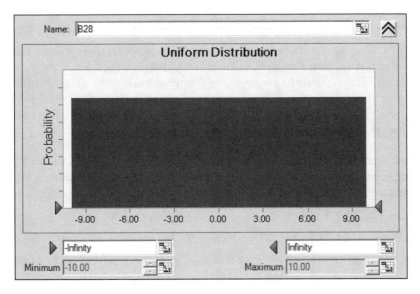

FIGURE A.25   Uniform distribution with $a = -10$ and $b = 10$.

PDF:

$$f(x) = \begin{cases} \dfrac{1}{b-a} & \text{for } a < x < b \\ 0 & \text{otherwise} \end{cases}$$

CDF:

$$F(x) = \begin{cases} 0 & \text{for } x < a \\ \dfrac{x-a}{b-a} & \text{for } a \geq x \geq b \\ 1 & \text{for } b < x \end{cases}$$

Mean:

$$\frac{a+b}{2}$$

Standard deviation:

$$\frac{b-a}{\sqrt{12}}$$

Excel function:

$$\text{CB.Uniform(Min,Max,LowCutoff,HighCutoff,NameOf)}$$

where Min $= a$, and Max $= b$.

Notes: The uniform distribution with $a = 0$ and $b = 1$ is used in generating variates from all other distributions in Crystal Ball. See Appendix B for details.

WEIBULL

The Weibull distribution is widely used in engineering practice to represent the lifetime of a system component composed of many parts that fails when the first of these parts fails. The Weibull has been applied to problems in the areas of tidal height, efficacy of medical treatment, insurance claims, maintenance of street lights, rock blasting, and spare part planning. For more about the Weibull distribution, see Prabhakar Murthy, Min, and Jiang (2004).

Parameters: Location, the location parameter, L, where $-\infty < L < \infty$; Scale, the scale parameter, s, where $s > 0$; and Shape, the shape parameter, β, where $\beta > 0$. See Figure A.26 for an example of the Weibull distribution with $L = 0$, $s = 1$, and $\beta = 2$.

PDF:

$$f(x) = \begin{cases} \dfrac{\beta}{s}\left(\dfrac{x-L}{s}\right)^{\beta-1} e^{-\left(\frac{x-L}{s}\right)} & \text{for } x \geq L \\ 0 & \text{otherwise} \end{cases}$$

CDF:

$$F(x) = \begin{cases} 1 - e^{-\left(\frac{x-L}{s}\right)^{\beta}} & \text{for } x \geq L \\ 0 & \text{otherwise} \end{cases}$$

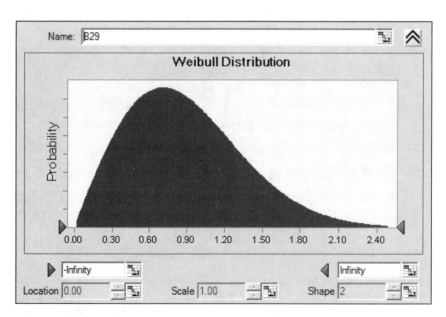

FIGURE A.26   Weibull distribution with $L = 0$, $s = 1$, and $\beta = 2$.

Mean:

$$L + s\Gamma\left[\frac{\beta + 1}{\beta}\right]$$

where $\Gamma[\cdot]$ is the gamma function defined in section A.2.

Standard deviation:

$$s\sqrt{\left(\Gamma\left[\frac{\beta + 2}{\beta}\right] - \left\{\Gamma\left[\frac{\beta + 1}{\beta}\right]\right\}^2\right)}$$

Excel function:

CB.Weibull(Loc,Scale,Shape,LowCutoff,HighCutoff,NameOf)

where Loc $= L$, Scale $= s$, and Shape $= \beta$.

Notes: The Weibull distribution with $\beta = 2$ is also known as the Rayleigh distribution.

YES-NO

The yes-no distribution describes a random occurrence with two possible outcomes, which are usually denoted by $x = 1$ (a "success") and $x = 0$ ("failure").

Parameters: Probability of Yes(1), the probability of a success, p, where $0 < p < 1$. See Figure A.27 for an example of the yes-no distribution with $p = 0.8$.

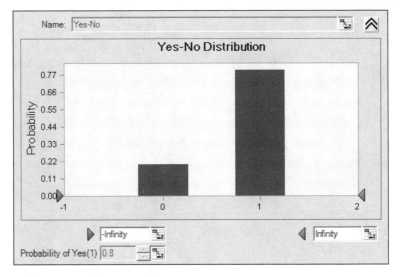

FIGURE A.27 Yes-no distribution with $p = 0.8$.

PDF:

$$f(x) = \begin{cases} 1-p & \text{for } x = 0 \\ p & \text{for } x = 1 \\ 0 & \text{otherwise} \end{cases}$$

CDF:

$$F(x) = \begin{cases} 0 & \text{for } x < 0 \\ 1-p & \text{for } 0 \leq x \leq 1 \\ 1 & \text{for } 1 \geq x \end{cases}$$

Mean:

$$p$$

Standard deviation:

$$\sqrt{p(1-p)}$$

Excel function:

CB.YesNo(Prob,LowCutoff,HighCutoff,NameOf)

where **Prob** $= p$.

Notes: The yes-no distribution is also known as the Bernoulli distribution, and is equivalent to the binomial distribution with $n = 1$.

Generating Assumption Values

This appendix provides a brief description of how Crystal Ball generates values from its assumptions, to which we refer in this appendix as random numbers and random variates. For our purposes, a *random number* is a computer-generated number that appears to be drawn from the uniform probability distribution with $a = 0$ and $b = 1$ (see Appendix A), independently of the other random numbers. A *random variate* is a computer-generated number that appears to be drawn independently from any other probability distribution.

Crystal Ball uses a variety of methods to generate independent random variates by transforming random numbers. The choice of transformation depends on several factors, such as the type and parameters of the distribution, as well as the sampling method used (Monte Carlo or Latin Hypercube). For illustration, the inverse transform random-variate generation method is described below, and references are given for the other methods Crystal Ball uses. For more information about generating random numbers and variates, see Bratley, Fox, and Schrage (1987), Fishman (2006), Glasserman (2004), Law and Kelton (2000), and the references listed in the Bibliography section of the *Crystal Ball User Manual*.

GENERATING RANDOM NUMBERS

Crystal Ball generates random numbers using a linear congruential generator (LCG). An LCG is defined by the recursive formula

$$Z_i = (aZ_{i-1} + c)(\text{mod } m) \tag{B.1}$$

where m is the modulus, a is the multiplier, c is the increment, and Z_0 is the seed. The operator "mod" in Expression B.1 represents *modulo reduction*, which means to take the remainder after dividing by the modulus. For example, $31(\text{mod } 8) = 7$, because 8 goes into 31 three times with a remainder of 7. Likewise, $3(\text{mod } 8) = 3$, $11(\text{mod } 8) = 3$, and $890(\text{mod } 8) = 2$.

Modulo reduction is used simply to ensure that the LCG delivers a sequence of integers, Z_i such that $0 \leq Z_i \leq m - 1$. After dividing each integer by the modulus, m, we get a sequence $U_i = Z_i/m$ for $i = 1, 2, \ldots, m - 1$ that appears to be iid $U(0, 1)$. If

$c > 0$, the recursion in Expression B.1 is called a *mixed* LCG. If $c = 0$, the recursion is called a *multiplicative* LCG.

Example LCG

To understand how LCGs work, consider the mixed LCG with $a = 5$, $c = 1$, $m = 8$, and $Z_0 = 3$,

$$Z_i = (5Z_{i-1} + 1)(\text{mod } 8),$$

which is in cells A3:C23 of file LCGExamples.xls shown Figure B.1. This simple LCG has three desirable features:

1. Because the LCG generates the $m = 8$ integers $\{0, 1, 2, 3, 4, 5, 6, 7\}$ before it repeats, the LCG is said to be *full period*.
2. The integers appear to be generated independently of each other in the sense that they do not occur in any readily identifiable systematic order, such as $\{7, 6, 5, 4, 3, 2, 1, 0\}$.
3. By specifying the seed, you can determine the rest of the stream of "random" numbers.

	A	B	C	D	E	F
1	**LCGExamples.xls**					
2	**Mixed LCG**					
3	**i**	**Z_i**	**U_i**		**Parameters**	
4	0	3	---		a	5
5	1	0	0.000		c	1
6	2	1	0.125		m	8
7	3	6	0.750		Z_0	3
8	4	7	0.875			
9	5	4	0.500			
10	6	5	0.625			
11	7	2	0.250			
12	8	3	0.375			
13	9	0	0.000			
14	10	1	0.125			
15	11	6	0.750			
16	12	7	0.875			
17	13	4	0.500			
18	14	5	0.625			
19	15	2	0.250			
20	16	3	0.375			
21	17	0	0.000			
22	18	1	0.125			
23	19	6	0.750			

FIGURE B.1 LCG defined by
$Z_i = (5Z_{i-1} + 1)(\text{mod } 8)$ with $Z_0 = 3$.

Because the stream of numbers appears random, but is actually deterministic and in the systematic order defined by the recursion, the values generated by an LCG are often called *pseudorandom numbers*.

The parameters must be chosen carefully to give an LCG full period. For example, make the LCG in Figure B.1 multiplicative by setting the increment, $c = 0$, and the LCG will generate the set of integers $\{3, 7, 3, 7, \ldots\}$, which makes the LCG less than full period. This is undesirable because it is inefficient, and can be misleading. If you use $m - 1$ random numbers from a mixed LCG that is less than full cycle, you will be using some of the random numbers more than once, so the estimates you obtain from the simulation will not be as precise as they would be based on $m - 1$ random numbers from a mixed LCG that is full cycle.

Now consider the multiplicative LCG with $a = 5$, $m = 7$, and $Z_0 = 3$,

$$Z_i = 5Z_{i-1} \quad \mod \ 7,$$

which is in cells A27:C47 of file LCGExample.xls shown Figure B.2. This multiplicative LCG generates the $m - 1 = 6$ integers 1 through 6. Clearly, if a multiplicative LCG somehow generated $Z_i = 0$ for any i, then all other Z_is would

	A	B	C	D	E	F
1	**LCGExamples.xls**					
26	**Multiplicative LCG**					
27	i	Z_i	U_i		Parameters	
28	0	3	---		a	5
29	1	1	0.143		m	7
30	2	5	0.714		Z_0	3
31	3	4	0.571			
32	4	6	0.857			
33	5	2	0.286			
34	6	3	0.429			
35	7	1	0.143			
36	8	5	0.714			
37	9	4	0.571			
38	10	6	0.857			
39	11	2	0.286			
40	12	3	0.429			
41	13	1	0.143			
42	14	5	0.714			
43	15	4	0.571			
44	16	6	0.857			
45	17	2	0.286			
46	18	3	0.429			
47	19	1	0.143			

FIGURE B.2 LCG defined by $Z_i = 5Z_{i-1}$ mod 8 with $Z_0 = 3$.

equal zero, too. Therefore, the multiplicative LCGs of most use are those that generate the integers 1 through $m - 1$, where m is a large number. Fortunately, researchers have developed LCGs with good statistical properties, and Crystal Ball uses one of these good LCGs in its algorithms.

Crystal Ball's LCG

Crystal Ball version 7.2 uses the prime modulus multiplicative linear congruential generator defined by

$$Z_i = (62089911 Z_{i-1})(\text{mod } 2^{31} - 1),$$

where the modulus $m = 2^{31} - 1 = 2,147,483,647$ is a prime number (i.e., evenly divisible only by itself and 1) chosen in conjunction with $a = 62089911$ to give the LCG good statistical properties and compatibility with personal computer architectures. For more information about choosing the parameters of an LCG, see Knuth (1998).

Crystal Ball's generator has period $m - 1 = 2^{31} - 2 = 2,147,483,646$, so is capable of delivering more than 2 billion distinct random numbers. By setting Seed in Run Prefs... you are determining Z_0. If Seed is set to 0, CB will determine the seed based on the number of milliseconds since Windows was last started on your computer.

Excel's Random Number Generator

Excel has a random number generator that it uses for its =rand() function. The first random number is:

$$r_i = \text{fractional part of } (9821 * r_{i-1} + 0.211327) \quad \text{for } i = 1, 2, \ldots$$

where $r_0 = .5$. Excel's random number generator will provide up to 1 million different numbers. Through a specification in an initialization file, you can have Excel determine its seed, r_0, from the system clock. See

http://support.microsoft.com/kb/q86523/

for more information.

Besides being able to generate only a small fraction of the number of random numbers Crystal Ball can produce, this generator has relatively poor statistical properties. For more information about random number generators and their statistical properties, see the Web site,

http://random.mat.sbg.ac.at/links/rando.html.

GENERATING RANDOM VARIATES

Crystal Ball uses random numbers in a variety of methods to generate random variates. The particular method used depends on the assumption's distribution function, and the type of sampling (Monte Carlo or Latin Hypercube) you have specified in the Run Preferences. The specific method used to generate random variates from each assumption is listed in Chapter 2 of the *Crystal Ball Reference Manual*. In this appendix, we will consider just one of the methods, inverse transformation, and see how Latin Hypercube sampling is used with it to make the sampling "more even."

Inverse-Transform Method

Suppose that you want to generate a random variate, x, from a distribution with CDF, $F(x)$. The inverse-transform method takes a random number, u, from the interval $(0, 1)$, and transforms it into a random variate, x, by using the inverse of X's distribution function, $F^{-1}(x)$.

For example, suppose X has the right triangular distribution with PDF

$$f(x) = x/50 \quad \text{for } 0 \le x \le 10,$$

shown in Figure B.3, and CDF

$$F(x) = x^2/100 \quad \text{for } 0 \le x \le 10,$$

shown in Figure B.4. This distribution is the same as a Crystal Ball triangular assumption with $a = 0$, $b = 10$, and $m = 10$ (see Appendix A), so we will designate

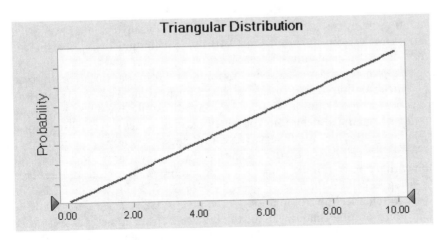

FIGURE B.3   Triangular PDF, $f(x) = x/50$ for $0 \le x \le 10$.

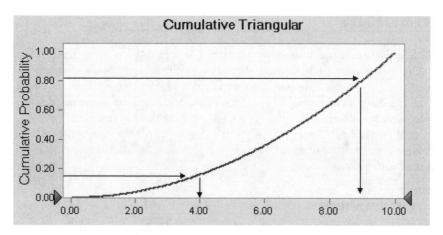

FIGURE B.4   Triangular CDF, $F(x) = x^2/100$ for $0 \leq x \leq 10$. This is the cumulative distribution function for the PDF given in Figure B.3. The figure also illustrates the inverse-transform algorithm. For $U = .16$, $F^{-1}(.16) = 10\sqrt{.16} = 4$, and for $U = .81$, $F^{-1}(.81) = 10\sqrt{.81} = 9$.

it as triangular(0,10,10). Given a value, u, generated by Crystal Ball's LCG, a corresponding value from the distribution of X is found by inverting the CDF as follows to get an expression for x as a function of u:

$$F(x) = u = x^2/100 \Rightarrow x = 10\sqrt{u}.$$

Figure B.4 illustrates the inverse transformation. For the value $u = .81$, the corresponding variate from the triangular(0,10,10) distribution is determined as $x = 10\sqrt{.81} = 9$; and for $u = .16$, the triangular(0,10,10) variate is $x = 10\sqrt{.16} = 4$. By generating many such values of u randomly between 0 and 1, we get a Monte Carlo sample from the triangular(0,10,10) distribution of X. See the file InverseTransform.xls for a demonstration.

The inverse-transform method also works for discrete random variables. In some cases, it is difficult or impossible to find a closed-form formula for $F^{-1}(x)$, so the inverse-transform method cannot be used. However, it is also possible to generate random variates from the distributions for which Excel provides inverse distribution functions. For example, the file InverseTransform.xls shows how a uniform(0,1) random number in cell **A9** is used to generate random variates from the beta distribution with parameters $\alpha = 2$, $\beta = 3$, $a = 0$, and $b = 10$ (see section A.2). This is done by using in cell **B9** the formula =BETAINV(A9,2,3,0,10). Excel's **BETAINV** function uses a numerical approximation to the inverse CDF, $F^{-1}(x)$, for the beta distribution. For more information about the inverse-transform method and other ways to generate random variates, see Chapter 8 of Law and Kelton (2000), or Chapter 3 of Fishman (2006).

LATIN HYPERCUBE SAMPLING

Latin Hypercube sampling (LHS) is a form of stratified sampling that Crystal Ball's authors have implemented to help ensure that all portions of the distribution are used to generate random variates, especially the tails. To illustrate how LHS works, consider Figure B.5, in which the triangular(0,10,10) CDF is stratified into five equal pieces by values of $F(x)$. Stratum A includes values of $F(x)$ between 0 and 0.2, stratum B includes values of $F(x)$ between 0.2 and 0.4, stratum C includes values of $F(x)$ between 0.4 and 0.6, stratum D includes values of $F(x)$ between 0.6 and 0.8, and Stratum E includes values of $F(x)$ between 0.8 and 1.0. Figure B.6 shows the PDF for the triangular(0,10,10) distribution with the same strata, A through E. By construction, each of the five pieces of the PDF has area 0.2.

With Latin Hypercube sampling enabled, Crystal Ball will randomly select one of the strata, then generate a random variate, u, within that stratum and compute the corresponding random variate x. On the next trial, it will randomly select a stratum that has not yet been selected, and compute the random variate x corresponding to the value of u selected. It will continue this until all five strata have been used, then will repeat the process until one of the stopping criteria is met.

If more trials are specified than the number of strata, then Crystal Ball will attempt to split up evenly the number of trials for which each stratum is sampled. This is why it is best in **Run Preferences** to make **Number of trials to run** on the **Trials** tab an integer multiple of **Sample size** on the **Sampling** tab. The value of **Sample size** is the number of strata into which the distribution is divided.

What is a Latin Hypercube? A *Latin square* has the property that each of the three symbols A, B, and C, appear only once in each row and column of a two-dimensional

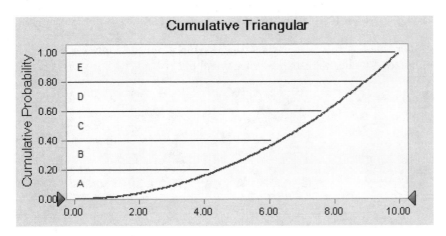

FIGURE B.5 Triangular(0,10,10) CDF, $F(x) = x^2/100$, for $0 \leq x \leq 10$, stratified into five equal pieces by values of $F(x)$. The defining values are: $F^{-1}(0.2) = 4.47$, $F^{-1}(0.4) = 6.32$, $F^{-1}(0.6) = 7.75$, and $F^{-1}(0.8) = 8.94$.

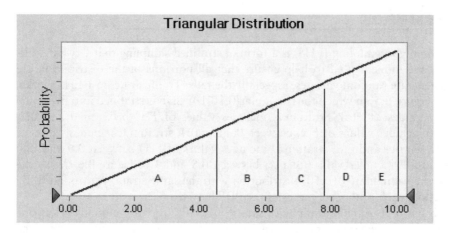

FIGURE B.6 Triangular PDF stratified into five equal pieces by area. The defining values are: $F^{-1}(0.2) = 4.47$, $F^{-1}(0.4) = 6.32$, $F^{-1}(0.6) = 7.75$, and $F^{-1}(0.8) = 8.94$.

matrix, as shown below.

$$\begin{bmatrix} A & B & C \\ B & C & A \\ C & A & B \end{bmatrix}$$

A *Latin cube* has the property that each symbol appears only once in each row or column of a three-dimensional matrix, as shown below in three layers of Latin squares.

$$\begin{bmatrix} A & B & C \\ B & C & A \\ C & A & B \end{bmatrix} \begin{bmatrix} C & A & B \\ A & B & C \\ B & C & A \end{bmatrix} \begin{bmatrix} B & C & A \\ C & A & B \\ A & B & C \end{bmatrix}$$

A *Latin Hypercube* has the property that each symbol appears only once in each row or column of a higher-than-three-dimensional matrix.

Variance Reduction Techniques

A s we saw in Chapter 12, one of the many uses of Monte Carlo simulation by financial analysts is to place a value on financial derivatives. You now know that you can sharpen the point estimate of the derivative's value by using the brute force method of increasing the number of trials run during a simulation. However, there are also other relatively simple changes that you can make to a model that provide dramatic increases in precision for a given number of simulation trials. Such changes made to a model are called variance reduction techniques. This appendix, based on Charnes (2002), shows how the variance reduction techniques of antithetic variates (AV) and control variates (CV) can be used to sharpen the precision of your estimate of the value of an Asian call option.

The best point estimate of the value of a derivative is usually the mean, or arithmetic average of the derivative's discounted payoff taken over all trials of the simulation. One measure of the sharpness of the point estimate of the mean is Mean Standard Error, defined as

$$\text{Mean Standard Error} = \sqrt{\frac{\text{Variance}}{\text{Trials}}}. \qquad \text{(C.1)}$$

The precision of the mean as a point estimate is often defined as the half-width of a 95% confidence interval, which is calculated as

$$\text{Precision} = 1.96 \times \text{Mean Standard Error.} \qquad \text{(C.2)}$$

Lower values of Precision in Expression (C.2) correspond to sharper estimates.

Increasing the number of trials is a brute force method of obtaining sharper estimates. This reduces the Mean Standard Error by increasing the value of Trials in the denominator of Expression(C.1). However, highly precise estimates with the brute force method can take a long time to achieve. So-called *variance reduction techniques* reduce Mean Standard Error by decreasing Variance in the numerator of Expression (C.1) and can be used to speed up simulations by achieving a specified level of precision with a smaller number of Trials.

In this appendix, we consider two variance reduction techniques, the method of antithetic variates and the method of control variates. The AV method is more widely applicable than CV, but when it can be used, the CV method is much more efficient.

The use of Monte Carlo simulation in pricing options was first published by Boyle (1977), but recently the literature in this area has grown rapidly. You can learn more about the use of variance reduction techniques from Fishman (2006), or Law and Kelton (2000). For a good discussion of variance reduction techniques applied to financial derivatives, see Boyle, Broadie, and Glasserman (1997), or Glasserman (2004).

USING CRYSTAL BALL TO VALUE AN ASIAN OPTION

As described in Chapter 12, an Asian option is also called an average option because its price is linked to the average value of the underlying asset on specific dates. Suppose the prices of the underlying asset are denoted by S_t, for $t \in \{0, 1, \ldots, T\}$, where T is the expiration date of the option. The agreed amount for which the underlying is traded is called the *strike price*, denoted by K. An average-price Asian option has a payoff at time T based on the difference between the strike price and the arithmetic average price of the underlying asset. Specifically, the payoff is $V = \max(A - K, 0)$, where $A = \sum_{t=1}^{T} S_t / T$. Financial analysts are often interested in determining the value of the option, denoted here as C_A.

In the Black-Scholes worldview, a fair value for an option is the present value of the expected value of the option payoff at expiration under a risk-neutral random walk for the underlying asset prices. Therefore, the formula used in a Crystal Ball model to generate daily asset prices on the ith trial of the simulation is

$$S_{t+1}^{(i)} = S_t \exp\left((r - \sigma^2/2)(1/252) + \sigma\sqrt{1/252}Z^{(i)} \right), \qquad (C.3)$$

for $t = 1, 2, \ldots, T$, where r is the risk-free rate of interest, σ is the annual volatility of the asset prices, and $Z^{(i)}$ is a standard normal random variate. Expression (C.3) assumes that there are 252 trading days in a year.

The general approach to using Crystal Ball to find the price of an average-price Asian option is straightforward (see the file AsianCallVarReduction.xls for specific details):

1. For each simulation trial, $i = 1, 2, \ldots, N$, simulate sample paths of the underlying asset prices, S_t, for $t = 0, 1, \ldots, T$ according to Expression(C.3).
2. Calculate the average price, A, of the underlying asset and payoff of the option at time T as $V^{(i)} = \max(A - K, 0)$.
3. Compute the present value of the cash flows of the option on each sample path, as $\widehat{C}_A^{(i)} = V^{(i)} e^{-rT/252}$.
4. Use the average of the present values over the sample paths,

$$\widehat{C}_A = \sum_{i=1}^{N} \widehat{C}_A^{(i)} / N,$$

as the point estimate of the option's value, and use the variance of the distribution of the values $\widehat{C}_A^{(i)}$ to obtain the precision of $\widehat{C}_A$ with Expression (C.2).

Crystal Ball takes care of the housekeeping details in the steps above, so that in practice all we need to do after running the simulation model for a given number of trials is look at the Crystal Ball Forecast window statistics to obtain the forecast cell mean, which is $\widehat{C}_A$, and the mean standard error, which is a measure of precision.

ANTITHETIC VARIATES

The method of antithetic variates for variance reduction is based on the fact that if $Z^{(i)}$ has a standard normal distribution, then so does $-Z^{(i)}$. Therefore, if we replace $Z^{(i)}$ in (C.3) with $-Z^{(i)}$, we also get a valid sample from the distribution of stock prices at time T. In using antithetic variates with the procedure given above, we construct two intermediate estimates in Step 3, $\widehat{C}_A^+(Z^{(i)})$ and $\widehat{C}_A^-(-Z^{(i)})$, then a final estimate, $\widehat{C}_A^{AV} = (\widehat{C}_A^+ + \widehat{C}_A^-)/2$ as the point estimate in Step 4. Because of the way we use $Z^{(i)}$ and $-Z^{(i)}$, the estimates $\widehat{C}_A^+$ and $\widehat{C}_A^-$ both have the same expected value; however, because the two estimates are negatively correlated, the distribution of $\widehat{C}_A^{AV}$ has a lower variance than the variance of either estimate by itself. Thus, antithetic variates gives an estimate that has the expected value we are trying to find, but with a smaller Mean Standard Error than the estimate obtained without using a variance reduction technique.

CONTROL VARIATES

The method of control variates replaces the evaluation of an unknown expected value with the evaluation of the difference between the unknown quantity and a related quantity whose expected value is known. Here, the unknown quantity of interest is the value, C_A, of an average-price Asian call option whose payoff at expiration is $\max(A - K, 0)$, where A is the arithmetic average of the underlying asset prices during the holding period. The related quantity with known expectation is the value, C_G, of an Asian option whose payoff is $\max(G - K, 0)$, where $G = \left(\prod_{t=1}^{T} S_t\right)^{1/T}$ is the geometric average. Because of the lognormality of the stock price model, an analytic expression is available for C_G, but not for C_A (see Kemna and Vorst 1990 for details).

The values of interest here are denoted as $C_A = \mathrm{E}\left[\widehat{C}_A^{(i)}\right]$, and $C_G = \mathrm{E}\left[\widehat{C}_G^{(i)}\right]$, where $\widehat{C}_A^{(i)}$ and $\widehat{C}_G^{(i)}$ are the discounted option payoffs for a single simulated path of the underlying for options that pay off on the arithmetic and geometric means, respectively. Because

$$C_A = C_G + \mathrm{E}\left[\widehat{C}_A - \widehat{C}_G\right],$$

an unbiased estimator of C_A is given by

$$\widehat{C}_A^{CV} = \widehat{C}_A + (C_G - \widehat{C}_G)$$

which becomes the point estimate to be used in Step 4 of section C.1. Using C_G as a control variate reduces variance because it "steers" the estimate toward the correct value.

COMPARISON

The spreadsheet file AsianCallVarReduction.xls contains a Crystal Ball model shown in Figure C.1 for estimating the value of an average-price Asian Call option, along with reports on the performance of the model for options having different strike prices and volatilities of the underlying asset. Figure C.2 shows the distribution of the discounted cash flows for simulations with no variance reduction, antithetic variates (AV), and control variates (CV) for an at-the-money Asian Call option having initial price = $55, strike price = $55, underlying volatility = 30%, and time to expiration = 126 days. All of these distributions have means that are estimates of the option's value, but only the distribution of values from the simulation with no variance reduction resembles the distribution of cash flows that might be generated by the option. The other three simulations yield distributions that have the desired mean, but the shapes of the distributions are not indicative of the potential cash flows of the option. However, the mean standard errors computed from each of the four distributions are comparable.

Table C.1 shows the mean, standard error, and percentage of reduction in standard error for each estimation method when the simulation model was run for $N = 1,000$ trials. The antithetic variates nearly doubled the precision (halved the standard error). The control variates method gave an estimate that is roughly twenty times more precise than (has a standard error error that is 4.8% of) that achieved with no variance reduction.

	A	B	C	D	E	F	G	H	I	J
1	**AsianCallVarReduction.xls**									
2										
3	Inputs			Time	Z	Price+	Price-		Geometric	
4	S_0	$55.00		0	0.00	$ 55.00	$ 55.00	Average	Payoff	PV(Payoff)
5	K	$55.00		1	0.00	$ 55.01	$ 55.01	$ 55.77	$ 0.77	$ 0.7301
6	Sigma	30.00%		2	0.00	$ 55.02	$ 55.02			
7	T (years)	0.5		3	0.00	$ 55.04	$ 55.04		Arithmetic	
8	R_f	10.00%		4	0.00	$ 55.05	$ 55.05	Average	Payoff	PV(Payoff)
9	a	5.75%		5	0.00	$ 55.06	$ 55.06	$ 55.77	$ 0.77	$ 0.7318
10	sig_a	17.32%		6	0.00	$ 55.07	$ 55.07			
11				7	0.00	$ 55.08	$ 55.08	Antithetic Variates (AV) Estimate		
12	Black-Scholes			8	0.00	$ 55.10	$ 55.10	Average-	Payoff(-)	PV(Payoff)
13	Sol'n for Geometric			9	0.00	$ 55.11	$ 55.11	$ 55.77	$ 0.77	$ 0.7318
14	Average Option			10	0.00	$ 55.12	$ 55.12			
15	d_1	0.29598		11	0.00	$ 55.13	$ 55.13	Control Variates (CV) Estimate		
16	d_2	0.17351		12	0.00	$ 55.14	$ 55.14			PV(Payoff)
17	N(d_1)	0.61638		13	0.00	$ 55.16	$ 55.16			$ 3.1796
18	N(d_2)	0.56887		14	0.00	$ 55.17	$ 55.17			
19	C(S,T)	$ 3.18		15	0.00	$ 55.18	$ 55.18			
20				16	0.00	$ 55.19	$ 55.19			
130				126	0.00	$ 56.53	$ 56.53			

FIGURE C.1   Crystal Ball model for estimating the value of an average-price Asian Call option.

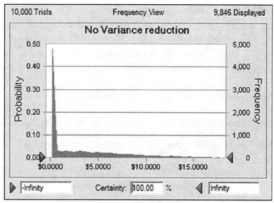

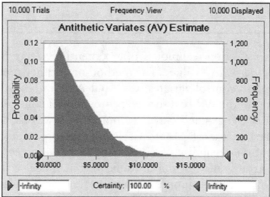

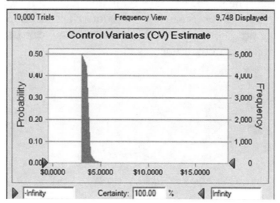

FIGURE C.2 Distribution of the discounted cash flows for simulations with no variance reduction, antithetic variates (AV), and control variates (CV) for an at-the-money Asian call option having initial Price = $55, strike Price = $55, underlying volatility = 30 percent, and time to expiration = 126 days.

TABLE C.1   Means, standard errors, and increases in precision from the simulation model in AsianCallVarReduction.xls using no variance reduction, antithetic variates (AV), control variates (CV) to obtain estimated values of an average price Asian call option having initial price = $55, strike price = $55, underlying volatility = 30%, and time to expiration = 126 days.

Estimation Method	Mean	Standard Precision Error	Increase
No Variance Reduction	3.3611	0.0476	1.00
Antithetic Variates (AV)	3.3580	0.0235	2.03
Control Variates (CV)	3.3102	0.0022	21.64

CONCLUSION

Variance reduction techniques offer potentially large increases in the precision of estimated derivative values. The method of antithetic variates (AV) is generally less effective than control variates (CV), but AV can be easily applied to more types of derivatives than CV because CV requires that a control variate is available, such as the value of the geometric-average option that was used here.

Interest in use of Monte Carlo methods for derivatives pricing is increasing because of the flexibility of the method in handling complex financial instruments. Monte Carlo simulation will continue to gain appeal as financial instruments become more complex, workstations become faster, and simulation software is adopted by more users. The use of variance reduction techniques along with the greater power of today's workstations can help to reduce the execution time required for achieving acceptable precision to the point that simulation can be used by financial traders to value derivatives in real time.

About the Download

INTRODUCTION

This appendix provides you with information on the contents of the download that accompanies this book.

ACCESSING THE DOWNLOAD

1. Visit http://textbook.crystalball.com
2. Enter the code given on the card at the back of this book

SYSTEM REQUIREMENTS

Please refer to the Decisioneering web site, www.crystalball.com, for the latest system requirements.

WHAT'S INCLUDED IN THE DOWNLOAD

The following sections provide a summary of the software and other materials included in the download

Excel Worksheets

Any Excel worksheets from the book are in the folder named "Content." These worksheets are provided for your reference so that you may track the course of the book using Microsoft Excel and build financial models of your own using these worksheets as templates. Note that each file, however, typically contains additional information in different worksheets within that file.

Note: Many popular spreadsheet programs are capable of reading Microsoft Excel files. However, users should be aware that a slight amount of formatting might be lost when using a program other than Microsoft Excel. Also, the Crystal Ball add-in works only with Microsoft Excel.

Crystal Ball Trial

Crystal Ball® software transforms Microsoft® Excel spreadsheets into dynamic models that solve almost any problem involving uncertainty, variability and risk. Included with this book is a time-sensitive license of Crystal Ball Professional that will expire 180 days from the date of installation. Crystal Ball Professional includes Monte Carlo simulation plus advanced capabilities of OptQuest®, to search for optimal solutions, CB Predictor™ to create accurate predictive models and Extreme Speed, to run simulations up to 100 times faster.

To access the software, follow the download instructions on the inserted card. If you experience difficulties downloading or installing the software, please contact Crystal Ball's Technical Support Dept. at helpdesk@crystalball.com or http://support.crystalball.com. Technical support is available only through e-mail and the Decisioneering web site. Crystal Ball and Decisioneering are registered trademarks of Decisioneering, Inc.

CUSTOMER CARE

Technical support is available only through email and the Decisioneering web site. For technical support, contact us at helpdesk@crystalball.com or http://support.crystalball.com.

arbitrage   The purchase of securities on one market for immediate resale on another in order to profit from a price discrepancy.

assumption   An estimated value or input to a spreadsheet model.

assumption cell   A value cell in a spreadsheet model that has been defined as a probability distribution using Crystal Ball's Distribution Gallery.

CDF   Cumulative distribution function, which gives the probability that a variable will fall at or below a given value.

certainty bands   In a trend chart, a graphic depiction of a particular certainty range for each forecast.

certainty level   The percentage of values in the certainty range compared to the number of values in the entire output distribution.

certainty range   The linear distance for the set of values between the certainty grabbers on the forecast chart.

coefficient of variability   also **coefficient of variance** or **coefficient of variation** A measure of relative variation that relates the standard deviation to the mean. Results can be represented in percentages for comparison purposes.

continuous probability distribution   A probability distribution that describes a set of uninterrupted values over a range. In contrast to the Discrete distribution, the Continuous distribution assumes there are an infinite number of possible values.

correlation   In Crystal Ball, a dependency that exists between assumption cells.

correlation coefficient   A number between −1 and 1 that specifies mathematically the degree of positive or negative correlation between assumption cells. A correlation of 1 indicates a perfect positive correlation, −1 indicates a perfect negative correlation, and 0 indicates there is no correlation.

cumulative frequency distribution   A chart that shows the number or proportion (or percentage) of values less than or equal to a given amount.

decision variable   A Crystal Ball variable in your model that you can control.

derivative security   A financial instrument whose price is derived from that of another financial security.

deterministic model   Another name for a spreadsheet model which yields single-valued results.

discrete probability distribution   A probability distribution that describes distinct values, usually integers, with no intermediate values. In contrast, the Continuous distribution assumes there are an infinite number of possible values.

display range   The linear distance for the set of values displayed on the forecast chart.

dominant   A relationship between distributions in which one distribution's values for all percentile levels are higher than another's. (see also *Subordinate*)

entire range   The linear distance from the minimum forecast value to the maximum forecast value.

forecast   A statistical summary of the assumptions in a spreadsheet model, output graphically or numerically.

forecast cell   A formula cell that has been defined as a forecast and refers either directly or indirectly to assumption cells.

forecast definition   The forecast name and parameters assigned to a cell in a Crystal Ball dialog.

forecast formula   A formula that has been defined as a forecast cell.

forecast value   also **trial** A value calculated by the forecast formula during an iteration. These values are kept in a list for each forecast, and are summarized graphically in the forecast chart and numerically in the descriptive statistics.

formula cell   A cell that contains a mathematical formula.

frequency   also **frequency count** The number of times a value recurs in a group interval.

frequency distribution   A chart that graphically summarizes a list of values by subdividing them into groups and displaying their frequency counts.

goodness-of-fit   A set of mathematical tests performed to find the best fit between a standard probability distribution and a data set.

grabber   also **certainty grabber** and **truncation grabber** A control that lets you use the mouse to change values and settings.

group interval   A subrange of a distribution that allows similar values to be grouped together and given a frequency count.

iteration   also **trial** A three-step process in which Crystal Ball generates random numbers for assumption cells, recalculates the spreadsheet model(s), and displays the results in a Forecast Chart.

kurtosis   The measure of the degree of peakedness of a curve. A normal distribution curve has a kurtosis of 3.

Latin hypercube sampling   In Crystal Ball, a sampling method that divides an assumption's probability distribution into intervals of equal probability. The number of intervals corresponds to the Minimum Sample Size option available in the Run Preferences dialog. A random number is then generated for each interval. Compared with conventional Monte Carlo sampling, Latin hypercube sampling is more precise because the entire range of the distribution is sampled in a more even, consistent manner. The increased accuracy of this method comes at the expense of added memory requirements to hold the full Latin hypercube sample for each assumption.

mean   The familiar arithmetic average of a set of numerical observations: the sum of the observations divided by the number of observations.

mean standard error   The Standard Deviation of the distribution of possible sample means. This statistic gives one indication of how accurate the simulation is.

median   The value midway (in terms of order) between the smallest possible value and the largest possible value.

mode   That value which, if it exists, occurs most often in a data set. In a continuous probability distribution, the mode is the number on the horizontal axis lying beneath the highest point on the pdf curve. In a discrete probability distribution, the mode is the value having the greatest probability of occurrence.

model sensitivity   The overall effect that a change in an assumption cell produces in a forecast cell. This effect is solely determined by the formulas in the spreadsheet model.

Monte Carlo simulation   A system which uses random numbers to measure the effects of uncertainty in a spreadsheet model.

PDF Probability density function that represents the probability that an infinitely small variable interval will fall at a given value.

probabilistic model A system whose output is a distribution of possible values. In Crystal Ball, this system includes a spreadsheet model (containing mathematical relationships), probability distributions, and a mechanism for determining the combined effect of the probability distributions on the model's output (Monte Carlo Simulation).

probability (Classical Theory) The likelihood of an event.

Probability Distribution also Distribution A set of all possible events and their associated probabilities.

rainbow option An option whose value depends on more than one source of uncertainty.

random number A mathematically selected value which is generated (by a formula or selected from a table) to conform to a probability distribution.

random number generator A method implemented in a computer program that is capable of producing a series of independent, random numbers.

range The difference between the largest and smallest values in a data set.

rank correlation also **Spearman's rank correlation** A method whereby Crystal Ball replaces assumption values with their ranking from lowest value to highest value using the integers 1 to N prior to computing the correlation coefficient. This method allows the distribution types to be ignored when correlating assumptions.

real option An option involving a real asset.

relative probability also relative frequency A value, not necessarily between 0 and 1, that indicates probability when used in a proportion.

reverse cumulative frequency distribution A chart that shows the number or proportion (or percentage) of values greater than or equal to a given amount.

risk The uncertainty or variability in the outcome of some event or decision.

seed value The first number in a sequence of random numbers. A given seed value produces the same sequence of random numbers every time you run a simulation.

sensitivity The amount of uncertainty in a forecast cell that is a result of both the uncertainty (probability distribution) and model sensitivity of an assumption cell.

sensitivity analysis The computation of a forecast cell's sensitivity with respect to the assumption cells.

skewed An asymmetrical distribution.

skewed, negatively A distribution in which most of the values occur at the upper end of the range.

skewed, positively A distribution in which most of the values occur at the lower end of the range.

skewness The measure of the degree of deviation of a curve from the norm of a asymmetric distribution. The greater the degree of skewness, the more points of the curve lie to either side of the peak of the curve. A normal distribution curve, having no skewness, is symmetrical.

spreadsheet model Any spreadsheet that represents an actual or hypothetical system or set of relationships.

standard deviation The square root of the variance for a distribution. A measurement of the variability of a distribution, i.e., the dispersion of values around the mean.

strike price The contractually agreed amount for which the underlying asset may be traded in an option contract.

subordinate A relationship between distributions in which one distribution's values for all percentile levels are lower than another's. (see also **Dominant**)

trial also **iteration** A three-step process in which Crystal Ball generates random numbers for assumption cells, recalculates the spreadsheet model(s), and displays the results in a Forecast Chart.

trial as used to describe a parameter in certain probability distributions. The number of times a given experiment is repeated.

truncation The specification of an upper limit, a lower limit, or both on the range of values to be generated from a Crystal Ball assumption.

value cell A cell that contains a simple numeric value.

variable A quantity that can assume any one of a set of values and is usually referenced by a formula.

variance The square of the standard deviation; i.e., the average of the squares of the deviations of a number of observations from their mean value. Variance can also be defined as a measure of the dispersion, or spread, of a set of values about a mean. When values are close to the mean, the variance is small. When values are widely scattered about the mean, the variance is larger.

virtual memory Memory which uses your hard drive space to store information after you run out of random access memory. Virtual memory supplements your random access memory.

References

Ameriks, J., Veres, R., and Warshawsky, M. J., "Making Retirement Income Last a Lifetime," *Journal of Financial Planning*, December 2001.

Ameur, H. B., L'Ecuyer, P., and Lemieux C. 1999. Variance Reduction of Monte Carlo and Randomized Quasi-Monte Carlo Estimators for Stochastic Volatility Models in Finance. In H. B. Nembhard, P. A. Farrington, D. T. Sturrock, and G. W. Evans, eds., *Proceedings of the Winter Simulation Conference*, IEEE, 336–343.

Amram, M., and N. Kulatilaka. 1999. *Real options: Managing strategic investment in an uncertain world*. Boston: Harvard Business School Press.

Anděl, J. 2001. *Mathematics of Chance*, New York: John Wiley & Sons.

Arnold, B. C. 1983. *Pareto Distributions*, Fairland, M.: International Cooperative Publishing House.

Aspray, W. 1990. *John von Neumann and the origins of modern computing*. Cambridge, Mass.: MIT Press.

Avramidis, A. N., and Hyden, P. 1999. Efficiency Improvements for Pricing American Options with a Stochastic Mesh, in H. B. Nembhard, P. A. Farrington, D. T. Sturrock, and G. W. Evans, eds., *Proceedings of the Winter Simulation Conference*, IEEE, 344–350.

Avramidis, A. N., and J. R. Wilson. 1995. Correlation-induction techniques for estimating quantiles in simulation experiments. In *Proceedings of the 1995 Winter Simulation Conference*, C. Alexopoulos, K. Kang, W. R. Lilegdon, and D. Goldsman, eds., IEEE, Piscataway, N.J.

Avramidis, A. N., and J. R. Wilson. 1996. Correlation-induction techniques for estimating quantiles in simulation experiments. Technical Report, Department of Industrial Engineering, North Carolina State University, Raleigh, N.C.

Ayyangar, A. A. K. 1941. "The Triangular Distribution," *Mathematics Student*, Vol. 9: 85–87.

Barraquand, J., and Martineau D. 1995. Numerical valuation of high-dimensional multivariate American securities. *Journal of Financial and Quantitative Analysis*, Vol. 30: 383–405.

Balakrishnan, N., 1991. *Handbook of the logistic distribution*. New York: Marcel Dekker, Inc.

Bell, S. 1962. *Approximating the Normal Distribution with the Triangular*. Sandia Corporation Report No. 494.

Bengen, W. P. 1994. "Determining Withdrawal Rates Using Historical Data," *Journal of Financial Planning*, October, pp. 14–24 (reprinted in 2004 Best of 25 Years series).

Bengen, W. P. 1996. "Asset Allocation for a Lifetime," *Journal of Financial Planning*, August, pp. 58–66.

Bengen, W. P. 1997. Conserving Client Portfolios During Retirement, Part III. *Journal of Financial Planning*, December, pp. 84–97.

Bernardo, A. E., and B. Chowdry. 2002. "Resources, real options and corporate strategy." *Journal of Financial Economics*, Vol. 63, No. 1 (January), 211–234.

Black, F., and M. Scholes. 1973. The pricing of options and corporate liabilities. *Journal of Political Economy*, Vol. 81: 637–654.

Blattberg, R. C., Getz, G., and Thomas, J. S. 2001. *Customer Equity: Building and managing relationships as valuable assets*. Boston: Harvard Business School Press.

Bortkiewicz, L. von. 1898. *Das Gesetz der Kleinen Zahlen*. Leipzig: Teubner.

Bowman, E. H., and G.T. Moskowitz. 2001. Real options analysis and strategic decision making. *Organization Science*, 12, No. 6 (November/December): 772–777.

Boyle, P. P. 1977. Options: A Monte Carlo Approach. *Journal of Financial Economics*, Vol. 4: 322–338.

Brabazon, T. 1999. Real options: Valuing flexibility in capital investment decisions. *Accountancy Ireland*, 31, No. 6 (December): 16–18.

Bratley, P., B. L. Fox, and L. E. Schrage. *A Guide to Simulation*, 2nd ed., New York: Springer-Verlag, 1987.

Brealey, R. A., S. C. Meyers, and F. Allen, 2006. *Principles of corporate finance*, 8th ed. New York: McGraw-Hill.

Boyle, P., M. Broadie, and P. Glasserman. 1997. Monte Carlo methods for security pricing. *Journal of Economic Dynamics and Control*, Vol. 21: 1267–1321.

Boyle P., M. Broadie, and P. Glasserman. 1995. Recent advances in simulation for security pricing. In C. Alexopoulos, K. Kang, W. R. Lilegdon, and D. Goldsman, ed., *Proceedings of the Winter Simulation Conference*, IEEE, 212–219.

Broadie, M., and P. Glasserman. 1997. Pricing American-style securities using simulation. *Journal of Economic Dynamics and Control*, Vol. 21: 1323–1352.

Broadie, M., and P. Glasserman. 1996. Estimating security price derivatives using simulation. *Management Science*, Vol. 42, No. 2: 269–285.

Brown, L. (ed.). 2002. *Shorter Oxford English dictionary on historical principles*, New York: Oxford University Press.

Caflisch R. E., W. Morokoff, and A. B. Owen. 1997. Valuation of mortgage-backed securities using Brownian bridges to reduce effective dimension. *Journal of Computational Finance*, Vol. 1, No. 1: 27–46.

Campbell, J. A. 2002. Real options analysis of the timing of IS investment decisions. *Information and Management*, Vol. 39, No. 5 (March): 336–344.

Charnes, J. M. 2000. Using simulation for option pricing, in *Proceedings of the 2000 Winter Simulation Conference* (J. A. Joines, R. R. Burton, K. Kang, and P. A. Fishwick, eds), Orlando, Fla.

Charnes, J. M. 2002. Sharper estimates of derivative values. *Financial Engineering News*, June/July (no. 26): 6–8.

Charnes, J. M., and P. P. Shenoy. 2002. A forward Monte Carlo method for solving influence diagrams using local computation. *Management Science*.

Childs, P. D., S. H. Ott, and A. J. Triantis. 1998. Capital budgeting for interrelated projects: A real options approach. *Journal of Financial and Quantitative Analysis*, September.

Cooley, P. L., C. M. Hubbard, and D. T. Walz, 2003. Does international diversification increase the sustainable withdrawal rates from retirement portfolios. *Journal of Financial Planning*, pp. 74–80.

Copeland, T. 2001. The real options approach to capital allocation. *Strategic Finance*, Vol. 83, No. 4 (October): 33–37.

Copeland, T., and V. Antikarov. 2001. *Real options: A practitioner's guide*. New York: Texere Publishing Limited.

Cortazar, G. 2000. Simulation and numerical methods in real options valuation. Working Paper. Pontificia Universidad Catolica de Chile—General.

Covello, V.T., and J. Mumpower. 1985. Risk analysis and risk management: An historical perspective." *Risk Analysis*, Vol. 5, No. 2: 103–120.

D'Agostino, R. B., and M. A. Stephens, eds. 1986. *Goodness-of-fit techniques*. New York: Marcel Dekker.

Dangl, T. 1999. Investment and capacity choice under uncertain demand. *European Journal of Operational Research*, Vol. 117, No. 3 (September 16): 415–428.

de Haan, L., and A. Ferreira. 2006. *Extreme value theory: An introduction*. New York: Springer.

Demirer, R., J. Charnes, and D. Kellogg. 2002. Influence Diagrams for Real Options Valuation. Submitted for publication.

Desai, A. M., and P. Tufano. 2002. Laura Martin: Real options and the cable industry. Harvard Business School Case and Teaching Paper Series, Case No.: 201–004, Teaching Note: 202–060 9.

Dixit, A. K., and R. S. Pindyck. 1994. *Investment under uncertainty*. Princeton, N.J.: Princeton University Press.

Duffie, D. 1996. *Dynamic asset pricing theory*, 2nd ed. Princeton, N.J.: Princeton University Press.

Dwyer, F. R. 1997. Customer lifetime valuation to support marketing decision making. *Journal of Direct Marketing*, Vol. 11, No. 4, Fall, 7–13.

Economides, N. 1999. Real options and the costs of the local telecommunications network. New York University, Center for Law and Business, Working Paper No. 99-007.

Elton, E. J., and M. J. Gruber. 1974. On the maximization of the geometric mean with lognormal return distribution. *Management Science*, Vol. 21, No. 4: 483–488.

Evans, M., N. Hastings, and B. Peacock. 1993. *Statistical Distributions*, 2nd ed. New York: John Wiley & Sons.

Falco, A., and J. D. Campo. 2001. Regulated investments and the valuation of capital investment strategies through a real options' approach. Working Paper, Universidad Cardenal Herrera CEU–Facultad de Ciencias Sociales y Juridicas and Universidad Complutense de Madrid–Departamento de Economia Financiera.

Fan, J. Q., and Q. W. Yao, 2003. *Nonlinear time series: Nonparametric and parametric methods*. New York: Springer.

Fishman, G. S. 2006. *A First Course in Monte Carlo*. Belmont, Calif.: Duxbury.

Freedman, D., R. Pisani, R. Purves, and A. Adhikari. 1991. *Statistics*, 2nd ed. New York: W. W. Norton.

Fu, M. C. 1995. Pricing of financial derivatives via simulation. In C. Alexopoulos, K. Kang, W. R. Lilegdon, and D. Goldsman, eds. *Proceedings of the Winter Simulation Conference*, IEEE. 126–132.

Fu, M. C., and J. Q. Hu. 1995. Sensitivity analysis for Monte Carlo simulation of option pricing. *Probability in the Engineering and Informational Sciences*, Vol. 9, No. 3: 417–446.

Fu, M. C., S. B. Laprise, D. B. Madan, Y. Su, and R. Wu, 1999. Pricing American options: A comparison of Monte Carlo simulation approaches. U. Maryland, College Park, Md.

Gamba, A. 2002. "Real options valuation: A Monte Carlo simulation approach." Faculty of Management, University of Calgary, Working Paper No. 2002/3.

Geske, R., and H. E. Johnson. 1984. The American put option valued analytically. *The Journal of Finance*, Vol. 39, No. 5: 1511–1524.

Glasserman, P., *Monte Carlo methods in financial engineering*. New York: Springer-Verlag, 2004.

Glasserman P., and X Zhao. 1999. Fast greeks by simulation in forward LIBOR models. *Journal of Computational Finance*, Vol. 3, No. 1: 5–39.

Glover, F. 1977. Heuristics for integer programming using surrogate constraints. *Decision Sciences*, Vol. 8: 156–166.

Glover, F. 1997. Tabu search and adaptive memory programming—advances, applications and challenges. In Barr, Helgason and Kennington, eds. *Interfaces in computer science and operations research*, Kluwer Academic Publishers.

Grant D., G. Vora, and D. Weeks 1997. Path-dependent options: Extending the Monte Carlo simulation approach. *Management Science*, Vol. 43, No. 11: 1589–1602.

Gupta, A. K., and S. Nadarajah. 2004. *Handbook of beta distribution and its applications*, New York: Marcel Dekker, Inc.

Guyton, J. T. 2004. Decision rules and portfolio management for retirees: Is the "safe" initial withdrawal rate *too* safe? *Journal of Financial Planning*, October, 54–62.

Haenlein, M., A. M. Kaplan, and D. Schoder. 2006. Valuing the real option of abandoning unprofitable customers when calculating customer lifetime value. *Journal of Marketing*, Vol. 70 (July): 5–20.

Hardy, M. 2006. Simulating Value at Risk (VaR) and conditional tail expectation. *Financial Engineering News*, Vol. 47, February.

Herath, H. S. B., and C. S. Park. 1999. Economic analysis of R&D projects: An options approach. *Engineering Economist*, Vol. 44, No. 1: 1–35.

Herath, H. S. B., and C. S. Park. 2002. Multi-stage capital investment opportunities as compound real options. *Engineering Economist*, Vol. 47, No. 1: 1–27.

Hertz, D. B. 1968. Investment Policies That Pay Off, *Harvard Business Review*, Vol. 46: 96–108.

Ho, K., M. A. Milevsky, and C. Robinson. 1994. "Asset allocation, life expectancy and shortfall." *Financial Services Review*, Vol. 3, No. 2, pp. 109–126.

Holton, G. A. 2003. *Value at risk: Theory and practice*. San Diego, Calif.: Academic Press.

Huchzermeier, A., and C. H. Loch. 2001. Project management under risk: Using the real options approach to evaluate flexibility in R&D. *Management Science*, Vol. 47, No. 1 (January): 85–101.

Huisman, K. J. M., and P. M. Kort. 2000. Strategic technology adoption taking into account future technological improvements: A real options approach. Tilburg University Center for Economic Research Working Paper No. 52.

Hull, J. C. 1997. *Options, futures, and other derivatives*. Upper Saddle River, N.J.: Prentice Hall.

Hull J., and A. White. 1993. Efficient procedures for valuing European and American path-dependent options. *Journal of Derivatives*, Fall: 21–31.

Hull, J., and A. White. 1987. The pricing of options on assets with stochastic volatilities. *Journal of Finance*. Vol. 42, No. 2: 281–300.

Ibbotson Associates. 2006. *Stocks, bonds, bills, and inflation: 2005 yearbook*. Chicago: Ibbotson Associates.

Isaac, R. 1995. *The pleasures of probability*. New York: Springer-Verlag.

Jennergren, L. P. 2006. A Tutorial on the McKinsey Model for Valuation of Companies. Stockholm School of Economics Working Paper Series in Business Administration No. 1998:1, Fifth revision, February 20.

Johnson, N. L., A. W. Kemp, and S. Kotz, 2005. *Univariate discrete distributions, 3rd ed.* New York: John Wiley & Sons.

Johnson, N. L., S. Kotz, and N. Balakrishnan. 1994. *Continuous univariate distributions, 2nd ed.* New York: John Wiley & Sons.

Joy C., P. P. Boyle, and K. S. Tan. 1996. Quasi-Monte Carlo methods in numerical finance. *Management Science*, Vol. 42, No. 6: 926–938.

Kellogg, D., and J. Charnes. 2000. "Real-options valuation for a biotechnology company." *Financial Analysts Journal*, May/June, 76–84.

Kemna, A. G. Z., and A. C. F. Vorst. 1990. A pricing method for options based on average asset values. *Journal of Banking and Finance*, Vol. 14: 113–129.

Klein, E. 1967. *A comprehensive etymological dictionary of the English language.* Amsterdam: Elsevier Publishing Company.

Knuth, D. E. 1998. *The Art of Computer Programming, Third Edition*, Volume 2: Seminumerical Algorithms. Reading, MA: Addison-Wesley, 1998.

Koller, T., M. Goedhart, and D Wessels. 2005. *Valuation: Measuring and managing the value of companies, 4th ed.*, Hoboken, N.J.: John Wiley & Sons.

Lander, D. M., and G. E. Pinches. 1998. Challenges to the practical implementation of modeling and valuing real options. *1998 Special Issue of The Quarterly Review Of Economics And Finance, Real Options: Developments and Applications.*

Law, A. M., and W. D. Kelton. 2000. *Simulation modeling and analysis, 3rd ed.* New York: McGraw-Hill.

Lemieux, C. and P. L'Ecuyer. 1998. Efficiency improvement by lattice rules for pricing Asian options. In D. J. Medeiros, E. F. Watson, J. S. Carson and M. S. Mannivannan, eds., *Proceedings of the Winter Simulation Conference.* IEEE: 579–585.

Longstaff, F. A., and E. S. Schwartz. 1998. Valuing American options by simulation: A simple least-squares approach. UCLA Working Paper.

Luenberger, D. G. 1998. *Investment science.* New York: Oxford University Press.

Macrae, N. 1992. *John von Neumann: The scientific genius who pioneered the modern computer, game theory, nuclear deterrence, and much more.* New York: Pantheon Books.

Maguire, M. 2003. Wall street made me do it: A preliminary analysis of the major institutional investors in U.S. newspaper companies. *The Journal of Media Economics*, Vol. 16, No. 4: 253–264.

Mann, P. S. 2007. *Introductory Statistics, 6th ed.*, New York: John Wiley and Sons.

McDonald, R. L. 2006. *Derivatives markets, 2nd ed.* Boston, Mass.: Pearson Education, Inc.

McGill, J. I., and G. J. Van Ryzin. 1999. Revenue Management: Research Overview and Prospects, *Transportation Science*, Vol. 33, No. 2 (May): 233–256.

McKay, M. D., R. J. Beckman, and W. J. Conover. 1979. A comparison of three methods for selecting values of input variables in the analysis of output from a computer code. *Technometrics*, Vol. 21, No. 2, 239–245.

McNeil, A. J., R. Frey, and P. Embrechts, 2005. *Quantitative Risk Management: Concepts, techniques and tools*, Princeton, N.J.: Princeton University Press.

Melicher, R. W., and E. A. Norton. 2006. *Finance: Introduction to institutions, investments, and management*, 12th ed. New York: John Wiley & Sons.

Metropolis, N. 1987. The beginning of the Monte Carlo method. *Los Alamos Science*, Special Issue (15): 125–130.

Metropolis, N., and S. Ulam. 1949. The Monte Carlo method. *Journal of the American Statistical Association*, Vol. 44, No. 247 (September), 335–341.

Microsoft Corporation. 2005. Random number generation, Article ID 86523 (Revision 1.3), obtained from http://support.microsoft.com/kb/. Accessed December 18.

Milevsky, M. A., K. Ho, and C. Robinson. 1997. Asset allocation via the conditional first exit time or how to avoid outliving your money." *Review of Quantitative Finance and Accounting*, Vol. 9: 53–70.

Morokoff, W. J. 1998. Generating quasi-random paths for stochastic processes. *SIAM Review*, Vol. 40, No. 4, 765–788.

Mun, J. 2002. *Real options analysis*. New York: John Wiley & Sons.

Neter, J., W. Wasserman, and G. A. Whitmore. 1993. *Applied statistics*, 4th ed., Needham Heights, Mass.: Allyn and Bacon.

Niederreiter, H. 1988. Low discrepancy and low dispersion sequences. *Journal of Number Theory*, Vol. 30: 51–70.

Niederreiter, H., and J. Spanier, eds. 1998. *Monte Carlo and quasi-Monte Carlo methods*. New York: Springer.

Oppenheim, L. 1977. *Ancient Mesopotamia*. Chicago: University of Chicago Press.

Owen, A. B. 1998. Monte Carlo extension of quasi-Monte Carlo. In E. F. Watson, D. J. Medeiros, J. S. Carson, and M. S. Mannivannan, eds., *Procs. of the Winter Simulation Conference*. IEEE, 571–577.

Ore, O. 1960. Pascal and the invention of probability theory, *American Mathematical Monthly*, Vol. 67, No. 5 (May): 409–419.

Patel, J. K., and C. B. Read. 1996. *Handbook of the normal distribution*, 2nd ed., New York: Marcel Dekker.

Pawlina, G., and P. M. Kort. 2002. Strategic capital budgeting: Asset replacement under market uncertainty. *Proceedings of the EFMA 2002 London meetings*.

Pilopović, D. 1998. *Energy risk*. New York: McGraw-Hill.

Pitman, J. *Probability*, New York: Springer-Verlag, 1993.

Prabhakar Murthy, D. N., X. Min, and R. Jiang. 2004. *Weibull models*. New York: John Wiley & Sons.

Priestley, M. B. 1981. *Spectral analysis and time series*. London: Academic Press.

Proctor, K. S., 2004. *Building financial models with Microsoft Excel: A guide for business professionals*. Hoboken, N.J.: Wiley Finance, 2004.

Pye, G. 2000. "Sustainable Investment Withdrawals," *Journal of Portfolio Management*, Summer, pp. 73–83.

Quine, M. P., and E. Seneta, 1987. "Bortkiewicz's Data and the Law of Small Numbers," *International Statistical Review*, Vol. 55, 173–181.

Reichheld, F. F. 1996. *The Loyalty Effect: The hidden force behind growth, profits, and lasting value*, Boston: Harvard Business School Press.

Rejda, G. E. 2003. *Principles of risk management and insurance*, 8th ed. Boston: Addison-Wesley.

Rubinstein, M. 2006. *A history of the theory of investments: My annotated bibliography*. Hoboken, N.J.: John Wiley & Sons.

Rubinstein, R. Y. 1981. *Simulation and the Monte Carlo method*. New York: John Wiley & Sons.

Samuelson, Paul A. 1969. Lifetime portfolio selection by dynamic stochastic programming. *Review of Economics and Statistics*, Vol. 51, No. 3 (August): 239–246.

Smith, J. E., and K. F. McCardle. 1999. Options in the real world: Lessons learned in evaluating oil and gas investments. *Operations Research*, Vol. 47, No. 1 (January/February), 1–15.

Stein, M. 1987. Large sample properties of simulations using Latin Hypercube sampling. *Technometrics*, Vol. 29, 143–151.

Stephens, M. A. 1979. EDF Statistics for Goodness of Fit and Some Comparisons. *Journal of the American Statistical Association*, Vol. 69, No. 347 (September), 730–737.

Stephens, M. A. 1976. Asymptotic results for goodness of fit statistics with unknown parameters. *The Annals of Statistics*, Vol. 4, No. 2 (March), 357–369.

Tasche, D. 2002. Expected shortfall and beyond. *Journal of Banking and Finance*, Vol. 26, 1519–1533.

Taudes, A., M. Feurstein, and A. Mild. 2000. "Options analysis of software platform decisions: A case study." *MIS Quarterly*, Vol. 24, No. 2 (June): 227–243.

Terry, R. 2003. The relation between portfolio composition and sustainable withdrawal rates. *Journal of Financial Planning*, May, pp. 64–78.

Tezel, A. 2004. Sustainable Retirement Withdrawals, *Journal of Financial Planning*, July.

Tilley J. A. 1993. Valuing American options in a path simulation model. *Transactions of the Society of Actuaries*, Vol. 45: 83–104.

Treischmann J. S., R. E. Hoyt, and D. W. Sommer. 2005. *Risk Management and Insurance*, 12th ed. Thompson.

Trigeorgis, L. 1996. *Real options: Managerial flexibility and strategy in resource allocation*. Cambridge, Mass.: MIT Press.

Tsay, R. S. 2002. *Analysis of financial time series*. New York: John Wiley and Sons.

Tseng, C. L., and G. Barz. 2002. Short-term generation asset valuation: A real options approach. *Operations Research*, Vol. 50, No. 2 (March/April): 297–310.

Tyson, D. 1997. *Scrying for beginners: Tapping into the supersensory powers of your subconscious*. St. Paul, Minn.: Llewellyn Publications.

Uryasev, S. 2000. Conditional Value-at-Risk: Optimization Algorithms and Applications. *Financial Engineering News*, Vol. 14 (February).

Vázquez-Abad, F. J., and D. Dufresne. 1998. Accelerated simulation for pricing Asian options. In D. J. Medeiros, E. F. Watson, C. J. S. and M. S. Mannivannan, eds., *Proceedings of the Winter Simulation Conference*. IEEE. 1493–1500.

Vose, D. *Risk analysis: A quantitative guide*, 2nd ed. West Sussex, England: Wiley, 2000.

Wilmott, P. 1998. *Derivatives: The theory and practice of financial engineering*. West Sussex, England: Wiley.

Wilmott, P. 2000. *Paul Wilmott on quantitative finance*. West Sussex, England: Wiley.

Zhang, G. 2000. "Accounting information, capital investment decisions, and equity valuation: Theory and empirical implications." *Journal of Accounting Research*, Vol. 38, No. 2, 271–295.